Why Economics is not yet a Science

EDITED BY
Alfred S. Eichner

M. E. SHARPE, INC.
Armonk, New York

To my colleagues at Rutgers

Both those who, like Paul
Davidson and Jim Street, share
my critical view of the orthodox
economic theory

And those who, by insisting
that students master this body
of theory, have bestirred me
to put together this collection
of essays.

,HB
71
.W47
1983

Library of Congress Cataloging in Publication Data
Main entry under title:

Why economics is not yet a science.

  Includes index.
  Contents: What do we mean by asking whether economics is a science? / E. Ray
Canterbery and Robert J. Burkhardt—Modern empiricism and quantum-leap theorizing
in economics / James A. Swaney and Robert Premus—Ideology, methodology, and neo-
classical economics / Peter Wiles—[etc.]
  1. Economics—Addresses, essays, lectures.
I. Eichner, Alfred S.
HB71.W47   1983   330   83-12859
ISBN 0-87332-249-5
ISBN 0-87332-265-7 (pbk.)

Printed in the United States of America

Why Economics is not yet a Science

CONTENTS

‖ ‖ ‖ ‖ ‖ ‖ ‖ ‖ ‖ ‖ ‖ ‖

Wassily Leontief

FOREWORD

‖ ‖ ‖ ‖ ‖ ‖ ‖ ‖ ‖ ‖ ‖ ‖ ‖

Academic economics

"A dismal performance. . . . What economists revealed most clearly was the extent to which their profession lags intellectually."[1] This editorial comment by the leading economic weekly (on the 1981 annual proceedings of the American Economic Association) says, essentially, that the "king is naked." But no one taking part in the elaborate and solemn procession of contemporary U.S. academic economics seems to know it, and those who do don't dare speak up.

Two hundred years ago the founders of modern economic science—Adam Smith, Ricardo, Malthus, and John Stuart Mill—erected an imposing conceptual edifice based on the notion of the national economy as a self-regulating system of a great many different but interrelated, and therefore interdependent, activities: a concept so powerful and fruitful that it gave impetus to Charles Darwin's pathbreaking work on his theory of evolution.

The central idea of what is now being referred to as Classical Economics attracted the attention of two mathematically trained engineers, Léon Walras and Vilfredo Pareto, who translated it with considerable refinement and elaboration into a concise language of algebra and calculus and called it the General Equilibrium Theory. Under the name of neoclassical economics this theory now constitutes the core of undergraduate and graduate instruction in this country.

As an empirical science, economics dealt from the outset with phenomena of common experience. Producing and consuming goods, buying and selling, and receiving income and spending it are activities engaging everyone's attention practically all the time.

[1] *Business Week*, 18 January 1982, p. 124.

Originally published as a Letter to the Editor in *Science*, Vol. 217, July 9, 1982, pp. 104-105. Copyright 1982 by the American Association for the Advancement of Science.

Even the application of the scientific principle of quantification did not have to be initiated by the analyst himself—measuring and pricing constitute an integral part of the phenomena that he sets out to explain. Herein lies, however, the initial source of the trouble in which academic economics finds itself today.

By the time the facts of everyday experience were used up, economists were able to turn for bits and pieces of less accessible, more specialized information to government statistics. However, these statistics—compiled for administrative or business, but not scientific, purposes—fall short of what would have been required for concrete, more detailed understanding of the structure and the functioning of a modern economic system.

Not having been subjected from the outset to the harsh discipline of systematic fact-finding, traditionally imposed on and accepted by their colleagues in the natural and historical sciences, economists developed a nearly irresistible predilection for deductive reasoning. As a matter of fact, many entered the field after specializing in pure or applied mathematics. Page after page of professional economic journals are filled with mathematical formulas leading the reader from sets of more or less plausible but entirely arbitrary assumptions to precisely stated but irrelevant theoretical conclusions.

Nothing reveals the aversion of the great majority of the present-day academic economists for systematic empirical inquiry more than the methodological devices that they employ to avoid or cut short the use of concrete factual information. Instead of constructing theoretical models capable of preserving the identity of hundreds, even thousands, of variables needed for the concrete description and analysis of a modern economy, they first of all resort to "aggregation." The primary information, however detailed, is packaged in a relatively small number of bundles labeled "Capital," "Labor," "Raw Materials," "Intermediate Goods," "General Price Level," and so on. These bundles are then usually fitted into a "model," that is, a small system of equations describing the entire economy in terms of a small number of corresponding "aggregative" variables. The fitting, as a rule, is accomplished by means of "least squares" or another similar curve-fitting procedure.

A typical example of a theoretical "production function" intended to describe the relationship between, say, the amount of steel produced, y_1, and the quantities of the four different inputs,

y_2, y_3, y_4, and y_5 needed to produce it is, for instance, described as follows:[2]

$$y_1{}^{P_1} = a_1 |G^2|{}^{P_1} + (1 - a_1) |G^3|{}^{P_1}$$

where:

$$-G^2 = [a_2 |y_2|^{P_2} + (1 - a_2) |y_3|^{P_2}]^{\frac{1}{P_2}}$$
$$-G^3 = [a_3 |y_4|^{P_3} + (1 - a_3) |y_5|^{P_3}]^{\frac{1}{P_3}}$$

or alternatively:

$$\ln |G^2| = 1/2 \ln |y_2| + 1/2 \ln |y_3|$$
$$\ln |G^3| = 1/2 \ln |y_4| + 1/2 \ln |y_5|$$

or, finally:

$$\ln y_1 = a_1 \ln |G^2| + (1 - a_1) \ln |G^3|$$

To ask a manager of a steel plant or a metallurgical expert for information on the magnitude of the six parameters appearing in these six equations would make no sense. Hence, while the labels attached to symbolic variables and parameters of the theoretical equations tend to suggest that they could be identified with those directly observable in the real world, any attempt to do so is bound to fail: the problem of "identification" of aggregative equations after they have been reduced—that is, transformed, as they often are—for purposes of the curve-fitting process, was raised many years ago but still has not found a satisfactory solution. In the meantime, the procedure described above was standardized to such an extent that, to carry out a respectable econometric study, one simply had to construct a plausible and easily computable theoretical model and then secure—mostly from secondary or tertiary sources—a set of time series or cross section data related in some direct or indirect way to its particular subject, insert these figures with a program of an appropriate statistical routine taken from the shelf into the computer, and finally publish the computer printouts with a more or less plausible interpretation of the numbers.

While the quality and coverage of official statistics have recently been permitted to deteriorate without eliciting determined protest

[2] L. R. Christensen, D. W. Jorgenson, L. J. Lau, "Transcendential logarithmic production functions," *Review of Economic Statistics*, 55, 28 (1972).

Table 1

Percentages of different types of articles published
in the *American Economic Review*

Type of article	March 1972 to December 1976	March 1977 to December 1981
Mathematical models without any data	50.1	54.0
Analysis without mathematical formulation and data	21.2	11.6
Statistical methodology	0.6	0.5
Empirical analysis based on data generated by the author's initiative	0.8	1.4
Empirical analysis using indirect statistical inference based on data published or generated elsewhere	21.4	22.7
Empirical analysis not using indirect statistical inference based on data generated by author	0.0	0.5
Empirical analysis not using indirect statistical inference based on data generated or published elsewhere	5.4	7.4
Empirical analysis based on artificial simulations and experiments	0.5	1.9

on the part of their potential scientific users, masses of concrete, detailed information contained in technical journals, reports of engineering firms, and private marketing organizations are neglected.

A perusal of the contents of the *American Economic Review*, the flagship of academic economic periodicals over the last 10 years, yields the picture in Table 1.

These figures speak for themselves. In a prophetic statement of editorial policy, the managing editor of the *American Economic Review* observed[3] 10 years ago that "articles on mathematical economics and the finer points of economic theory occupy a more and more prominent place than ever before, while articles of a more empirical, policy-oriented or problem-solving character seem to appear less frequently."

Year after year economic theorists continue to produce scores of mathematical models and to explore in great detail their formal properties; and the econometricians fit algebraic functions of all

[3] G. H. Borts, *American Economic Review*, 62, 764 (1972).

possible shapes to essentially the same sets of data without being able to advance, in any perceptible way, a systematic understanding of the structure and the operations of a real economic system.

How long will researchers working in adjoining fields, such as demography, sociology, and political science on the one hand and ecology, biology, health sciences, engineering, and other applied physical sciences on the other, abstain from expressing serious concern about the state of stable, stationary equilibrium and the splendid isolation in which academic economics now finds itself? That state is likely to be maintained as long as tenured members of leading economics departments continue to exercise tight control over the training, promotion, and research activities of their younger faculty members and, by means of peer review, of the senior members as well. The methods used to maintain intellectual discipline in this country's most influential economics departments[4] can occasionally remind one of those employed by the Marines to maintain discipline on Parris Island.

WASSILY LEONTIEF

[4] M. W. Reder, *Journal of Economic Literature*, 20, 1 (1982).

PREFACE

The idea for this book first occurred to me in the late winter of 1980-81 after Fred Lee, then a graduate student at Rutgers, showed me an earlier version of the paper by Peter Earl which is included in this collection. The paper struck a responsive chord, beset as I then was in a running controversy both with a large number of my colleagues at Rutgers and with the economics section of the National Science Foundation on the very issues raised by Earl's paper. Why, I was asking my colleagues at Rutgers, should the graduate students be exposed, in the required core courses, only to the mainstream theory when many of its key propositions cannot be empirically demonstrated? And why, I was asking the staff of the National Science Foundation, was only mainstream research being funded when that line of inquiry was proving to be so barren? The Earl paper seemed to shed important light on both those questions.

I then remembered the essay by Peter Wiles which had appeared in the *Journal of Post Keynesian Economics* the year before. It had seemed, when I first read it, to go right to the heart of what is wrong with economics. Now, my enthusiasm for it undiminished, it seemed the perfect companion piece to the Earl paper. Richard Chase had previously sent me a copy of the essay included in this volume, and I was then preparing the paper on "Post Keynesian Theory and Empirical Research" which I would give at Ottawa University later that spring at a conference on Keynes and Sraffa (see the January-July, 1982, issue of *L'Actualite Economique*) and which appears, in a quite different version, as the concluding, title essay in this volume. Only a few other papers would need to be added, I realized, to make for a substantial, and powerful, critique of economics as an academic discipline.

It proved relatively easy to obtain those additional papers. John Blatt had already written a chapter on the misuse of mathematics by economists which he had been forced to leave out of a book on optimal control theory. He readily agreed to revise that chapter for this collection. Ray Canterbery and Bob Burkhardt had meanwhile been working on a philosophical critique of economics, and, after seeing a draft of their study, I asked if they would prepare a condensed version for this volume. They said they would. Since both the behavioralist and post-Keynesian perspectives were already represented, I then approached Ron Stanfield, who was working on an interpretative study of Kary Polanyi, about contributing an essay for this volume written from an institutionalist perspective. Ron not only submitted the essay which appears in this volume under his name; he also sent me a copy of an essay by Jim Swaney and Bob Premus, which I then added to the collection. Finally, after Wassily Leontief's letter appeared in *Science*, I asked if he would allow it to be republished as the foreword to this volume, and he promptly gave his consent.

That it has been relatively easy to put together this collection reflects, I believe, a pervasive feeling among a large number of economists—even though they are only a minority of the profession—that there is something so fundamentally wrong with economics that, until the error is corrected and economics placed on a different footing, little advance in economic knowledge can be expected. This feeling is accompanied by the belief that there is little hope economics will reform itself—at least not without substantial pressure from without—and that therefore the necessary change must come from within. Criticisms are rejected, not because they lack intellectual merit, but, rather, because they go against the grain of the prevailing orthodoxy. No appeal to the evidence will succeed. Only the evidence which accords with a priori belief is acknowledged. Economics has, in this respect, become a closed system of ideas, more like a religion than a science.

It is for this reason that the essays in this collection are directed primarily at those outside economics—even though it is hoped that minds within the profession, especially younger ones, are still open to persuasion. One audience is the larger lay public. It is this group which suffers the most from economics in its present form, not just in terms of the resources consumed in supporting those who hold teaching and research positions in the field but also in terms of the damage done by there not being a better understanding of how the economy works. The even more important audience, however, is the broader community of scientists. It is this group which is most directly threatened when ideas falsely masquerade as science, and it is this group which must respond accordingly. Just as it has been necessary for scientists to oppose "creationism" and other corruptions of biology and geology, so too it is necessary that they invoke whatever sanctions they can against the mislabeling of economics in its present form as science.

What follows is a rather harsh indictment of economics. Hopefully it will not be misconstrued as an attack on the integrity of individual economists. Certainly it is not meant to be. Nor is it meant to suggest that all the work presently being done by economists is scientifically worthless. Indeed, a great deal of it—all that avoids the orthodox theory and even some that only pays lip service to that theory—is quite valuable. Still, even with these qualifications, the indictment which follows is likely to anger, and indeed infuriate, many of our colleagues. Unfortunately, it cannot be helped. Harsh truths cannot be spoken without sometimes offending. The real question is whether the indictment is justified. This question must be left to the broader community of scientists to decide.

ALFRED S. EICHNER
CLOSTER, N.J.
JULY, 1983

Why Economics is not yet a Science

1

INTRODUCTION

Economics as a discipline is in crisis.

On this point there is a surprising consensus among a large number of economists who agree on little else.[1] The theory on which the governments of the economically advanced countries relied for so long to assure growth and stability no longer seems to work. That theory is some distillation—some would say bastardization —of the ideas put forward by Keynes in *The General Theory*. It is not that governments, by following Keynesian policies, can no longer reverse a decline in economic activity if they want to. It is rather that those policies are likely to be accompanied by a secular rise in the price level, touching off a wage-price spiral that is difficult to halt even after Draconian measures have been take to slow down the economy. The resulting stagflation is a phenomenon for which the prevailing theory in economics can offer no satisfactory explanation.

The crisis in economics has now become a crisis for the world economy. Governments, unsure of what policies to follow, have allowed their own economies, and therefore the world economy, to drift into a dangerous state of mounting unemployment and low growth even as inflation continues to erode the purchasing power of their currencies. Meanwhile, an increasingly fragile world financial structure, a legacy of the flirtation with monetarist nostrums combined with an unregulated Eurocurrency market, has brought the world economy to the brink of another major collapse, similar

---

[1] See, for example, Joan Robinson, "The Second Crisis in Economic Theory," *American Economic Review*, May 1972; Wassily Leontief, "Theoretical Assumptions and Unobserved Facts," *American Economic Review*, March 1971; John R. Hicks, *The Crisis in Keynesian Economics*, Basic Books, 1974; Daniel Bell and Irving Kristol, eds. *The Crisis in Economic Theory*, Basic Books, 1980.

to that which spawned the Keynesian revolution in economic policy at an earlier time. It is in this context that the question of why economics is not yet a science is of more than just parochial concern to economists.

The prevailing view among economists is that their discipline, if not already a science, is well on the way to becoming one. Even critics are likely to argue that, with but a slight change in either emphasis or approach, economics will eventually be able to provide an answer to stagflation and other economic puzzles. The thrust of the essays in this volume, many of them not previously published, is quite different. They suggest that the malaise runs much deeper, that as long as economists continue to "do economics" in the same old way—the only way now considered acceptable within the profession itself—the rest of society had better be wary of the advice it accepts from them.

Canterbery and Burkhardt, in the first essay which follows, indicate that there are two quite different ways in which the term "science" can be used. One is in the Kuhn-Lakatos sense of an overarching paradigm with a hard core to which most practitioners in the field would subscribe and which is the basis for the "normal science" they typically pursue. The other is in the logical-positivist sense of knowledge-claims being tested against experience, of the various propositions not yet falsified constituting a logically coherent whole, and of the theory's explanatory power steadily increasing over time. Canterbery and Burkhardt then go on to note that, while economics is clearly a science in the Kuhn-Lakatos sense, it is far from being a science in the logical-positivist sense— even though the latter is the view of science most economists profess to hold. In support of this argument, they present evidence on how few is the number of universities represented by published articles in the leading journals—the principal means of communicating within the discipline—and how seldom it is that the key propositions of the dominant neoclassical theory are rigorously tested in those articles. In their view, economics has become a narrow, stagnant, closed system of ideas.

In the next essay, Swaney and Premus also argue that economics as a discipline fails to meet the logical-positivist criteria for being considered a science—except that they emphasize the failure of economists to follow the methods of science at the initial, and critical, theory formulation stage. Models are elaborated, using

mathematics and other tools of deductive analysis, on an eviden-
tial base which consists of little more than casual empiricism,
hunches, and unrealistic assumptions. To apply the testing procedures called for by the logical-positivists to a body of theory developed in this manner represents a caricature rather than a realization of the scientific method. What is unrecognized by the majority of economists, they point out, is how intimately connected
are theory formulation and data collection, and how difficult it is
to carry out meaningful empirical tests of a theory which is inade-
quately grounded in reality. Swaney and Premus conclude that
economics relies upon methods at the theory formulation stage
which are excessively deductive and that this then leads to empirical work which is largely inefficient and unproductive. To illustrate their point, they examine the recent work which has been
done in the fields of migration and monetary economics.

Wiles, in the third essay, focuses even more sharply on the deductive methods relied upon so heavily by economists. First,
however, he distinguishes between an ideology and a methodology. An ideology, he says, is "a general and coherent *Weltanschauung*, felt passionately and defended unscrupulously." When
the sacred propositions upon which the ideology rests run counter
to the evidence, a special methodology will be developed, he says,
so that the sacred propositions can still be sustained. Wiles argues
that the neoclassical theory which dominates conventional economic thought is not an ideology. Although there is a *Weltanschauung*, an all-encompassing view of society as consisting of rational human beings competing independently of one another in
the marketplace, there are no sacred propositions. The one-time
ideological insistence on the moral as well as economic virtues of
free trade has been replaced by a mere fascination with the problem of optimal resource allocation. There are, however, sacred procedures. These procedures involve a special methodology which,
though still used by some economists to defend *laissez-faire* principles, should not be mistaken for an ideology. The special methodology is axiomatic reasoning, and it is a methodology, Wiles
argues, far removed from that of science. This axiomatic methodology, together with excessive abstraction and an insistence on
economic determinism, constitutes the "Ricardian vice," and it
makes economics a quasi-scientific intellectual activity. It also
makes economists blind to the factors producing inflation, factors
which to the noneconomist seem obvious.

Earl elaborates at some length on a point briefly touched on by Wiles—why the ideas of economists, though so sharply at variance with economic reality, continue to be transmitted from one generation of economists to the next. In his analysis, Earl dispenses with the usual premise that economists are committed to discovering the truth and instead adopts the behavioralist assumption that economists are interested primarily in career and other individualistic goals. He then proceeds to show how a concern with advancement through the academic hierarchy described by Canterbery and Burkhardt in the first essay can force the neophyte economist to work within the dominant neoclassical tradition, even though this is likely to limit significantly the contribution he or she can make to economic knowledge. Among the factors at work which Earl mentions is the need to turn out articles rapidly, articles which will more readily be accepted by older colleagues, and therefore articles which are more likely to be published in journals and considered favorably by appointments and promotions committees. Earl uses this behavioralist approach to show not only why the dominant neoclassical theory retains its preeminent position within the academy but also why the empirically more relevant behavioralist approach which he favors has been virtually ignored by economists. Not the least important of these reasons is that the behavioralistic approach, like the similar institutionalist approach favored by Swaney and Premus, eschews axiomatic reasoning.

Chase, in the fifth essay, examines economics on its own preferred grounds—as a body of axiomatic theory—thus picking up on the main point raised in several of the earlier essays. He indicates that, even insofar as being logically consistent is concerned, the dominant neoclassical theory is seriously flawed. The so-called Keynesian revolution, whatever its success in contributing to greater realism in economics, has only compounded the problem of coherence. The fact is that the ideas put forward by economists under the heading of microeconomics are at variance with the ideas put forward under the rubric of macroeconomics. While this has been the case ever since the Keynesian revolution, it now turns out that, as revealed by the Cambridge capital controversy, not even the deductive arguments arising from the microfoundations of neoclassical theory about the ability of markets to organize production optimally can be shown to be necessarily true. In response to this criticism, neoclassical economists are forced to defend the theoretical edifice they have erected with the argument that reswitching and capital reversal, the anomalies pointed out by post-Keynesian critics, are empirically unimportant. How strange it is that a group of knowledge-claimants which denies that its own theories need meet any empirical test—unlike a true science—should argue for rejecting a telling criticism of those theories on empirical rather than on logical grounds.

Nothing is more central to the belief of economists that theirs is a scientific discipline based on logical deduction than the widespread reliance on—some would say addiction to—mathematics. Blatt thus strikes at the heart of this conceit when he points out, in the sixth essay, that the use made of mathematics by economists is largely inappropriate. A mathematician rather than an economist by training, Blatt examines the recent fascination of economists with optimal control theory, a technique which he sees as encompassing most of the uses which are made of mathematics by economists. This technique, appropriate to other fields such as space exploration, is a dangerous one when applied to economic and other social problems because the results are not sufficiently "robust" to protect against the possibility that the underlying model has been misspecified. And indeed there is good reason to believe that the model economists generally rely upon is, at best, incomplete—if not actually wrongheaded. Neither the utility functions nor the production functions which are such an integral part of that model can be specified, and this is true because it is questionable whether they even exist. "All this," says Blatt, "is *not* the application of mathematics to the economic problems of the real world. Rather, it is the application of highly precise and elaborate mathematics to an entirely imaginary and fanciful economic cloud cuckoo land." Blatt attributes this misuse of mathematics by economists to what he terms the "Scriptures" of mathematical economics, the principal culprit being Samuelson's *Foundations of Economic Analysis*.

For Stanfield, the problem in economics is even more fundamental. The dominant neoclassical theory asks the wrong question. This has been true ever since Lionel Robbins persuaded his fellow economists that rational choice, or the optimal allocation of scarce resources, is the central problem that needs to be addressed within their discipline. The focus on the problem of rational choice is responsible for the mathematical formalism which characterizes economics, and it involves what can be termed the "economistic fallacy." This is the tendency to raise to a universal principle the specific workings of market capitalism. The economistic fallacy is an example of what Whitehead called the error of misplaced concreteness. "The economistic fallacy," says Stanfield, "identifies an abstract model with reality and considers empirical behavior only insofar as that behavior corresponds to the "formalistic model." Instead of asking how resources can be optimally allocated, and thus focusing on "economizing" behavior, economics ought to be inquiring into how different societies provide for their material needs and thus the varying ways they succeed in solving their economic problem. This latter approach, the one advocated by institutionalist economists, leads to a comparative method of analysis and to a concern with social rather than market values.

The editor of this volume, in the concluding essay, takes up the question first posed by Veblen more than eighty years ago—Why is economics not yet a science? The formal answer is that economics, despite having failed to empirically substantiate most of its key propositions, nonetheless continues to base its theoretical arguments on those very propositions. The key theoretical constructs for which there is little or no empirical support are (1) a set of convex indifference curves for every household reflecting the relative preferences for any two goods; (2) a set of continuous, or smooth, isoquants representing all the combinations of labor and other inputs needed to produce any particular good; (3) a set of positively sloped supply curves for the industrial sector of the economy; and (4) a set of marginal physical product curves for all the inputs used in the production process, especially the "capital" inputs. It is these four constructs which constitute the neoclassical core of economic theory and the microeconomic half of the neoclassical synthesis developed by Hicks and Samuelson. While the lack of empirical support for its key propositions is the formal reason economics is not yet a science, this still leaves the question of why economists continue to cling so tenaciously to those propositions. The answer put forward, as an elaboration of the themes to be found in several of the earlier essays, is two-fold: Neoclassical theory is the one thing most economists have in common, providing them with a common language and, in the form of a fictionalized market, a common metaphor. It is also the mystery that sets them apart from the untutored masses, even those learned in the other social sciences, and it is the means of filtering out the disbelieving. Still, this is only the role which the neoclassical theory plays in enabling the economics profession to continue reproducing itself without change. There is also the support which the same body of theory gives to a set of ideas which have been instrumental in the development of Western civilization—and thus the role the theory plays in preserving the political values of the larger society. The neoclassical theory is the basis for the notion that a market economy is a self-regulating mechanism, and it is this notion which then makes it possible to deny the need for any but a minimal involvement by the government in the economy. So intent are economists on being able to continue making this argument that, rather than abandon it—along with the theory which underlies it—they are willing to sacrifice any hope of economics becoming a science. Thus economics is not yet a science because, to those who constitute the "establishment" within the profession, it is more important to limit the power of the state than to understand how the economic system works. The tragedy is that the political argument can readily be separated from the economic analysis—with the two both strengthened as a result.

* * *

There are two assumptions implicit in the title of this volume. One of these assumptions—that economics is not yet a science—has already been identified, and the support for that proposition will be found in the essays which follow. The other assumption is that economics, though not yet a science, could one day become one. In some ways, this is likely to be the most controversial point of all.

When, in the essays which follow, it is implied that economics should become a science, it is not scientism the authors have in mind. Scientism involves paying lip service to the forms science takes while ignoring the substance. It is reflected in the use of arcane terms for the sake of arcane terms, the use of mathematics for the sake of mathematics, and the use of laboratory or similar "controlled" experiments for their own sake—all because arcane terms, mathematical language, and "controlled" experiments are seen as the hallmark of a true science. As such, scientism is the bane of all the social sciences, including economics.

Instead, what is meant by science in the essays which follow is a body of coherent theory for which there is at least some empirical support and no considerable evidence to the contrary. Unfortunately, by this standard, economics is not yet a science—and no amount of additional mathematical proofs will make it different. It is empirical relevance rather than mathematical rigor which is presently lacking in economics. Without empirical relevance, economics cannot hope to become a science.

Of course, even after distinguishing scientism from science, some may reject the latter. In certain cases, they reject it because they are more comfortable with a settled dogma—call it a religion or an ideology—than they are with what is little more than a powerful technique for uncovering error, and thus a potential threat to any settled dogma. The only argument which can then be made for the society's supporting as a whole the activity by which a settled dogma is further refined and its message broadly disseminated, even though it is not necessarily true, is that the dogma nonetheless has a certain utilitarian value—that it represents what the anthropologists term a "useful myth." Indeed, the notion that a market economy is a self-regulating mechanism can be viewed as such a myth. This, however, is not the argument which is usually made for subsidizing, at least with public funds, the research activities of economists and for including the discipline itself within the university curriculum. The argument that is usually made on behalf of economics is instead that, like any science, it is able to contribute to the growth of socially useful knowledge. The distinction between a useful myth and useful knowledge is therefore a critical one. Those who want to argue for refining and disseminating useful myths, whatever their specific content, are of course entitled to do so; however, their claim on public funds and their place in the academy are questionable.

Still others, however, would reject the mantle of science, not because they favor dogma—quite the contrary—but rather because they prefer to see economics grouped instead among the humanities. In part, this is simply a preference for the "poetic" truth to be found in the best of literature over the intellectual sterility reflected in much of what passes for scientific work, especially in the social sciences. As such, it is simply part of the reaction to the predominant scientism in those fields. But it also, more often than not, reflects the view, as Canterbery and Burkhardt note in the essay which next follows, that the subject matter of economics just does not lend itself to scientific analysis. As such, it needs to be considered along with the similar premise—though quite different line of reasoning—of those who, while agreeing that it would be desirable if economics could meet the criteria for being classified as a science, doubt that this is possible and therefore argue for holding economics, as a "social" rather than a "physical" science, to a lower standard.[2]

The belief that economics does not lend itself to scientific analysis because it is concerned with human behavior has considerable support in the history of Western philosophy. A similar idea was reflected in the arguments of the medieval church that the "natural scientists" should confine themselves to fauna and flora, leaving to the ecclesiastical authorities all matters that touched on human beings and their chances of ultimate salvation. The Darwinian and Freudian revolutions, not to mention the Marxian, have since shown how unwise it is to attempt to analyze the behavior of human beings in isolation from their environment. Today the argument is not so much that the scientist lacks the necessary theological training to fully comprehend human behavior but rather that the tools the scientist is able to bring to the task are inadequate. This belief is based on several different arguments.

There is first the unpredictability of individual behavior. Supported by the findings of post-Freudian psychology, one might argue that the response of the individual to any given situation can never be predicted with accuracy, thereby precluding the types of tests by which the natural sciences are able to substantiate their theories. The point, though correct, is not really so devastating to the hopes of economics eventually becoming a science once it is recognized that economics, like the other social sciences, has the much more modest goal of being able to predict, and hence explain, the behavior of social groups as distinct from individuals. It is not the response of the individual that economics as a discipline needs to be able to model but rather the response of the individual as part of a larger social system and thus the economic behavior of social groups. Of course, the currently prevailing theory in eco-

---

[2] See, for example, Donald N. McClosky, "The Rhetoric of Economics," *Journal of Economic Literature*, June, 1983.

nomics, with its focus on "rational economic man" and its blindness to the importance of social organization, easily lends itself to the mistaken belief that it is the behavior of individuals that economics is supposed to be able to explain. Still, there is no reason to carry over this mistaken view of what economics is actually all about to an unwarranted pessimism about what economics can eventually become.

Even with the focus on group as distinct from individual behavior, there is the large number of factors likely to play a role in any given situation—so many, in fact, that controlled experiments become all but impossible. Citing the multiplicity of forces which influence group behavior, one can still argue that economics cannot be expected to carry out the types of tests which are the hallmark of the natural sciences. Again, the point is well taken but hardly conclusive. It is the empirical validation of theory, and not the reliance on controlled experiments, which is the hallmark of any science; and there are a number of other means, statistical and historical analysis among them, by which a theory can be empirically validated. In this respect, the standard applied to economics and the other social sciences should be that which prevails, not in physics and chemistry, but, rather, in meteorology, geology, and biology.

Then there is the dynamic, interactive nature of much that occurs in the economic sphere. Pointing to a rich body of historical evidence, it is possible to argue that economic phenomena will never be adequately explained by the types of relatively simple functional relationships economists are able to incorporate into their mathematical models. Indeed, it is possible to go even beyond this criticism to argue that the mechanistic view which permeates all of economic theory simply fails to capture the complexity of actual economic processes. This, however, is only an argument against relying on simplistic models, based on one-way cause-and-effect relationships (or even, as in the case with the neoclassical core of the prevailing theory in economics, models in which there are no causal relationships whatsoever). It is not a sufficient reason for believing that more sophisticated models cannot be developed. Here, economics and the other social sciences might profitably follow the example of biology, which, in the wake of the cybernetic revolution, has abandoned simple mechanistic models for complex ones with numerous feedback loops.

Finally there is the fact that, most troublesome of all, the particular social system which is the focus of economic analysis is not immutable but rather continues to evolve and change over time. Again drawing on a rich body of historical material, it is possible to argue that, as an outstanding example of the Heisenberg principle, the closer economists come to being able to understand how the economy actually works, the more rapid will be the rate at which the system changes, propelled by that better understanding. This insight, however, need not defeat the hope of economics one day becoming a science. It simply means that, under the best of circumstances, economics like the other social sciences is likely to be better at explaining the past than in predicting the future. It does not mean that economics need lack all explanatory power or, to the extent that the past repeats itself, that it need even lack any predictive power.

The point is that whether economics can eventually become a science should not be settled by default. Until economists accept the same restrictions as their colleagues working in meteorology, geology, and biology, among other disciplines, one cannot be sure that economics will not one day become a science. So far, the methods of science have not failed workers in other fields of inquiry; there is no reason to believe that the same techniques, if properly applied, will not succeed in economics. It is this last point, implicit in many of the essays which follow, that makes the collection as a whole more than just a pessimistic assessment of economics at the present time.

*   *   *

The essays in this volume have for the most part been written by economists themselves. The two exceptions are the essays written in whole or in part by a mathematician and a philosopher, both of whose professional interests overlap with those of economists. The essays are thus a disclaimer—and a warning—from those on the inside (albeit representing only a minority position) to those on the outside, especially anyone forced to rely on the advice of economists. The warning is that there is something so fundamentally wrong with the way economics as a discipline has evolved that what economists have to say on any given subject— when the analysis is based on the neoclassical core of conventional economic theory—is hardly to be trusted. Indeed, this statement is more than just a warning. It is a cry of outraged protest over what economics has become: Rather than providing solutions to the world's economic problems, it has become a prime source of those difficulties. Few persons outside economics will need to be convinced of this point. To many people in positions of power, both in government and in the private sector, the intellectual bankruptcy of economics at the present time is only too painfully obvious. Still, it is one thing to know experientially that something is not quite right and another thing to know intellectually *why* it is not quite right. The essays in this volume represent an effort to explain the latter.

The essays, however, also reflect the belief that, however disreputable the state to which economics has now sunk, this need not be the permanent case. The present sorry condition of economics has not arisen because the problems are necessarily insoluble or because economics as a discipline is incapable of providing the answers. It is rather that economics has evolved into something quite different from a science.

The essays which follow attempt to pinpoint where economics has gone wrong. As can be seen from the variety of arguments made, all with at least some validity, there is no single source of error—and thus no single reform which can place economics back on the right path. Still, the essays do suggest that a transformation is possible and that in this way, with all those features of present-day economics which violate the spirit and substance of scientific inquiry thoroughly expunged, answers to the world's pressing economic problems may one day be found. It is, of course, at that point that economics will have finally become a science. This is the message of hope, and of optimism, which the collection as a whole is intended to convey.

E. Ray Canterbery and
Robert J. Burkhardt

2

WHAT DO WE MEAN BY ASKING WHETHER ECONOMICS IS A SCIENCE?

The question of whether economics is a science is far more complex than one might at first believe. The answer has as much to do with our understanding of what we mean by the word "science" —how the word is applied, and perhaps what we'd like it to mean —as with comparing the "scientific results" of economics with those of "real sciences" like physics or astronomy. It is generally thought that there are two opposing camps as to whether economics is a science. On the one hand, there are those who maintain that economics is essentially a science. Economics, it is argued, meets all the defining characteristics of science, whatever those might be. In their weaker moments, adherents to this position may admit that it is perhaps more accurate to say that economics only approximates being a science. To describe it as a science merely implies a standard which economists continuously seek to realize in practice but which, at the present time, is realized in neither the whole of economics nor any part of it. Or, as the adherents to this "pro-position" might say, economics has certain basic features of a science, as physics and agronomy and biology do; yet, like these other disciplines, it is not "completely scientific" in the way it goes about generating theories and then testing them. Immaculate conceptions are, after all, historically rare.

The other identifiable party to this debate maintains that economics is not a science. Actually, if the "pro-position" stated above has been somewhat simplified and differences ignored, this simplification is even more apparent in the "con-position" described next. Those who claim that economics is *not* a science do so for a number of different reasons. One group includes those

This is part of the joint product of a grant from the National Science Foundation (Grant No. 05577-16566). Any opinions, findings, and conclusions are those of the authors and do not necessarily reflect the views of the NSF.

who were once idealists, committed to the view that economics is ideally and potentially a science. Now, however, jaded through experience, they are convinced that economics either lost the vision, didn't try, or failed miserably in the effort. Also among the economics-is-not-a-science ranks are new and different idealists. They maintain that the very nature of economics, as a *social* science, precludes it from ever being a "real science" like physics or astronomy. Typically, "cons" of the latter persuasion don't lament the plight of economics at all. Instead they praise it: damned be the day that a science of human behavior should explain, predict, or experiment. Economists should be content to "understand" human nature.

There is a seldom recognized "third" position in the debate, however—one which views the adherents of the two other camps as simply talking past each other. This third position maintains that the other two groups are both right and both wrong—though for different reasons. It depends, essentially, on whether the adherents to those two positions are talking descriptively or normatively, analytically or sociologically, historically or nonhistorically. Clearly, both camps use terms like "science," "explanation," "verification," "laws," "theories," and so forth. Yet, when we consider what philosophical commitments each group begins with, we can see that the words do not have exactly the same meanings to the two sides.

Thus, in this essay it is useful to first consider what philosophers of science mean when they say "science" and what criteria they submit for its application. Next we will consider how these views relate to the question of whether economics is a science, and, finally, we'll try to answer the question: Is it?

I

The question of whether economics is a science could not have arisen prior to the twentieth century. From ancient times through the nineteenth century, the standards according to which a body of suppositions, theories, explanations, and predictions could be judged as "adequate" might have been changing. Still, the mere organization of a body of theories in some logical fashion, aimed— accurately or not—in the direction of knowledge, sufficed to qualify it as a science. The latter term was understood to mean organized cognition. Again, a certain progress, if one calls it that, can be said to have occurred in the kinds of standards designating "good explanations," or good theories. Early criteria, such as "in accord with revealed truth" gave way to the standard "formulated according to the natural light of reason" and, later, "testable by experience." Still, the claim to be a "science" was not reserved for particular kinds of theories or subject matter. Consider the "science of witchcraft" and physiognomy, judged legitimate sciences in their times and places.

A self-conscious conception of science emerged only with the rise of the logical positivist school of philosophy in the early 1900s. This philosophical system offered not only criteria for evaluating particular theories and explanations, but also ones for evaluating whole areas of investigations as well. Depending upon the subject matter, or upon the type of explanation offered, systems of organized cognition directed toward an all-encompassing "knowledge" or "truth" were rejected, or at least told to repent their nonscientific ways. Philosophy was among the first to feel the axe; ethics later; religion, of course, had to fall; still later, sociology, anthropology, and political economy felt the pressure. The logical positivists, not to be confused with so-called "positivists" like Milton Friedman in economics, made their weight felt.

Hollis and Nell[1] neatly catalogue the major tenets of the logical positivist position. These are:

1. Claims to knowledge of the world are justified only by experience;

2. Whatever is known by experience could have been otherwise;

3. All cognitively meaningful statements are either analytic (their truthfulness determined solely by the meanings of the words) or synthetic (their truthfulness determined by facts of experience);

4. Synthetic statements, being refutable, cannot be known a priori;

5. Analytic statements have no factual content;

6. Analytic truths are true by convention;

7. A causal law is an adequately confirmed empirical hypothesis;

8. A test of a theory is the success of its predictions;

9. Judgments of value have no place in science;

[1] M. Hollis, and E. Nell, *Rational Economic Man* (Cambridge: Cambridge University Press, 1975), p. 10.

10. Sciences are distinguishable by their subject matter and not by their methodology.

A further canon must be added to these. It is that science, according to logical positivists, must necessarily *progress* if it follows the above ten commandments. Through the process of continual theory-formation and testing according to experience, "unscientific" theories will be systematically discarded while true, scientific theories and laws will be shown to be true, and accumulated.

The logical positivist had a mission, which was to unify science under these canons. It was soon realized, however, that the repeated efforts to bring diverse though legitimate areas of inquiry, such as physics and biology, and sociology and botany, under the positivist umbrella were fraught with problems. Some were internal to the project of the positivists itself; some more "external." One internal problem, which in part stemmed from the practical consequences of applying the canons, especially 1 and 7, and in part from the fact that no scientist actually does follow all of those rules, led philosopher of science Karl Popper to introduce the notion of "falsifiability" in order to save the sinking positivist ship.[2] As it turns out, this rescue mission was about as effective as throwing an anchor to a drowning sailor.

Popper argued that the insistence on empirical verification of all statements (all synthetic statements, that is) isn't realistic. It's too stringent a demand, yields certain paradoxes, and, in the final analysis, isn't the way science operates. Science is instead a moving picture of conjectures, refutations, new conjectures, and so forth, governed by the principle of falsifiability. Rather than try to prove theories true, scientists should—and do—really try to prove them false. At the very least, one should be able to imagine what it would be like for the theory in question to be false in order to retain it as a candidate for a true or workable theory. Otherwise, the theory in question is probably a piece of a priori reasoning, perhaps even a fiction. Popper retains a commitment to empirical, synthetical science, but with a major modification. We should be concerned as much with the process of scientific discovery and theory-creation as with the structure and status of the statements that we claim to be scientific.

[2] Karl Popper, *The Logic of Scientific Discovery* (London: Hutchinson, 1959), and *Conjectures and Refutations* (London: Routledge and Kegan Paul, 1963).

There is a good bit more to Popper's line of argument. He included an attempt to develop, aggressively, a logic for falsification, a normative "how-to" for systematically rejecting theories. Its major importance, however, is that it introduced a pragmatic side to the positivist project, with recognition of what we might call "sciencing"—the doing of science—and the essentially normative nature of the canons for sciencing.

The pragmatic character of much scientific research and discovery became a focal point for disputes about the nature of "real science." The positivists argued that, even with a principle of falsification supplanting that of verification, real science retains the logical structure outlined in the positivist canons. Others, especially Thomas Kuhn[3] and Imre Lakatos[4] maintained that the whole of science was process, research programs, and paradigms. Taking their clue from historical studies of science, especially the "model" science of physics, philosophers of science like Kuhn and Lakatos argue that science never actually adheres to the positivistic canons. Instead, the canons are ex post facto creations of the positivists. In fact, the historian-pragmatists contend, science is really definable not by either its content or its empirical methodology but rather by what scientists who are accepted as scientists by other scientists hold it to be. Science is whatever scientists do.

The importance of this kind of claim vis-à-vis the positivists is threefold. First, in Kuhn's view a sociological analysis is more instructive than a logical construction for understanding the nature of science. Second, both Kuhn and Lakatos, and perhaps Popper as well, maintain that the criteria for science, as opposed to fiction or philosophy or religion, are established not from "on high," but instead from within the ranks of the practicing scientists. In this sense logical positivism becomes a Trojan horse. And third, the criteria that the positivists proposed mark only one *kind* of science, not "science itself"—and a false and misleading view of that one kind of science at that. (W. V. O. Quine, a philosopher of science and logic, has persuasively argued that the analytic-synthetic distinction that stands at the foundation of empiricist science is an il-

[3] Thomas Kuhn, *The Structure of Scientific Revolutions* (Chicago: University of Chicago Press, 1970); see also M. N. Richter, *Science as a Cultural Process* (Cambridge MA: Schenkman, 1972), pp. 77-83.

[4] Imre Lakatos, and Alan Musgrave, *Criticism and the Growth of Knowledge* (Cambridge: Cambridge University Press, 1970), pp. 92-195.

legitimate distinction. Thus positivists, even committed ones in the scientific community, are operating on the basis of a fiction.)[5]

The key to Kuhn's view of science lies in his concept of the scientific paradigm. Though variously defined, a scientific paradigm is best described as an outstanding scientific achievement, one that some scientific community has acknowledged as supplying the foundation for further scientific practice. It has some of the characteristics of a world view shared by a spectrum of society, at least for the limited world of scientific research and experiment. The paradigm must be attractive enough to win in competition with other potential paradigms. At the same time, the paradigm must be sufficiently "open-ended" to leave unresolved all sorts of problems that its adherents can solve.

Paradigms thus are comprehensive and open-ended at the same time: problems generated by the paradigm remain unsolved, but the paradigm holds out the prospect of successful solutions if people simply follow the well-trodden paths of previous researchers in the community. The paradigm thus provides a certain security for those working under it, as it serves to define who, in a broader scientific context or in society at large, are like-minded and indeed "really scientists."

Sociologically, some of the marks of a paradigm are that adherents all tend to hold the same level of academic degree; all have similar kinds of education, both technical and cultural; they all read the same literature, especially journal articles, so that they can communicate with each other in a way that is relatively free of ambiguity, at least on basic terms.

In terms of the structure of science, Lakatos adds considerably to Kuhn's analysis. Lakatos sees that the paradigm, or "research program," contains two main components, the "hard core" and the "protective belt." The hard core is that portion of the paradigm that scientists have already decided is irrefutable. The protective belt is that portion that contains a degree of flexibility, as certain hypotheses are tested and rejected, others introduced, tested, and rejected. The protective belt represents the area in which Popperlian falsifiability or positivist verifiability operates. Some theories, or "explanations," never reach that point, except in periods of crisis, or what Kuhn calls a "scientific revolution." In that

[5] W. V. O. Quine, *Word and Object* (Cambridge MA: MIT Press, 1960).

unusual case, the fundamental achievement, or the fundamental world view, is challenged—and rejected. Kuhn points to the shift from Ptolemaic geocentrism to Galilean heliocentrism as a case in point.

In Kuhn's, Lakatos', and even Popper's analysis of science, a distinction must be made between a normative conception of science and a descriptive one. The positivists engaged in "persuasive definition" by using the name "science" only for those knowledge-directed organized systems that adhered to their canons, while Popper showed that the positivist criteria were both too strong and too weak—too strong as a description of science, and too weak as normative criteria. Kuhn and Lakatos augment Popper's analysis by suggesting that a "meaning of science," in either a normative or a descriptive sense, must rest upon a recognition that there are forces at work in the doing of science by scientists that make science in one respect at least an indescribable phenomenon. A particular paradigm has to be looked at, to a large extent, on its own terms to see what qualifies it to be called scientific and what does not. Normatively, we can of course maintain that all science should "look like" a particular paradigm, in terms of its structure, its assumptions, and its rules for conducting research. Even that, however, may be no more than to claim, from within a paradigm, that other paradigms are not "real science."

II

There are very few "olde-type positivists" in the philosophy of science anymore. Most philosophers of science have at least nodded in the direction of Kuhn's sociological and Lakatos' dynamic analyses. They see the canons positivists apply to "science" as values —not necessarily ethical, moral, religious, or political, but values nonetheless. They are "scientific values." The problem, when it comes to defining science, is this: are the "scientific values" of falsifiability, keeping analytic and synthetic distinctions straight, and maintaining a value-free quest for greater understanding possible?

What is interesting is that even pragmatist philosophers of science think that, to a large extent, the "values" of the positivist program are basically sound and that, within limits, it is possible to live according to them. Science, that is, can be practiced fairly well if knowledge-claims are tested against experience, say in the lab; if law-like statements are subjected to falsification-instances; and if moral values are at least kept to a minimum in the practice of theory-formation and the choice of research puzzles. Granted, a full or perfect adherence to the positive ideals would be impossible; still, they would be kept firmly in mind. The pragmatist argues that, to a large extent, adherence to these ideals has worked in the past to produce a certain movement, if not progress, in science. And, by attempting to act in accordance with these ideals, especially falsifiability, we have made even paradigm shifts, or changes in the hard core.

Economics, however, is an illuminating instance of how the values of the positivists, even as ideals and not as descriptive criteria of real science, are not always attained in disciplines that claim to be scientific. In fact, economists seem to pay only lip service to the positivist ideals, going off and doing their own thing irrespective of whatever normative criteria philosophers of science—or indeed other kinds of scientists—have found to be sound, or at least functional. In this respect, economics may be a science, but only in the bold-faced Kuhnian sense of there being a paradigm within which economists practice and according to which they self-referentially define their activity as science. Economics may thus be a pre-positivist "system of organized cognition"—much in the same way, perhaps, as Ptolemaic geocentrism.

If we look at the dominant paradigm in economics, we see, in fact, that the discipline has not progressed very far; and, despite a certain avowal of positivist values, the protective belt functions there more like a chastity belt than even Kuhn and Lakatos would consider acceptable for a practicing science.

The paradigm of orthodox economics takes its lead from Adam Smith's *Wealth of Nations*. Orthodox economists recognize that, although Smith's work is "wrong" in spots, it is nonetheless based on a great truth, the self-regulating nature of the market, which marks the book as the initial achievement in economics. Alfred Marshall's *Principles* follows in a direct evolutionary path with Paul Samuelson's *Foundations* and J. R. Hick's *Value and Capital* providing a present-day cul-de-sac. We hardly need to recapitulate the way in which the ideas reflected in Smith's invisible hand, the maximization hypothesis, the propensity of man to truck and barter, and so forth have been buttressed and tightened throughout the past two centuries. Nor do we need to note how numerous are the research puzzles and problems that have been generated at the protective belt, so that challenges to the fundamental world view have rarely if ever been taken seriously, at least by "real economists." Even the so-called "Keynesian revolution," a presumed paradigm shift, has been successfully aborted insofar as Keynes's vision has been co-opted to a large extent by the dominant neoclassical orthodoxy.[6]

Still, a look at the paradigm from a sociological perspective can show some interesting trends and can set the stage for understanding why it is that positivist values do not succeed even as ideals for the economist. One major reason is the academic prestige structure so important to economists, since academics such as Milton Friedman and Paul Samuelson are among the leading figures. The academic publish-or-perish system, the value of "pure research," and the fact that the doctoral degree is the major license to practice all justify this emphasis on academia.

The most prestigious form of publication is a quantitative theoretical article in a "number-one" journal, such as *The American Economic Review*, a journal of the American Economic Association. While workers in some academic disciplines (e.g., history, anthropology) prefer books and monographs, economists since World War II, like physicists, prefer the journal article. Journal articles are cited far more than other publications.[7] While many of those who are at the apex of the profession, including Nobel Prize winners like Milton Friedman and Paul Samuelson, have also written popular books and articles, their professional prestige derives primarily from their technical writings. Popular pieces are simply frosting on the cake. In fact, Samuelson concluded his 1961 Presidential Address before the American Economic Association by saying: "In the long run, the economic scholar works for the only coin worth having—our own applause." Later, he claimed to have meant that economists should work honestly and not for public approval.[8] Still, the need for peer recognition is something that

[6] For this story, see E. Ray Canterbery, *The Making of Economics*, 2nd ed. (Belmont CA: Wadsworth, 1980).

[7] See C. Michael Lovell, "The Production of Economic Literature: An Interpretation," *Journal of Economic Literature* 11 (March 1973): 27-55.

[8] See Leonard Silk, *The Economists* (New York: Basic Books, 1976), p. 230.

economists share with other scholars and scientists who engage in ceremonial rituals that confer status on their elite, maintain discipline, and guarantee immortality. Scientists find it difficult to bear ostracism and isolation from their colleagues, even those who live at a distance. Courage (or recklessness) is the hallmark of those who dissent from Lakatos' hard core or Kuhn's normal science.

The strict hierarchy of the economics profession is especially stark in contrast to the emphasis upon individual choice, free entry (and exit), and free competition of the price theory paradigm. Leijonhufvud has used the metaphors of the caste system and the pecking order to describe the system of relations between the subfields of economics, relations between economists and other "tribes" of academics, and ties between senior and junior economists.[9]

In the profession, there is a structure of awards. Prizes in addition to the Nobel Prize are given, including the John Bates Clark medal to the most outstanding economist under forty. The presidency of the American Economic Association (AEA) is a position that carries with it a mild measure of patronage, since the president-elect of the association heads the convention program committee in arranging the program around a central theme. This does not always bias results in favor of Ph.D.'s from his school, according to Robert Eagly, an economist who has studied these professional patterns, but it may.[10] As Eagly points out, the annual conventions of the American Economic Association are not "open conventions." In sharp contrast to the conventions of many other scientific professions, the AEA has no public call for papers and no competition among prospective authors. Who appears on the program (and who is assured publication in the highly vaunted *Papers and Proceedings* of the Association) is narrowly restricted.

The same tendency toward what Eagly calls "democratic centralism," apparently a euphemism for market concentration and control, is reflected in the journals, which are, after all, edited and refereed by established scholars following a particular mode of operation. (One usually qualifies to be a referee upon publication in the particular journal.) Moreover, the population of those publish-

[9] Axel Leijonhufvud, "Life Among the Econ," *Western Economic Journal* (1973): 327-337.

[10] Robert V. Eagly, "Contemporary Profile of Conventional Economists," *History of Political Economy* (1974): 76-91.

ing *American Economic Review* articles is more or less the same as that of the AEA convention participants.

Economics as a field has, to a great extent, been sheltered from the winds of social change. There is still a high demand for economists by government and quasi-governmental agencies, businesses, and, consequently, universities. At the same time, the hierarchical "democratic centralism" of the American Economic Association has insulated it from student revolt in relative contrast to what has happened in other academic professional societies. In the Modern Language Association, a major professional society of humanities scholars, there was a coup at the business meeting. In the American Anthropological Association, students and other members gained the right to vote and helped pass radical resolutions at business meetings although the resolutions sometimes failed to be ratified by the full membership. By contrast, at the American Economic Association meetings, those who protest are vocal but orderly.

While articles by radicals appear regularly in major anthropological journals, George Borts, the editor of the *American Economic Review* from 1969 through 1980, claims that few worthy radical articles were submitted. He noted: "I am still waiting for comments on the Radical Critique of the Council of Economic Advisors Report, an invited paper which appeared December 1975. Despite a good deal of verbal comment which I was privileged to receive, this paper has not generated any significant attention from authors."[11] In his departing Editor's Report, Borts adds a second gratuitous insult to the injury. "The radical political economists, post-Keynesians, and Marxists have their own journals. If their methodologies are fruitful, I would expect economists of all persuasions to use them."[12] All this ignores the obvious: "Radicals," including Marxists and post-Keynesians, presume that their submissions will not be acceptable to the normal science or mainstream reviewers of the "leading" journals and therefore they do not submit.

[11] "Report of the Editor, AER," *American Economic Review: Papers and Proceedings* (February 1977): 451-452. Borts repeated this claim in his final report, but added Marxist and post-Keynesian authors to those who submitted a few bad papers, all of which were rejected.

[12] "Report of the Editor, AER," *American Economic Review: Papers and Proceedings* (May 1981): p. 460.

In this sense, one needs to realize that a "radical" in economic science is any scholar unfaithful to the dominant paradigm. For those "radicals" sufficiently naive to make submissions, there is the problem of acceptance. After making clear his strong personal hand in turning down papers, Borts states his own preference for "the rational, choice theoretic aspects of whatever behavior is under investigation. This is in keeping with the type of research that is being done in the profession."[13] In general, the Establishment in economics ignores its radicals and does not take them seriously. It does not have to.

There have been a relatively small number of institutions that have granted Ph.D.'s in economics and the top universities have a marked tendency to hire their own PH.D.'s or those from other high-ranking institutions. Of the Ph.D.'s granted in economics between 1935 and 1969, the sixteen top-ranked universities accounted for more than half. The most distinguished departments (according to the widely cited 1966 Cartter study)—in rank order, Harvard, Massachusetts Institute of Technology, University of Chicago, Yale, University of California at Berkeley, Stanford, and Princeton—hire each other's graduates.[14] Furthermore, the ranking of departments is strongly dependent upon the number of articles published in the "leading" journals. Two of the leading journals are at Harvard, one is at Chicago, and *The American Economic Review* was edited by a University of Chicago Ph.D. between 1969 and 1980. The holders of doctorates from these schools also are among the majority of authors in the leading journals and among convention participants. Our updated version of this research confirms that this trend continues. Of the full-length articles in Harvard's *Quarterly Journal of Economics* in 1973 through 1978, one-third were authored by Harvard graduates. Of the full-length articles during the same period in Chicago's *Journal of Political Economy*, one-fifth were authored by the University's graduates. Although the *American Economic Review* was located at Brown University, Chicago graduates ranked first in authorship and Harvard graduates third. These data are detailed in Tables 1, 2, and 3. Almost one-half of the members of the editor-

[13] Ibid., p. 459.
[14] Allan Cartter, *An Assessment of Quality in Graduate Education* (Washington: American Council on Education, 1966).

Table 1

Ph.D. Affiliation of *QJE* Authors, 1973-1978

Ph.D. grantor	Number	Percent
Harvard	34	33.3
Stanford	11	10.8
MIT	10	9.8
Yale	8	7.8
University of Chicago	6	5.9
University of California (Berkeley)	4	3.9
Columbia	3	2.9
Princeton	3	2.9
Cambridge	2	2.0
University of Wisconsin	2	2.0
University of Rochester	2	2.0
All others (1 each)	17	16.7
Totals	102	100.0%
Affiliation unknown	(62)	

Table 2

Ph.D. Affiliation of *JPE* Authors, 1973-1978

Ph.D. grantor	Number	Percent
University of Chicago	44	20.7
MIT	22	10.3
Harvard	21	9.9
Yale	18	8.5
Columbia	10	4.7
University of California (Berkeley)	8	3.8
Johns Hopkins	7	3.3
Stanford	6	2.8
University of Wisconsin	5	2.4
Princeton	5	2.4
Oxford	4	1.9
UCLA	4	1.9
University of Pennsylvania	3	1.4
University of Michigan	3	1.4
University of London	3	1.4
All others (2 or less)	50	23.5
Totals	213	100.3%*
Affiliation unknown	(60)	

*Total greater than 100% because of rounding.

Table 3

Ph.D. Affiliation of *AER* Authors, 1973-1978

Ph.D. grantor	Number	Percent
University of Chicago	28	14.0
MIT	21	10.7
Harvard	14	7.1
Stanford	12	6.1
Yale	12	6.1
Columbia	11	6.1
University of California (Berkeley)	10	5.1
Princeton	8	4.1
University of Pennsylvania	6	3.1
North Carolina State	6	3.1
University of Wisconsin	5	2.6
Johns Hopkins	5	2.6
Brown	5	2.6
University of Rochester	4	2.0
University of London	4	2.0
New School for Social Research	4	2.0
University of Virginia	3	1.5
UCLA	3	1.5
Purdue	3	1.5
Southern Illinois	3	1.5
All others (1 article each)	29	14.8
Totals	196	100.3%*
Affiliation unknown	(52)	

*Total greater than 100% because of rounding.

ial board of the *AER* during these years were from three schools, in rank order Chicago, MIT, and Harvard. About 70 percent of the board members were from Cartter's seven distinguished departments, and some 57 percent of the members of the nominating committees (for officers of the association). Is it any wonder that the departments are "distinguished"? Thus the "best" departments are those who publish in their own journals, which are "best" since they publish the "best" departments. This academic incest would be considered genetically unsound if it involved biological reproduction.

To be fair, our school publication data should be adjusted by

Table 4

Publication Shares Relative to Ph.D. Population Shares

	"Merit" ratio by leading journal*		
Ph.D. grantor	AER (Brown)	JPE (Chicago)	QJE (Harvard)
MIT	7.0 (1)	6.8 (1)	6.4 (2)
Stanford	4.0 (2)	1.8 (4)	7.1 (1)
Yale	3.6 (3)	5.0 (2)	4.6 (3)
University of Chicago	3.3 (4)	4.7 (3)	1.4 (6)
Princeton	2.2 (5)	1.2 (6)	1.6 (5)
University of California (Berkeley)	1.0 (6)	0.7 (7)	0.2 (8)
Columbia	0.8 (7)	0.6 (8)	0.4 (7)
University of Pennsylvania	0.8 (8)	0.4 (9)	0.0 (10)
Harvard	0.7 (9)	1.4 (5)	3.2 (4)
University of Wisconsin	0.3 (10)	0.3 (10)	0.2 (9)

*The share or percentage of authors of a particular Ph.D. affiliation divided by the share or percentage of total U.S. economics Ph.D. output (1920-1961) by the same institution.

the number of economic graduates from the schools in question to provide a "merit" ratio. Once adjusted for the number of graduates, Chicago's ranking drops from 1 to 3 in its own journal and Harvard drops from 1 to 4 in its journal (see Table 4). Chicago is fourth in the *AER*; Harvard drops to ninth. If the percentage of authors equaled the percentage of Ph.D. output for a particular department, publication frequency would be based upon population only. However, Wisconsin, which has produced nearly twice the share of graduates as Chicago, has very low ratios in these leading journals. A similar pattern applies to Columbia University. Does this mean that the Chicago graduate is 16 times as brilliant as Wisconsin's and 8 times as ingenious as Columbia's? If a common standard for acceptance of papers applies, one also wonders why the representation of a department is unequal across journals.

It is difficult to know what to make of all this. One thing is clear—if we apply neoclassical price theory. Fees are required upon the submission of papers to the *AER* and the *JPE*. Moreover, the *AER* is the organization journal for the profession and is purchased by all members. Yet, in the period studied, 54, 58, and 74 percent of the authors in the *AER*, *JPE*, and *QJE* respectively were graduates of Cartter's seven "distinguished" departments. All three journals drew from the same population. It is economically inefficient to print three separate journals for the output of only seven academic departments and unfair to the masses who pay submission fees in competition for the remaining minority space and thus subsidize the handful of departments. Finally, the membership of the AEA is subsidizing a Board of Editors drawn almost exclusively from the same seven sisters.

The "truth," therefore, resides in seven academic departments whose membership constitutes a small share of the registry of all economists. This small number of individuals dominates the "leading" journals, publications financially supported by the admiring apostles of economics who genuflect when encountering a "leading" author but otherwise ignore the journals' contents. Journals are to be published in by the few and subscribed to by the many. Were it not for the need for subscribers one might conclude that most economists are superfluous.

This picture of a pro-business-competition profession which itself behaves oligopolistically is softened somewhat by the realization that, while the different universities work in similar ways, their theoretical approaches and policy conclusions are not identical. While different universities are characterized by different approaches (e.g., the University of Chicago representing the "monetarist" approach), economists *do* read and do battle in the journals. Nonetheless, in studies of journal citations, certain tendencies towards parochialism can be noted. The faculty of a particular university department is cited more by those who were students there than by outsiders, again a practice common to other disciplines. Ideological and theoretical preferences are passed on from the professors to the students. While the difference in favorable and unfavorable citations of outside authorities is not great when all universities are considered, the doctoral students of certain schools have greater antagonisms than do others. For instance, Chicago students are more unfavorable to Harvard than others, and some holders of MIT doctorates are similarly antagonistic to Chicago faculty. All in all, the studies show that, while British and American economics are marked by a common basis, there is also considerable parochialism.[15] Often economists end up talking mainly to each other and not to the world.

[15] See Eagly, op cit. Also see G. Stigler and C. Friedland, "The Citation Practices of Doctorates in Economics," *Journal of Political Economy* (June 1975):

The sociology of the profession explains in large part why, at the level of theory or hypothesis testing, the positivist program simply does not exist, even as a "value." The tendency is to continue to support theories that themselves support the paradigm, without even attempting, or at least rarely attempting, to falsify the results of a hypothesis testing a theory. In an examination of 542 full-length "empirical" articles in the major orthodox economics journals from 1973 to 1978,[16] we found that only three articles actually attempted to falsify the hypothesis proposed; since the hypotheses were (necessarily) in accordance with the fundamental presuppositions of the orthodoxy, it at least appears that there is little, if any, serious concern for challenging fundamental presuppositions.

More interesting than the fact that hypotheses in these cases were nearly always accepted is the kinds of hypotheses that were accepted. Nearly all tended to support, in relatively uncontroversial fashion, the paradigm's major tenets, the "hard core" in Lakatos' term. A complete summary of these would be beyond our scope, but a sample appears in the attached appendix.[17]

We will allow these hypotheses to speak for themselves except to focus on one illuminating subfield of the paradigm. Approximately one out of every five articles appearing in the *American Economic Review* and the *Journal of Political Economy* combined was in one specialty, human capital, which falls within the rubric of the choice-theoretic nexus of economics. The premises of the human capital school—quite distinct from those of Wisconsin's human resources school, which studies similar phenomena—are consistent with the general defense of free markets. Gary Becker's hypotheses from "The Theory of Marriage: Part 1" (see Appendix, *Journal of Political Economy*) will suffice to illustrate the point. His first hypothesis is that the gain of men and women from marrying compared to remaining single is shown to depend positively on

---

477-480. Stigler is a Professor of Economics at the University of Chicago. For comparison with anthropology, see Beverly McElliott Hurlburt, "Status and Exchange in the Profession of Anthropologist," *American Anthropologist* (February 1976): 272-285.

[16] From E. Ray Canterbery and R. J. Burkhardt, "Economics: The Embarrassed Science," National Science Foundation EVIST Research Report, 1979. Appendix 10A.

[17] Ibid., Appendix 10D.

their incomes, human capital, and relative difference in wage rates. His second hypothesis is that men differing in physical capital, education or intelligence (aside from their effect on wage rate), height, race, or many other traits will tend to marry women with like measured values of these traits. The third hypothesis is that correlation between males for wage rates or for traits of men and women that are close substitutes in household production will tend to be negative. In short, the research constitutes an exercise in economic optimization within the household.

In this and the following examples, what is purportedly being tested is not ideally being assessed. First, the behavioral assumptions are taken on faith. Second, the hypotheses—that could be formulated from quite different assumptions—are presumed rather to derive directly from those behavioral characteristics taken on faith. Third, the empirical trackings claimed to support the hypotheses (and—it is falsely presumed—the behavioral assumptions) are not inconsistent with the affirmation of the hypotheses but neither are they in conflict with any number of other quite distinct behavioral assumption sets. In other words the human capital pioneers are nominally operating in the protective belt but they accept the assumptions of the core, fail to test those assumptions, and therefore both protect and extend the core.

Another specific application is Isaac Ehrlich's "The Deterrent Effect of Capital Punishment: A Question of Life and Death" in the *American Economic Review*, in which he affirms the hypothesis that capital punishment does have a deterrent effect on crime. This finding apparently was considered so remarkable that essentially the same article was also published in the *Journal of Political Economy*. Ehrlich extended his earlier study by concluding that punishment *in general* and capital punishment in particular have a restraining effect on murders.

Still another example is Ray C. Fair's racy "A Theory of Extramarital Affairs." Professor Fair develops a model that, he claims, explains the allocation of an individual's time among work and two types of leisure activity: time spent with spouse, and time spent with a paramour. In the event the reader supposes that the human capital theorist might run out of fields to invade, one more example suffices to show that no issue is sacred, including the sacred. Corcy Azzi and Ronald Ehrenbery write about "Household Allocation of Time and Church Attendance" in the *Journal of*

Political Economy. Their hypothesis? Religiosity, the individual's religious commitment and participation in church-related activities, can be explained by a multi-period utility maximization model of household allocation of time that includes implications about the division of participation between husband and wife in the shape of the household's life-cycle religious participation profile. In all cases the hypotheses were accepted.

Situations like this suggest that the "empiricist" nature of science, which the positivists proposed, breaks down when it comes to "real testing." But further, to reflect on the positivist ideal, economists continue to maintain that they "know" the results of even "rigged" testing, or partial verification without any attempts at falsification. What is more, the maximization hypothesis that sets the tone and content for much of the work that appears in journals is simply accepted as an empirical fact, thereby violating the positivist notion that definitions, i.e., analytic truths, have no factual content. And, "supply and demand" is continually invoked as an explanation, although extensive qualifying clauses and ceteris paribus assumptions once again discredit its "empirical" nature.

One feature of orthodox economics that is positivist in its appearance is the statement that analytic truths are true by convention, that is, by agreement among practitioners in the science. If indeed positivism were accepted as a normative conception of science, such analytic truths as the maximization hypothesis, rational economic man, supply and demand, and diminishing returns would perhaps be self-consciously embraced as values, and for certain political, moral, methodological, or other reasons. Friedman, at least has suggested a pragmatic value in accepting these constructs on faith—they generate predictions.[18] However, even failing predictions—as indeed many are—do not lead to a rejection of these and of conventional truths in favor of *more* pragmatic ones. One can only believe that they are accepted for other than purely practical or "scientific" reasons. And surely our analysis of the sociology of the profession bears this out.

III

We began by asking what we have to mean by a "science" to say whether or not economics is one. We can now restate that question

[18] Friedman, *An Essay on Positive Economics* (Chicago: University of Chicago Press, 1953).

by asking, What do we have to say of economics to say whether or not economics is a science? That is, Is economics really a science under any of the descriptive or normative definitions of science from philosophers of science?

The essence of science is, according to the "pro" camp or the economists who claim that economics *is* a science, definable by the positivist vision. This vista is a normative prescription, what good science *should* be. According to the logical positivists, science is empirical, testable, synthetic, value-free; and science is defined by having a certain kind of logical relational structure, with determinate content. Definitions are regarded as either practical, operational ones or simply stipulations on how certain terms are to be understood. Above all, however, once hypotheses or theories emerge, they are subject to falsification, whether they challenge old theories or not or whether, in being tested, a "basic theory" is rejected. Economists faithful to their own prescription, therefore, will be open to the potential falsifiability of even cherished hypotheses like the maximization hypothesis, and the laws of supply and demand.

Those "cons" who maintain that economics is a science in principle but not in practice ally themselves with those wavering "pros" who maintain that we are not there *yet*, despite our following the ten commandments of logical positivism. The "cons" are more impatient and lament the fact that even after two centuries—that include higher mathematics—"yet" hasn't arrived. It all seems futile to these "cons."

The less sympathetic "cons" will maintain that, as practicing economists, all they are doing is "social philosophizing," spinning theories as ideologies or, perhaps, as "moral fictions." Others, outside the profession, might be less charitable: Economists are not doing science, but simply giving the illusion that they are knowledge-directed or organized in their cognition. Indeed, the issues of the predictability of human behavior versus free will, or of social control versus a more "naturalist" view of social life, might implicate any social science that pretends to be a science as radically misconceiving itself and human beings.

The Kuhnian view describes science as its own history without giving any explicit advice as to how the history should have proceeded. If Kuhn is right, the claims of all the pros and cons are right on their own terms, but still mistaken. If we define "science" normatively, we answer the question of whether economics is a science before we formulate it. Human activities are not identifiable before the fact as of one kind or another. We should look at what counts as science, both for scientists and for everyone else. In this regard whatever economists do is science, unless they claim to be doing something else.

Is economics a science? Economists do not in practice follow their own normative commandments for science and thus economics is not a science in terms of their own criteria. However, economics has a paradigm and devout practitioners, so that economics is a science in a Kuhnian sense of having a single overarching paradigm to which most practitioners in the field subscribe. But so what?

IV

There is a critical problem that Kuhn's analysis encounters, that of the notion of the progress of science. As we noted, the ideal science discards false theories, accumulates more information, generates new explanations and so forth. Above this, the current science or present paradigm must be in some sense "better" than the previous science. Kuhn's analysis extends the notion of progress somewhat, to focus upon the question of "progress through paradigms."

Clearly, in one respect, there is progress *within* a paradigm. Researchers develop "new frontiers" within the context of shared basic assumptions. New puzzles are generated from old, and solved; more theories and hypotheses are advanced. For economics, it is clear that the Smithian–Marshallian paradigm has generated more and more data, explanation, predictions, mathematical formulas, puzzles, and solutions. Within the orthodoxy, within the neoclassical paradigm, there has been "progress."

Kuhn's point, however, is that the idea of scientific progress, from paradigm to paradigm, makes little sense. If the orthodoxy defines scientific progress, only in-house or inside-paradigm changes constitute scientific advances. Perhaps all we can say is that there has been a certain amount of "progress away" from some assumptions or world views. However, if those who judge prior paradigms do so with the criteria of their own, the contest is rigged. This is an even greater problem when evaluating the tenets of a potential new paradigm. For example, if an orthodox neoclassical is the judge for the "scientific nature" of a post-Keynesian paradigm, it will always fall short of "scientific standards"—unless the neo-classical is able to step outside his or her own paradigm and apply criteria that are independent of the orthodoxy (see, e.g., the criteria of Eichner, this volume). Paradigms can only define truth *within them*, as they define the limits of acceptable discourse, acceptable practice. The rank-ordering of paradigms requires an Olympian vista.

In the final analysis, all we can say is that, at present, orthodox economics is the dominant paradigm. Clearly, there are challenges and questions, both from within and from without. Perhaps it is the specter of a "new paradigm" which even allows the question to be raised as to whether economics is a science, and what that must mean. Since science is paradigm and paradigm is the science, however, one can only maintain that present challenges to the dominance of orthodox economics are only attempts to show that there are problems—some within and some social—which those trained within the community find insoluable. If a scientific revolution is at hand, though, it is not because theirs is not a scientific paradigm. Rather, it is because it is not *our* paradigm. We hope ours is more reliable. We hope ours meets criteria bigger than any singular paradigm. Even so, the orthodoxy will not enter the railway carriage until the unmistakable scent of revolution is in the air or else they arrive at the station in their coffins. The shift in paradigms only once in each generation is not due to mere chance.

APPENDIX

Sample from hypotheses empirically tested in leading general journals of economics, 1973-1978*

American Economic Review
December 1973, Vol. 63, No. 5
   Welch, Finis, "Black-White Difference in Returns to Schooling," pp. 893-907.

*Journals studied are *American Economic Review, Journal of Political Economy, The Economic Journal,* and *The Quarterly Journal of Economics.* The hypotheses presented constitute a non-random sample from the 340 empirical articles in these journals for the 1973-78 period. All hypotheses are available at cost from the authors.

Ho$_1$: Much of the gain associated with observed rise in the relative earnings of blacks in the United States is associated with tightening labor markets.

Ho$_2$: Part of this gain results from a coverage of completion levels.

Ho$_3$: The quality of schooling is an important variable.

Conclusion: Ho's [hypotheses] accepted.

March 1975, Vol. 65, No. 1

Gramm, Wendy Lee, "Household Utility Maximization and the Working Wife," pp. 90-100.

Ho$_1$: The marginal product of women's time in producing home goods is largest for households with young children.

Ho$_2$: The presence of the first child seems to be very important in explaining labor supply decisions of the wife. The second child does not seem to have a large effect on the wife's labor supply decision.

Ho$_3$: The age of the household is a factor affecting the labor supply decisions of the married female in this sample and this factor is distinct from the effect of the various ages of her children.

Conclusion: Ho's accepted.

June 1975, Vol. 65, No. 3

Ehrlich, Isaac, "The Deterrent Effect of Capital Punishment: A Question of Life and Death," pp. 397-417.

Ho: Capital punishment does have a deterrent effect on crime.

Conclusion: Ho accepted.

June 1976, Vol. 66, No. 3

Shishko, Robert, and Bernard Rostker, "The Economics of Multiple Job Holding," pp. 298-308.

Ho$_1$: The supply of moonlighting labor increases with the moonlighting wage rate and falls with primary job earnings.

Ho$_2$: Family size (a proxy for consumption) is significant and positively related to moonlighting hours. Furthermore, as is consistent with the life-cycle consumption hypothesis, age, which can be considered an inverse proxy for unmet family needs, shows a significant negative relationship to moonlighting hours.

Conclusion: Ho's accepted.

Frank, Robert H., "Why Women Earn Less: The Theory and Estimation of Differentials Overqualification," pp. 360-373.

Ho: The earnings differential between male and female can be attributed to a supply-side phenomenon, the overqualification differential, which measures the average fraction by which wives' earnings are reduced purely as a result of having followed their husband to a particular geographic location.

Conclusion: Ho accepted.

Journal of Political Economy
January/February 1973, Vol. 81, No. 1
Taubman, Paul J. and Terence J. Wales, "Higher Education, Mental Ability and Screening," pp. 28-55.

    Ho: Education adds to income by screening people with low education out of high-paying occupations.

Conclusion: Ho accepted.

Part 1, March/April 1973, Vol. 81, No. 2
Feldstein, Martin, "The Welfare Loss of Excess Health Insurance," pp. 251-279.

    Ho: American families are in general overinsured against health expenses. If insurance coverage were reduced, the utility loss from increased risk would be more than outweighed by the gain due to lower cost and the reduced purchase of excess care.

Conclusion: Ho accepted.

July/August 1973, Vol. 81, No. 4
Becker, Gary S., "The Theory of Marriage: Part 1," pp. 813-846.

    Ho_1: The gain to a man and woman from marrying compared to remaining single is shown to depend positively on their incomes, human capital, and relative difference in wage rates.

    Ho_2: Men differing in physical capital, education or intelligence (aside from their effect on wage rates), height, race, or many other traits will tend to marry women with like measured values of these traits.

    Ho_3: The correlation between males for wage rates or for traits of men and women that are close substitutes in household production will tend to be negative.

Conclusion: Ho's accepted.

August 1975, Vol. 83, No. 4
Peltzman, Sam, "The Effect of Automobile Safety Regulation," pp. 677-725.

    Ho: Safety regulation has no effect on the highway death toll and may have increased the share of this toll borne by pedestrians and increased the total number of accidents.

Conclusion: Ho accepted.

December 1977, Vol. 85, No. 6

Gronau, Reuben, "Leisure, Home Production and Work—The Theory of the Allocation of Time Revisited," pp. 1099-1123.

Ho: An increase in the market wage rate is expected to reduce work at home, while its effect on leisure and work in the market is indeterminate. An increase in income increases leisure, reduces work in the market, and leaves work at home unchanged.

Conclusion: Ho accepted.

Smith, Vernon, "The Principle of Unanimity and Voluntary Consent in Social Choice," pp. 1125-1139.

Ho: The existence of significant direct (and indirect) opportunity cost of thinking, calculating, and signaling makes strategizing in social choice uneconomical. Competitive behavior in such cases is a rational response.

Conclusion: Ho accepted.

Becker, Gary, Elizabeth M. Landes, and Robert T. Michael, "An Economic Analysis of Marital Instability," pp. 1141-1187.

Ho: Marital dissolution can be analyzed using a utility maximizing framework which incorporates uncertainty about the outcome of marital decisions.

Conclusion: Ho accepted.

The Economic Journal

September 1976, Vol. 86, No. 343

Hart, P. E., "The Dynamics of Earnings, 1963-73," pp. 551-565.

Ho: With cohort data, there is evidence that the inequality of earnings before taxes increased, but increases in inequality were usually accompanied by a clear tendency for the earnings of the poorer paid to increase proportionally more on the average than the earnings of the better paid.

Conclusion: Ho accepted.

QJE

February 1974, Vol. 78, No. 1

Straszheim, Mahlon R., "Housing Market Discrimination and Black Housing Consumption," pp. 17-43.

Ho: Racial discrimination in housing markets can be explained in terms of Blacks' responses to higher prices and to supply rationing arising from the existence of entry barriers to white submarkets.

Conclusion: Ho accepted.

May 1974, Vol. 88, No. 2

Darby, Michael P., "The Permanent Income Theory of Consumption: A Restatement," pp. 229-250.

Ho_1: The econometric techniques previously used to estimate the weight of current income in the determination of permanent income have suffered from severe upward bias.

Ho_2: The permanent income model can be formulated in terms of a simple perpetual inventory of an all-inclusive concept of wealth.

Conclusion: Ho's accepted.

February 1977, Vol. 91, No. 1

Beebe, Jack H., "Institutional Structure and Program Choice in Television Markets," pp. 15-37.

Ho: Steiner's suggestions that under limited channels monopoly will provide a more diverse program mix, greater consumer surplus, and greater total surplus than will competition depend critically on his strict viewer preferences assumption.

Conclusion: Ho accepted.

James A. Swaney and
Robert Premus

3

MODERN EMPIRICISM AND QUANTUM-LEAP THEORIZING IN ECONOMICS

I. Introduction

The literature on economic methodology has revolved around logical positivism, addressing its application to economic inquiry, its policy relevance, its implicit functions and goals, and its weaknesses. The literature has primarily focused on the logical structure of theory and the ideal approach to economic inquiry, with orthodoxy emphasizing logical positivism and heterodoxy emphasizing inductive development of theory.[1] These foci on how economists ought to behave, while important, have been to the neglect of how economists actually behave.[2] In other words, the economic methodology literature has been preoccupied with theoretical discussion of the appropriateness of methodological models with insufficient discussion of the actual processes used by economists to construct theories.

This preoccupation has been partially remedied by Benjamin Ward's *What's Wrong with Economics* (35) and Wilber and Harrison's "The Methodological Basis of Institutional Economics: Pat-

Reprinted from the *Journal of Economic Issues*, Vol. 16, No. 3, September 1982, pp. 713-730, by special permission of the copyright holder, The Association for Evolutionary Economics.

The opinions expressed in this paper do not necessarily represent the opinions of Wright State University or the Joint Economic Committee, U.S. Congress, the institutions with which the authors are connected respectively.

The authors would like to thank Marc R. Tool and J. Ron Stanfield for many helpful suggestions on a previous version.

[1] For the long-running debate on how economists should pursue knowledge, see Boland (1), Friedman (8), Rotwein (27), Machlup (21), Hill (14), Margenau (23), and Northrup (25).

[2] The "positive-normative" connotation is borrowed from Ward (35, p. 190).

tern Model, Storytelling, and Holism" (36). Ward argues that the primary activity in all social science is storytelling, that formalism has failed, and that open recognition of these facts would facilitate progress in economic science. Wilber and Harrison argue that both institutionalists and orthodox economists engage primarily in storytelling, respectively using the "pattern model form" and what might descriptively be termed the "incognito form." They agree with Ward that formalism has failed, yet they conclude: "The formal models of standard economics have their use, even by institutionalists, for certain types of problems" (36, p. 85). Formalism is more appropriate than the pattern model "when one or two factors or laws determine what is to be explained and when these factors or laws are better known and understood than the specific instance" (36, p. 85). Apparently, formalism's general failure in economics (as a science, but not as a storyteller) is the result of attempts to apply logical positivism where it cannot work.

While social and natural sciences differ in important respects, and while these differences severely limit the appropriateness of natural science methodology for the social science,[3] there is more to the story. We argue that logical positivism's failure is also due to economists' failure to actually follow the methodology of logical positivism where it *is* appropriate.[4]

Economic theories often resemble, in their logical structure, theories in the natural sciences, but the process economists use to construct their theories is peculiar to the discipline. While the underlying causes of this peculiarity are many, the primary outcome is ineffective or counterproductive policy.[5] Unlike other sciences, economics—primarily but not exclusively neoclassical economics —places excessive emphasis on the development of fully formu-

---

[3] In addition to the works previously noted the reader is referred to the cogent review of many authors and the original presentation of differences between natural and social science contained in T. W. Hutchison's *Knowledge and Ignorance in Economics* (16), particularly chapters two and three.

[4] We intentionally skirt, in addition to discussion of the differences between natural science and social science, the issue of how, other than through trial and error, the areas appropriate for logical positivism are to be identified. By focusing on the problem of how logical positivist methodology is (not) applied in economics, we also intentionally avoid discussion of the appropriate (and inappropriate) uses of various forms of storytelling. Our purpose is only to address the process of (would-be) logical positivism in economics.

[5] See the discussion of these causes in Section III.

lated theoretical systems without sufficient empirical grounding of behavioral assumptions and antecedent conditions: Economists "are virtually the only would-be scientists who are content to use stale, second-hand data collected chiefly by government agencies for other purposes" (32, p. 241).[6] Thus, most of the problems encountered in identifying empirical relationships, which later become necessary in the process of theory testing and policy formation, are ignored. Often developed with only a judicious use of mathematics, economic theory consequently lacks empirical import and policy usefulness in comparison to theory in the natural sciences.

We begin our analysis with a brief discussion of progress in natural sciences (Section II), employing Thomas S. Kuhn's model of scientific progress, followed by discussion of the process of theory construction in natural sciences (Section III). This process involves conscious interaction between realism and abstraction when one is systematically progressing from lower to higher order theoretical formulations within normal sciences. In Section IV, the application of methodological principles in economics is discussed. Two representative case studies suggest that the process of abstracting in economics can best be described as a "quantum leap" from the factual domain to the theoretical domain rather than as a systematic departure from reality as frequently occurs in the natural sciences. A major conclusion of the paper—presented in Section V—is that the efficiency of the logical positivistic methodology, in terms of generating valid abstract models with substantive policy content, would be greatly enhanced if economists would place more initial emphasis on establishing empirical relationships among variables within a framework that incorporated institutional barriers, changes in technology, and individual and social norms and goals.

II. Progress in the natural sciences

The methodology of the natural sciences is diverse and philosophers of science disagree over how scientific progress occurs.[7] The

---

[6] Implicit in this statement is the assumption that logical positivism's appropriate (but not necessarily exclusive) role in economics is in developing theory for policy purposes.

[7] For the literature in this debate, see Lakatos and Musgrave (18), Popper (26), and Kuhn (17).

processes of scientific progress will continue to be debated, but for the purposes of this paper Thomas Kuhn's distinction between normal and abnormal science will suffice.[8] Normal science, where most science is conducted, consists of progress by accretion. Inquiry is directed toward finding the missing pieces of the paradigm-defined puzzle. In the terminology of logical positivism as enunciated by Carl Hempel and Paul Oppenheim (13), the "General Laws" of the science, when applied logically to the "Antecedent Conditions," allow one to deduce accurate descriptions (as ex post explanations or ex ante predictions) of relevant empirical phenomena. The paradigm, then, consists of the General Laws which, in combination with alternative Antecedent Conditions, define the realm of inquiry.

When logical deduction yields a prediction which is repeatedly refuted by empirical testing, a seed which may eventually produce scientific revolution has sprouted. If this violation of paradigm-induced expectation, or anomaly, inhibits important practical applications or clearly calls into question explicit and fundamental generalizations of the paradigm (17, p. 82), a crisis, or abnormal science, will ensue. Alternative paradigm-aspirants will compete. If one of these world views eventually supplants the paradigm from which the anomaly arose, scientific revolution has occurred.

In pre-paradigm or immature science, there is no generally accepted paradigm and therefore no potential for revolution. But there is also nothing to direct inquiry. "Early fact-gathering is a far more nearly random activity than the one that subsequent scientific development makes familiar (and) is usually restricted to the wealth of data that lie ready to hand" (17, p. 15). Hence, immature science is characterized by an absence, if not of General Laws themselves, of the links which connect and organize these General Laws into a coherent view of the subset of reality under scrutiny. Logical positivism, then, does not apply to an immature science because the embryonic condition of the Explanans (General Laws in combination with Antecedent Conditions) renders logical deduction of Explanandum (hypothesis) impossible. Thus, nor-

---

[8] The choice of Kuhn (17) for a typology of scientific progress is twofold: First, Kuhn's conception is familiar to most economists; second, we believe Kuhn's original schema as employed in the following discussion could be replaced with his more recent concept of disciplinary matrices or with the schema of Popper or Lakatos without altering our analysis.

mal science is assumed in the following discussion because logical positivism does not apply to pre-paradigm or abnormal science.

III. The process of theory construction in natural sciences

Theoretical systems are developed in an attempt to understand and explain for the purposes of predicting and controlling the environment. In normal science, theory construction usually proceeds in stages from lower order (descriptive) concepts to higher order (theoretical) concepts, within the boundaries of perception, problem definition, and unquestioned general laws given by the discipline's extant paradigm. Potentially available data are prescreened by the view of reality implicit in the paradigm, but the remaining quantity of conceivably relevant data is nevertheless immense due to the complexity of reality. Even the normal scientist is confronted with a paradoxical demand for simplicity and realism. His or her first challenge is to organize the relevant but raw descriptive (or protocol) data, which consist of the complexity of observations of reality organized only by the world view of the paradigm, into the "common and crucial elements" relevant to the problem at hand. Thus, certain facts associated with the phenomenon being analyzed will be discarded in the abstracting process used to organize the protocol data.

The abstracting process proceeds in an orderly manner if the scientist is cognizant of the facts which he is eliminating. In particular, it is an orderly and systematic process when the interactive effects between the common and crucial elements and those considered peripheral to the problem at hand are known. The retention of certain elements and rejection of others involve judgments which are necessarily shaped by the basic tenets of the ruling paradigm. By defining and redefining the realm of common and crucial elements, the scientist eventually reaches a level of theory development wherein protocol data are organized. From these delimited, organized protocol data the scientist develops (abstracts) the constructs upon which higher level theory is based.

Empirical terms and relationships constructed during the first step of theory development serve as a foundation for higher level theory development. As this development proceeds, the theory is tested on a related set of protocol data where the hypotheses are expected to apply. Hence, tentative identification of common and crucial elements both *allows* and *commands* inclusion of additional protocol data. If those elements that were previously cast aside are in fact insignificant, the inclusion of a broader range of phenomena will not sacrifice theoretical accuracy, and the theory will be shown to be more general and inclusive. However, if a mistake has been made—if significant elements have been cast aside —attempts to apply the theory to a broader range of phenomena will fail, and the scientist will retreat to a lower theoretical level to reexamine the set of common and crucial elements. If this reexamination is successful, theoretical development can once again progress to a higher level and encompass previously peripheral phenomena. Hence the generality of high theory is achieved by gradually building from new data of a specific phenomenon toward an increasingly general and inclusive set of hypotheses.

Furthermore, the "incessant give and take" (30, p. 45) between fact and theory which is involved in this process produces higher level theory which is simpler as well as more inclusive, because peripheral elements have been discarded. While simpler, the constructs of higher level theory will in one sense be less "realistic." That is, in the process of developing theoretical terms and hypotheses which are more inclusive (explain more of reality), the detail of empirical reality is sacrificed. Thus, higher level theoretical concepts begin to take on the appearance of purely mental constructs. However, so long as the "incessant give and take" continues, the pitfall of losing contact with reality by overgeneralizing will be avoided.

The link between theoretical constructs and realism is found in the organization of the original protocol data which initiate the process of identification of the common and crucial elements of the phenomenon under investigation. It is from the original protocol data that the "bridge principles" (12, pp. 74-75), or rules of measurement necessary for applying the theoretical constructs, are derived. Of course, the more a posteriori knowledge that the theoretician possesses about the phenomenon that he or she is attempting to explain (i.e., the more delimited the original protocol data or the broader the historical experience[9] of the researcher), the less difficulty he or she will have in establishing bridging devices between the logical consequences of higher level theory and ac-

---

[9] This term, taken from Schumpeter, is explained in the following section.

tual circumstances. Such knowledge generally increases over time since remaining problems become narrower and more precisely defined as the paradigm matures.

Normally, not all the theoretical constructs are capable of being applied directly. Some are merely verbalizations of the original cognitive act or "vision" (30, p. 41) while others represent linkages with the extant paradigm. However, according to the philosophy of modern empiricism, this presents no problem in science as long as the constructs' meanings within the context of the theory are antecedently understood. This distinguishes modern empiricism from the ultra-empiricist position, which maintains that all concepts in science must be "operationally defined."[10]

IV. Economic methodology in process

The methodology of logical positivism is capable of contributing to effective public policy formation. As pointed out in the introduction, this statement should not be construed to mean that logical positivism is the sole appropriate approach to economic problems. Our point is that the apparent failure of logical positivism in economics is not solely the fault of the methodology; also, it is the fault of economists who label their work "produced by the process of logical positivism" when they in fact subvert the process by shortcutting.

Were it not for the fact that a good economic theory does not improve with age, an analogy with wine making would be appropriate. While the good winegrower will spend years learning the skills of cultivation and wine making, the "do-it-yourselfer" will purchase everything needed to make wine in the kitchen in a matter of weeks. Similar shortcutting which occurs in economics we call "quantum-leap theorizing." Much as the "do-it-yourself" wine maker puts trust in the local grocer, the economist puts trust in bad data, usually from the government. While the kitchen wine maker may or may not recognize as unhealthy the yeast energizer used to speed fermentation, the economist, often knowingly, overlooks poisonous data inaccuracies (24). The driving motive

---

[10] See Rudner (28), Hempel (12), and Scheffler (29) for cogent discussions of the modern empiricists' justification of the use of nonoperational concepts in scientific analysis and for discussions of the ultra-empirical position on this matter.

and results of the kitchen logical positivist are also similar to the kitchen wine maker: expedient production at the expense of quality.

While not generally considered to be in the school of logical positivism, John Dewey's methodological approach more nearly approximates natural science logical positivism than does the kitchen variety. Dewey argued that, to be appropriate, ends are never given but are subject to modification as analysis proceeds; hence, "ends-in-view" (34, p. 283). "[T]he only situation in which knowing is fully stimulated is one in which the end is developed in the process of inquiry and testing" (6, p. 146). Modern empiricism confirms this position during the initial stages of theory development with its insistence on empirical selection of the common and crucial elements and the recurrent building of bridges of correspondence between raw protocol data and the conceptual systematization thereof. Dewey's correct contention was that scientific analysis required a "conjugate correspondence" between "factual and conceptual subject matter" (5, p. 491). In the language of modern empiricism, bridges must be built between empirical elements and theoretical concepts in the scientific process. In Dewey's language,

> [I]f there is one lesson more than any other taught by the methods of the physical sciences, it is the strict correlativity of fact and ideas. Until social inquiry succeeds in establishing methods of observing, discriminating and arranging data that evoke and test correlated ideas, and until, on the other side, ideas formed and used are (1) employed as *hypotheses*, and are (2) of a form to direct and prescribe operations of analytic-synthetic determination of facts, social inquiry has no chance of satisfying the logical conditions for attainment of scientific status. (5, p. 491)

Scientific status had not yet been achieved by the social sciences in the 1930s. Dewey argued that, in matters of policy formation,

> it is commonly assumed that the problems which exist are already definite in their main features. . . . The consequence of this assumption is that the work of analytic discrimination, which is necessary to convert a problematic situation into a set of conditions forming a definite problem, is largely foregone. (5, p. 493)

In other words, policy formation was based on theories which were insufficiently rooted in empirical reality. This was seen as evidence of the immaturity of social science.

> The immature state of social inquiry may thus be measured by the extent

> to which these two operations of fact-finding and of setting up theoretical ends are carried on independently of each other, with the consequence that factual propositions on the one side and conceptual or theoretical structures on the other are regarded each as final and complete in itself by one or another school. (5, p. 507)

Having progressed beyond this stage of development, economics as a science continues to fall short of a methodology which consistently produces scientific progress.

When a logical positivistic approach is called for in economics, the scientific process, following Schumpeter, should consist of a vision, a verbalization or conceptualization of that vision which facilitates organization of raw (protocol) data, collection of further facts (common and crucial elements) along with abandonment of irrelevant facts, and, pari passu, via bridging devices, the addition of further relations and concepts (higher level theoretical constructs) and elimination of irrelevant and inaccurate hypotheses.

> Factual work and "theoretical" work, in an endless relation of give and take, naturally testing one another and setting new tasks for each other, will eventually produce *scientific models*, the provisional joint products of their interaction with the surviving elements of the original vision, to which increasingly more rigorous standards of consistency and adequacy will be applied. This is indeed a primitive but not, I think, misleading statement of the process by which we grind out what we call scientific propositions. (30, p. 42)

In normal science, visions are at least framed in the context of the extant paradigm and, as Schumpeter argued, visions tend to be imbued if not distorted by ideology (30, p. 42). The "crushing out" of ideologies is a time-consuming and never ending task (30, p. 44), and "we shall not be able to live up to the program" of how economists should proceed (30, p. 14). Yet Schumpeter was sharply critical of economists' performance (30, pp. 18-19), arguing that insufficient "historical experience" and inadequate statistical knowledge were common among economists. Regarding historical experience, which is composed of both "an adequate command of historical *facts* and an adequate amount of historical *sense*" (30, p. 13), Schumpeter argued that

> most of the fundamental errors currently committed in economic analysis are due to lack of historical experience more often than to any other shortcoming of the economist's equipment. (30, p. 13)

Regarding statistical methods:

It is impossible to understand statistical figures without understanding how they have been compiled. It is equally impossible to extract information from them or to understand the information that specialists extract for the rest of us without understanding the methods by which this is done—and the epistemological backgrounds of these methods (30, p. 14).

It is during the initial stages of the scientific process that both of these weaknesses are most glaring in contemporary economics. The painstaking effort necessary to analyze systematically interactions within the protocol data, thereby providing the basis for establishing bridge principles at a later stage of theory development, is largely bypassed. Instead, a common practice in economics is essentially to invert the scientific process by developing fully formulated theoretical structures based on casual empiricism, hunches, and unrealistic assumptions. The "applications" of theory which follow ignore or misrepresent important aspects of reality, resulting in irrelevant if not destructive policy prescriptions.

The first stage of theory development in normal economic science, then, is typically a quantum leap from reality to theory. Economists typically engage in nonscientific behavior to develop their theories, and only then do they begin to employ the modern empiricist scientific process as described by Carl Hempel and other logical positivists. *After* the fully formulated theoretical systems have been unscientifically developed, economists *then* attempt to link the theory's logical consequences to real phenomena by a process of model verification. The result is that model verification in economics is frequently a highly subjective trial-and-error process involving numerous applications of econometric methods. It is a trial-and-error process because the econometric models are not based on reality, but rather contain the nonscientific biases of the theoreticians. A voluminous and often controversial empirical literature on the subject consequently emerges. This process may eventually result in a sorting out of the common and crucial elements and a forging of a qualified consensus of opinion, but it is a far cry from logical positivism as practiced within normal natural science.

In applying theoretical concepts developed through quantum-leap methods, continued redefinition and new concept introduction occurs *after* theoretical systems are highly developed. In this manner theories do evolve and take on new forms as new facts are discovered. However, a more straightforward procedure—consistent with the application of scientific methods in the natural sciences—would be to place more emphasis at the initial stage of theory development on the use of inductive methods to analyze the institutional, cultural, social, and technological interactions of the phenomena. With this incessant give and take between data and concepts, redefinition and new concept introduction would occur *during* theory building and would therefore be part of the process. Hence, theory developed beyond the initial stage would have structurally inherent bridging devices necessary for empirical verification. As human behavior changes over time, the theory would continually require vision, but realism would not have to be sacrified for simplicity.

Furthermore, with a "sub-quantum-leap" process of theory development, the final product would be substantially different from the higher level theory developed by the quantum-leap method. In general, the sub-quantum-leap method would yield, in comparison to quantum-leap theorizing, superior policy recommendations.

The thesis that economics, as a rule, relies upon the excessive use of deductive methods at the initial stages of theory development, and that such a method is a relatively inefficient and imprecise process, can be evaluated by an analysis of the "state of the art." To do this, we restrict our discussion to the application of methodological principles in migration and monetary economics. These subdisciplines are characterized by extensive theoretical and empirical work that we take to be indicative of the nature of the scientific process in other subdisciplines of economics.

A. Migration economics

In attempting to understand human migration behavior, economists have applied utility theory within a human investment framework. Migrants are assumed to respond to economic opportunity differentials among aerial units. And when the frictions of space, political institutions, imperfect knowledge, and differential amenity variables (e.g., climatic conditions) are assumed away—by a quantum-leap abstraction process—the resulting geographical population distribution is optimal in the sense that national product is maximized. Thus, population mobility displays desirable normative properties because it facilitates the efficient allocation of resources over space.

When the pure (deductive) theory of migration is tested for relevance, bridge principles identifying migration flows and measures of economic opportunities such as wages and unemployment are identified. In this process, basic assumptions relating to the costs of migration, information flows, public sector variables, and amenities are relaxed (identified) to make the model realistic. Empirical knowledge of the interrelationships among explanatory variables and the interdependence of migrants' "utility functions" are at best vaguely perceived. Nevertheless, through a process of successive testing and model respecification (introducing new concepts, postulating alternative functional forms and refined measurements) the relevant facts concerning the common and crucial elements, and hence the irrelevant facts, begin to become empirically discernible.

However, after he surveyed the massive post-1970 empirical literature on migration behavior, Michael Greenwood's (10) concluding remarks strongly suggest that the common and crucial elements are only vaguely discernible in the migration literature. The magnitude of effects, the direction of causality among explanatory variables, definitions, and functional forms vary among the numerous tests. Thus, on the determinants of migration Greenwood concluded:

> One of the most perplexing problems confronting migration scholars is the lack of significance of local unemployment rates in explaining migration. (10, p. 411)
>
> . . . .
>
> Migration does occur from low to high income regions, but some debate remains regarding the relative importance of origin and destination characteristics in explaining migration. Appreciable differences have been uncovered in the magnitudes in which income and other factors influence various population or labor force subgroups in their decisions regarding whether and where to migrate. (10, p. 411)
>
> . . . .
>
> A number of studies suggest significant differences in the migratory behavior of whites and nonwhites. However, the conclusions of many of these studies may be misleading because of a failure to control for age and education, and in some instances for employment status. . . . To attribute the observed behavioral differences to race or to discrimination has frequently been inappropriate. (10, p. 411)
>
> . . . .
>
> Crucial questions that remain to be analyzed . . . involve the importance

of welfare and of the quantity and quality of public services in general on the decision to migrate, particularly on the decisions of low-income persons. (10, p. 412)

Also, controversy over single-equation versus simultaneous-equation models remains unresolved. Greenwood illustrates the potential gravity of this problem:

> An assumption that underlies the many single-equation, multiple regression approaches to migration is that while the various explanatory factors influence migration, migration does not in turn influence these factors. If this assumption does not in fact hold, the parameter estimates of the various models possess a simultaneous-equations bias that may be great enough to vitiate the findings. (10, p. 412)

Finally, lacking empirical import, migration models have little relevance in the policy arena. This is consistent with Greenwood's observation:

> What is perhaps most striking about the massive literature on the determinants of interregional migration is the lack of direct policy implications. (10, p. 412)

B. Monetary economics

Empirical models in monetary economics provide a second case in point for the basic thesis of this paper, namely, that deductive systems developed by quantum-leap abstraction procedures, as a "first approximation" of reality, are likely to be both extremely difficult to validate in the presence of actual circumstances and, concurrently, void of policy direction.

Central to the efficacy of monetary policy (defined in terms of efficiency of control over monetary aggregates) is a stable demand function for money or, at least, a predictable demand function for money under a wide variety of circumstances. Being a crucial link in the transmission process, econometric research in monetary economics has developed an extensive empirical literature on the determinants of the demand function for money. Thus, analysis of the process of developing a demand function for money serves to indicate the normal process of theory development in other areas of monetary economics.

Boorman and Havrilesky (2, p. 285), after surveying numerous empirical works in applied monetary theory, concluded that the *consensus* of monetary economists is "that the interest rate plays a significant role in the determination of the public's demand for money," but this conclusion depends upon a particular definition of money and interest rates as well as the time period of analysis. Likewise, income was found to affect the demand for money in numerous tests, but this conclusion is contingent upon the definition of income (permanent or current) and upon the time period involved. Moreover, there appears to be little agreement concerning appropriate functional relationships, and the controversy over single-equation versus simultaneous-equation systems has not been resolved. Thus, probably the most definitive empirical proposition that has been derived from the vast monetary theory literature is that:

> there is no empirical basis for the liquidity trap hypothesis; the proposition that the demand for money function becomes infinitely elastic at some low level of interest rates. (2, pp. 285-286)

Of course, economic conditions may not have presented the circumstances to adequately test the liquidity preference hypothesis. However, this suggests that whether or not it exists under certain nonexistent conditions is trivial.

Because of the present "state of the art" in monetary economics, a greater emphasis on measurement, concept definition, and establishing empirical laws might be expected. This may be occurring to some extent, but it is not indicative of recent theoretical developments in monetary economics. For example, instead of the traditional view of money as a "consumer good" that facilitates the exchange process, money is now being viewed as a "producer's good" that enters as a factor of production into the aggregate production function. However, with the lack of significant empirical knowledge of aggregate production functions and uncertainty about which definition of money is relevant, it is not surprising that the rigorously deduced consequences of theoretical models representative of this approach are of questionable relevance for empirical research.

A more efficient approach and one far more consistent with the methodology of modern empiricism would be to spend considerably more time in the empirical domain analyzing the actual behavior of the phenomena under investigation. For example, economists have been unable to understand the behavior of banking institutions and monetary authorities because they spend a great part of their time studying actions and inferring purposive behavior. Thus, when the money supply is increased this might be interpreted as a deliberate attempt to change monetary policies, but, in fact, money supply growth may be linked to growth in the economy. The usual assumption of exogeneity of the money supply may be unrealistic. We contend that study of the institutional framework in which money is created would lead to more fruitful empirical formulations of money supply behavior.

In summary, disagreements over relevant variables, the functional relations of these variables, estimation procedures, and interpretations of empirical works are combined with a general vagueness of concepts in both the migration and the monetary literature. We interpret this generally poor state of empirical knowledge[11] as reflecting a peculiar and inefficient application of the scientific process, namely, the repetitive econometric applications of models in an attempt to "discover" facts that are relevant (irrelevant) to the common and crucial elements of theories which are insufficiently grounded in empirical reality.

V. Summary and conclusions

We began our analysis in Section II with a discussion of the process of theory construction in natural sciences. There we argued that, during normal science, abstraction is an orderly and systematic *process* which requires eliminating facts within the domain of inquiry that are irrelevant to the problem at hand. Normal science views selection of the common and crucial elements of a theory as an empirical question that must be resolved at each stage of abstraction. In general, theoretical models, logical consequences of those models, and rules of correspondence are developed by a process of "systematic abstraction." Thus, as a general rule, hypotheses are postulated with considerable a posteriori knowledge of processes and interactions within the empirical domain—a process we have described as sub-quantum-leap theorizing.

Our analysis of the scientific process as applied to migration and monetary economics suggests that in economics quantum-leap theorizing provides the theory, which is then refined by a process of

---

[11] The references cited provided only a very general overview of the migration and monetary literature. Although they hardly do justice to the important technical developments in the field, they are indicative of the application of methodological principles in economics.

successive testing and adjustment through a gradual discovery of factual circumstances. Interactive elements that are either (1) irrelevant to the theory, (2) possibly relevant to the theory but not initially incorporated into the theory's set of primitive terms, or (3) relevant and consistent with the theory's logical consequences are discovered during this process of refinement. Thus, factors that are endogenous to the common and crucial elements are gradually identified and systematized by a repeated application of econometric and other statistical methods.

The trial-and-error approach to theory development and policy formulation is by no means limited to the migration and monetary economics literature. Professor Wassily Leontief, in recent testimony before the Joint Economic Committee, U.S. Congress, echoed these same sentiments when he commented on the current status of the various macroeconomic theories underlying policy making in Washington. According to Leontief,

> The factual validation and implementation of these theories is based on what is often referred to as "casual empiricism" or on construction of more and more intricate econometric models. In these models, increasingly ingenious but still utterly unreliable methods of indirect statistical inference are employed in vain to compensate for the lack of hard, systematically organized factual information. (19, p. 2)

Continuing, he adds:

> At the present time it is the inability—or occasionally the reluctance of official statistical organizations—to collect and systematize large masses of readily available specialized information, not the lack of analytical tools, that seems to hinder effective practical implementation of the planning as contrasted with the traditional trial-and-error approach to policy formation in the economic field. (19, p. 7)

Finally, according to Leontief,

> creation and maintenance of a comprehensive data base would permit a drastic reduction in the amount of guesswork, and one might add, of idle theorizing that is involved in our policymaking process now. (19, pp. 8-9)

In principle, the economist's method of quantum-leap theorizing could lead to empirically relevant theories through successive testing, but apparently this procedure has not been successful in establishing theories with significant empirical import. We suggest that these severe inefficiencies in theory development in economics will continue to exist if economists insist on a continued inversion of the application of scientific principles. Thus, the continued proliferation of theories, rather than indicating economics is pre-paradigmatic science, suggests that the dominant neoclassical paradigm is such a complete and dominating world view that it inhibits inductive development of theories which reflect economic reality. In short, economists all too frequently leap from their oversimplified view of the nature of man and their naive view of the institutional framework as a God-given constant to elegant and sophisticated theories which are void of constructive policy content. It is through this quantum-leap process that overgeneralization occurs and "realism" in the sense of policy relevance is lost. The "conjugate correspondence" and "incessant give and take" between the empirical and conceptual realm, between fact and theory, should be part of the theory development process, not just an ex post appendage thereto.

In conclusion, current economic methodology is within the mainstream of modern empiricism in the sense that hypotheses are evaluated in terms of the canons of science; however, this paper questions the efficiency of the actual process of theory development in economics and argues for a more systematic evaluation of the role of social and economic institutions within the context of economic theory.

The methodology suggested herein argues against both the excessive reliance on government documents for data and the direct application of formal economic theory to these data to test hypotheses about human and institutional behavior. This is the principal method used by many economists to find empirical support for their previously developed models. The failure to obtain firsthand knowledge of human behavior in the institutional context in which hypotheses about human behavior are being tested is an inverted form of empiricism. For example, a considerable body of literature has been developed to examine the role of welfare assistance on the location decisions of the poor. Welfare is generally defined as AFDC [Aid to Families with Dependent Children] payments and the poor are generally defined as the black migrant population. The AFDC payments are presumed to reflect the diverse bundle of welfare benefits available to the poor and the poor migrant population is presumed to be reflected in the black migrant population. These are both heroic assumptions that we consider a quantum leap from the factual domain to the theoretical domain.

We argue that a far more fruitful approach to hypothesis formulation and testing would be to place far greater emphasis on examining the historical and institutional environment confronting poor migrants. This approach suggests that the historical method, interviews, case studies, experiential learning, and questionnaire studies have a far more important role to play in economic science than they have been afforded. The counter arguments that these methods are too cumbersome and that data requirements are too large are untenable in light of recent advances in computer technology and information processing. Such arguments are based not on net benefit determinations, but rather, as Leontief makes clear, on ingrained habits of behavior:

> [The] lack of necessary factual information [is due to the] continuous unwillingness of academic economists to give up their traditional reliance on abstract mathematical formulas—linked to reality only by a very fragile bridge of indirect statistical inference. . . . (20)

The methodology suggested in this paper has important implications for graduate training in economics. Universities can do much to improve the educational process and place economics more in line with modern empirical methods. Students in economics cannot conduct controlled experiments to the extent that they are conducted in the natural sciences, but they can be given an opportunity to acquire experience by working as interns in a business or public environment. Greater familiarity with primary data and with habits of human behavior relevant to the problem at hand would lead to more fruitful hypotheses and more rapid advances in economics as a science.

Finally, the peculiar application of methodological procedures in economics has contributed to the excessive trichotomization of economics into pure theory, applied theory, and institutional analysis. This trichotomization has unnecessarily inhibited the developments of both applied theory, via removing institutions from the domain of pure theory, and institutional analysis, via the healthy distrust of orthodoxy's version of empiricism. Applied theory has been unnecessarily juxtaposed against institutional analysis, thereby hindering communication and knowledge development.

Our analysis suggests that it is quite appropriate to object to purely deductive theory whenever such theory is offered as science. Such objections have been previously voiced primarily on the grounds that these approaches tend to be biased, self-serving, or apologetic. The objection raised here is that any purely deductive approach to theory formulation, while it may tell a convincing story, will be scientifically weak and will lead to misguided policy. If quantum-leap theorizing within normal economic science is increasingly replaced by sub-quantum-leap theorizing, both the efficiency of the scientific process and the level of effective communication between applied theory and institutional analysis will be enhanced.

REFERENCES

1. Boland, Lawrence A. "A Critique of Friedman's Critics," *Journal of Economic Literature* 17 (June 1979) pp. 503-522.

2. Boorman, J. T., and Thomas M. Havrilesky. *Money Supply, Money Demand and Macroeconomic Models.* (Boston: Allyn and Bacon, Inc., 1972).

3. Brody, Baruch, ed. *Readings in the Philosophy of Science.* (Englewood Cliffs, N.J.: Prentice-Hall, Inc., 1970).

4. Caldwell, Bruce. "Positivist Philosophy of Science and the Methodology of Economics," *Journal of Economic Issues* 14 (March 1980) pp. 53-76.

5. Dewey, John. *Logic: The Theory of Inquiry.* (New York: Holt, Rinehart and Winston, 1938).

6. Dewey, John. *Reconstruction in Philosophy.* (New York: Henry Holt and Company, 1920).

7. Feyerabend, Paul K. "How to Be a Good Empiricist—A Plea for Tolerance in Matters Epistemological." In *Readings*, Brody, ed. (1970) pp. 325-335.

8. Friedman, Milton. *Essays in Positive Economics.* (Chicago: University of Chicago Press, 1954).

9. Goodman, Nelson. *Fact, Fiction, and Forecast.* (New York: Bobbs-Merril Co., 1965).

10. Greenwood, Michael J. "Research on Internal Migration in the United States: A Survey," *Journal of Economic Literature* 13 (June 1975) pp. 397-433.

11. Gurwich, Aron. "Social Science and Natural Science" in Robert L. Heilbroner, ed. *Economic Means and Social Ends.* (Englewood Cliffs, N.J.: Prentice-Hall, Inc., 1969) pp. 37-55.

12. Hempel, Carl G. *Philosophy of Natural Science.* (Englewood Cliffs, N.J.: Prentice-Hall, Inc., 1966).

13. Hempel, Carl G., and Paul Oppenheim. "Studies in the Logic of Explanation." In *Readings*, Brody, ed. (1970) pp. 8-27.

14. Hill, Lewis. "A Critique of Positive Economics," *American Journal of Economics and Sociology* 27 (July 1968) pp. 259-266.

15. Hutchison, T. W. *Knowledge and Ignorance in Economics.* (Chicago: University of Chicago Press, 1977).

16. Kuhn, Thomas S. "Second Thoughts on Paradigms." In Frederick Suppe, ed., *The*

Structure of Scientific Theories. (Chicago: University of Illinois Press, 1974).

17. Kuhn, Thomas S. *The Structure of Scientific Revolutions.* (Chicago: University of Chicago Press, 1970).

18. Lakatos, Imre, and Alan Musgrave. *Criticism and the Growth of Knowledge.* (Cambridge and New York: Cambridge University Press, 1970).

19. Leontief, Wassily. "The American Economy and Its Prospects," Statement submitted to the Joint Economic Committee of the United States Congress, January 19, 1982.

20. Leontief, Wassily. "If Mr. Reagan's Policies Flop, Then What?" *The New York Times,* February 22, 1981.

21. Machlup, F. "Operational Concepts and Mental Constructs in Model and Theory Formation," *Giornali Degli Economisti E Annali De Economia* (September-October 1960) pp. 553-582.

22. Mannheim, Karl. *Ideology and Utopia.* (New York: Harcourt, Brace, and World, 1936).

23. Margenau, Henry, "What Is a Theory." In S. R. Krupp, ed., *The Structure of Economic Science.* (Englewood Cliffs, N.J.: Prentice-Hall, Inc., 1966), pp. 23-28.

24. Morgenstern, Oskar. *On the Accuracy of Economic Observations.* (Princeton, N.J.: Princeton University Press, 1963).

25. Northrup, F.S.C. *The Logic of the Sciences and the Humanities.* (New York: The World Publishing Company, 1947).

26. Popper, Karl. *The Logic of Scientific Discovery.* (New York: Basic Books, 1959).

27. Rotwein, Eugene. "Empiricism and Economic Method: Several Views Considered," *Journal of Economic Issues* 7 (September 1973) pp. 361-382.

28. Rudner, Richard S. *Philosophy of Social Science.* (Englewood Cliffs, N.J.: Prentice-Hall, Inc., 1966).

29. Scheffler, Ismael. "Prospects of a Modest Empiricism, I and II," *Review of Metaphysics* 10 (1956-57) pp. 383-400, 602-625.

30. Schumpeter, Joseph A. *History of Economic Analysis.* (New York: Oxford, 1954).

31. Shubik, Martin. "A Curmudgeon's Guide to Microeconomics," *Journal of Economic Literature* 8 (June 1970) pp. 405-434.

32. Silk, Leonard. *The Economists* (New York: Avon, 1978, originally published by Basic Books, 1976).

33. Tarascio, Vincent T., and Bruce Caldwell. "Theory Choice in Economics: Philosophy and Practice," *Journal of Economic Issues* 13 (December 1979) pp. 983-1006.

34. Tool, Marc R. *The Discretionary Economy.* (Santa Monica, California: Goodyear, 1979).

35. Ward, Benjamin. *What's Wrong with Economics?* (New York: Basic Books, 1972).

36. Wilber, Charles K., with Robert S. Harrison. "The Methodological Basis of Institutional Economics: Pattern Model, Storytelling, and Holism," *Journal of Economic Issues* 12 (March 1978) pp. 61-89.

Peter Wiles

4

IDEOLOGY, METHODOLOGY, AND NEOCLASSICAL ECONOMICS

It was as if an inscription over the gates of science should run: No Observation Without Explanation; *and another one over the turnstiles should read*: Facts not admitted unless accompanied by respectable Hypotheses. Should the latter fail to satisfy the authorities, both will be requested to leave the premises immediately. (Haynes, 1980)

... doctrinaire psychoanalytic theory is a confidence trick and a terminal product as well—"something akin to a dinosaur or a zeppelin in the history of ideas, a vast structure of radically unsound design and with no posterity." (Medawar, 1981)

... the only coin worth having, the praise of our fellow economists (Paul Samuelson, lecture at the City University, London, December 2, 1980).

Caring more for the patient than for achievement on the operating table, of which often the surgeon is the sole beneficiary, I refuse to admire technique for itself alone. (Gueullette, 1956, p. 1)

1. Ideology defined

1.1. An ideology is defined here as a general and coherent *Weltanschauung*, felt passionately and defended unscrupulously. It contains *sacred propositions* of a factual sort. In the face of contrary evidence, the words in these propositions will be redefined, or the philosophical status of the propositions will even be changed, in order not to abandon the original concatenation of words. A special methodology and vocabulary will also grow up, the use of which confines the devotees to problems and approaches

Reprinted from *Journal of Post Keynesian Economics*, Winter 1979-80, Vol. 2, No. 2, pp. 155-180, improved after reading Rousseas 1981 and Dow 1981.

that cannot threaten the sacred propositions. *In the long run, without a protective methodology and a limited vocabulary, an ideology cannot last.* Before scientific method was agreed upon, special methodologies were legion. Now they arise only to protect ideologies. This is my main message. I treat both methodology and vocabulary as separate from the factual propositions in the *Weltanschauung*, but of course the former can become as sacred as the latter.

1.2. Ideology is of less importance than methodology in what follows. But let us learn to handle this definition of it by examining several related things that are not quite an ideology. A scientist's obstinate personal commitment to a particular theory is not an ideology. His theory is not a world view, and he has no special methodology or vocabulary. All he has is a sacred proposition, unscrupulously defended. Indeed his sacred proposition may be true and new—in which case, scrupulous or otherwise, he is a persecuted pioneer.

Not every *Weltanschauung* is an ideology. For many people have a conscious, general collection of views which, though not self-contradictory, are not actually coherent, and which they are willing to abandon piece by piece in deference to new evidence or argument. Alternatively, people may be foolish fanatics whose beliefs are too inconsistent to be termed an ideology.

The self-serving commitment of young professionals to the ideology of their elders is not itself an ideology, but exactly what it seems to be: behavior adopted in the hope of promotion and social approval. Put these individuals in another milieu, and they change their thinking. The true ideologue, on the other hand, avoids uncomfortable environments or enters them deliberately in a spirit of missionary self-sacrifice. This unscrupulous behavior on the part of the young, however, reminds us that every self-respecting ideology acquires a social power base and uses monetary, legal, military, and other inducements to perpetuate itself. We do not enter here into this very important side of the matter.[1]

Can an ideology simply be correct? Does there exist a group of propositions fulfilling the criteria of section 1.1 that are nevertheless all true? Nonexistential theorems cannot be demonstrated. All we need say here is that such a group of propositions has not yet been discovered.

[1] But see the contributions by Earl, Canterbery and Burkhardt, and Eichner herein.

2. The role of methodology

2.1 We have already delivered our main message: no special methodology, no permanent ideology. This implies that some correct, general methodology exists, and I would now argue that the correct general methodology is simply scientific method, as taught in textbooks of the history of science, or of logic, and practiced— or so they tell us!—by natural scientists. As Schumpeter points out (1954, pp. 7-9) this methodology is not static, and we cannot legislate for the future. But I have more confidence than Schumpeter in the slowness and small extent of future change and insist absolutely that no valid element in one methodology contradicts a valid element in another. In this sense *all correct methodologies are one*, and, very specifically, this is true of the natural and the social sciences taken together.

I disagree wholly, therefore, with the view that the social sciences require a different methodology from the natural sciences. Specifically, however, the social sciences deal with objects that act according to their *memories*. This is indeed different from all natural sciences except animal ethology, since the fact that objects under study have memories constantly changes the statistical universe and thus enormously complicates the scientist's task. For this purpose new methods are needed, and it becomes evident that the old methods are a special case, valid only for the study of objects that cannot remember. As is so often true in such cases, this does not refute the old methods, or introduce any contradiction whatsoever between new and old. Moreover, since the new is more complicated than the old, and based upon it, it behooves the social scientist to master the methodology of the natural scientist.

However, Schumpeter is extremely misleading with regard to methodology. For a historian of "analysis," as he constantly reminds us, he is very coy about it. Nay, more. On page 43 he flatly contradicts my "main message" above, since he seems to recognize no methodological problem special to economics (pp. 1-9). By dismissing Ricardo's methodology as the "Ricardian vice" (p. 473), he implies that there is virtue elsewhere. He is throughout excessively conciliatory and inclined to paper over cracks. His copious references to Marx treat him as if he were just another economist, and Marx's "Platonism" is explicitly excluded from consideration (see footnote 3 below). Schumpeter also plays down the *Methoden-*

streit, which is in fact a perfect illustration of my "main message." For it was held at the time that Ricardo, with his method of "abstraction," had proved the advantage of free trade for everyone, and certainly free trade was in all respects an ideology (see section 4.7). But German academe was romantic, nationalist, and protectionist, so it sought a less abstract methodology on which to found its wholly separate ideology. Since Ricardo's logic was incontestable, it has to be shown to be inapplicable.[2]

2.2. Methodology is a dull subject, especially when things are going right and a science is productive. At such times the question tends to attract dullards: "those who can, do; those who can't, teach." But interest revives when a science dries up. Another cause of *Streit*, and even of *Methodenstreit*, is a shortage of funds and posts. Salary and status attract the best minds, and so such individuals must, when faced with cuts, consider methodology as a principle of allocation.

Why is this last case so probable? His methodology *defines* a scientist, an academic, any sort of intellectual. Painters are cubists, abstract impressionists, or whatever; novelists are stream-of-consciousness, absurdist, and so on. It matters much less what they paint or describe: the way they do it determines their enemies, their guru, their patron, the colleagues who should be their friends, their good and their bad reviews, where they exhibit or publish, etc. In sum, *le style c'est l'homme*. But what is style? Why, simply a short, obsolete word for methodology. We have styles of doing things when the best way of doing them is not obvious. Insofar as "best" is itself a subjective concept and prey to fashion, style may be with us forever, even in economics.

Yet an enormous amount of human capital is invested in a style. It is the style, more than the facts, that we learn. Style is difficult, and its mastery is an achievement. It is not surprising that those who practice a given methodology support each other, for all their stock rises or falls together.

2.3. So birds of a feather flock together. But birds are territorial: they defend the perimeters of the region they have occupied—

---

[2] This is most ironic, since Friedrich List has already defended German economic nationalism sufficiently by very Ricardian means: the infant industry argument. Thus the founder of the German school was a Ricardian! Few today would wish to deny the validity of his special case or exclude him from the neoclassical synthesis.

not indeed against other species but against individuals of their own kind who belong to other groups. To abandon the metaphor, we develop a methodology to research certain problems and answer certain questions. Intruders into "our" area with strange methodologies endanger all this human capital, whereas "people like us," who only make "creative extensions" of our own methodology, show its vitality and give us reflected prestige. Hence, the strong "craft demarcations" that disfigure intellectual and university life (a craft is of course itself a methodology).

3. Other illustrations of the role of methodology

3.1. It may help, before proceeding to neoclassical economics, to consider two relevant cases in which a methodology has been influential upon an ideology.

3.2. Christian theology is of all theologies the most cerebral, actually academic. Yet Christian doctrine cannot be proved scientifically. So the methodologies of professors of Christian theology contain elements unknown to science. We meet a new connection between our minds and reality: faith. Faith works in parallel to the five senses, and the (sacred) propositions it delivers to us cannot be verified by them. Most of these sacred propositions are indeed collected in a long book, which is itself protected by faith from the Higher Criticism. But faith was so strong that it saw nothing to fear in logic (fides quaerens intellectum) and so in the end the Higher Criticism became bolder and bolder. The reply of faith now tends to be that the sacred propositions, taken literally for so many centuries, are actually metaphors, still spiritually regenerative and historically once necessary. In our language, the "concatenation of words" remains untouched, but the words' philosophical status is changed.

On the more strictly scientific front, again, we meet a strange methodological axiom: teleology. Every part of nature, every historical event, has purpose. The final cause is this ultimate purpose, which "attracts"; other causes may "repel," but not the final one. This cause is God's plan, which is known only to faith. This notion is Aristotelian and very moderate; if the teleological cause is ultimate enough, most sciences can live in the intermediate terrain. But there have also been outbreaks of a much more antiscientific methodology: the Platonic. According to Plato, the Ideas of things, known to us a priori and indeed innately, are superior to the chaos of mere actual things known to us through science, technology, history, and everyday life. Moreover, it is on this upper-class level of reality that things are indeed decided, since ideas are related to each other by logical entailment, and causality is the reflection of this entailment among the lower-class things on whose plane we live. We owe to St. Augustine and the Gnostics such intrusions into the Aristotelian stream of Christian philosophy. The matter is of importance to us here because Marx (see below) was a Platonist. But it is not our purpose to polemize with either Plato or Christianity, let alone completely to describe them, and we pass immediately to Marx.

3.3. Marx also made the Platonic distinction between what he called "abstractions" (not Ideas) and humdrum reality.[3] His "values," in *Capital*, Book I, demonstrate the exploitation of the proletariat, since capital is unproductive (but privately owned) and appropriates the surplus value produced by labor. These values, whereby exchange ratios are the ratios of direct labor content alone, are Ideas: they correspond to no observed reality whatsoever. His Book III "production prices," which tacitly admit the productivity of capital and yield exchange ratios according to the money cost of labor and capital together, are mere sublunary facts. Marx, as a good Platonist, is not very worried by the contradiction, since Platonism permits very loose and undefined relations between upper-class and lower-class philosophical levels—and certainly forbids the quantitative testing of assertions about these relations. Thus by the time we have arrived at Book III we see just how divorced from the facts is Book I; but its rhetoric stands. The theory of surplus value has ceased to explain reality and has become already a sacred proposition.

Over and above the Platonism of ideas as more real than phenomena, Marx takes over the dialectic—Hegel's special tricky, manipulable logic. Since it plays no role in the BookI/Book III distinction or in the theory of surplus value itself, we shall pass it over here.

---

[3] It is my assertion that Marx is a Platonist. He would have denied this, admitting only his discipleship to Hegel. But Hegel's single Idea is more like God, while Marx's abstractions are numerous, like Plato's Ideas. Cf. Rousseas, 1981, and Wiles, 1981.

4. The essence of neoclassicism

4.1. We distinguish neoclassicism here from Austrian and Chicago economics in particular. Neoclassicism is part *Weltanschauung*, part congenial methodology. But the former, though coherent, is not general nor is it passionately felt; it is the latter that is passionately felt, though by a paradox it contains within it sufficient empiricism to wreck an ideology.

4.2. The *Weltanschauung* tells us that society consists essentially of independent individuals, each strongly motivated to seek his own "economic" interest and to do so rationally. Competition keeps good social order; its absence demands social intervention. Demand and supply are reasonably price elastic, so price signals are effective; but externalities are very common and demand social intervention. Unemployment has Malthusian or Keynesian causes and requires the respective social cures implied. We know what the liberal state ought to do, and that it can do it. Public and private property can easily be managed according to the same rules, so property is not an issue.

So moderate a position implies no particular attitudes toward drugs, social services, education, and so on. It does not pry into intrafamily relations or imply that this school of psychology is right and that one wrong. It recognizes limits to the reach of economics. It allows wide differences among its practitioners on peripheral issues such as how to vote or what income distribution to advocate. Note how extremely important some of these issues are: surely the last two, for example, would not be peripheral to a real ideology.

4.3. The methodology, however, is much tighter. Neoclassical economics consists of a highly idiosyncratic, protective, restrictive, lockstep methodology that, surprisingly, leaves its practitioners free to believe almost (but not quite) anything. The methodology studies intensively a narrow range of facts which it mercilessly preselects. *It is an only partly scientific methodology without an attached ideology.* The passions that used to characterize the latter in the classical period, however (see below), now attach themselves to the former.

Thus the plodding ox of a commonplace, understated, and tolerant *Weltanschauung* has been yoked to the racehorse of an axiomatic methodology. This is a unique state of affairs in the world of the intellect. It makes of economics a very peculiar subject indeed. Not nearly enough attention has been paid either by economists or by historians of science to this extremely odd situation. Let us try to explain it.

4.4. Regretfully, I find Gunnar Myrdal's explanation[4] mostly incorrect. His factual account of what is wrong with economics accords almost completely with my own, but he argues that it has happened because of the impossibility of avoiding value judgments in the social sciences and the refusal of economists to recognize this. Now, first, this is a non sequitur. The "Ricardian vices" (Schumpeter's phrase) that Myrdal correctly describes have no obvious connection with anyone's values and indeed afflict the most left-wing economists, including Marxists; yet these people's attitude toward values is quite unorthodox. Nor does Myrdal attempt to supply a more subtle connection between the value problem and the resulting methodology. Second, the avoidance of value judgments is not impossible, merely very difficult. It is possible in all matters at least to *approach* objectivity—nay, with time, to approach it asymptotically. Economists are completely right to strive toward this goal. They are even right to be optimistic about it, and Myrdal's pessimism does great harm.

In fact, he even borders on the quicksand of *Wissenssoziologie*, that "undiscovered country from whose bourn no traveller returns." For if it is *in principle* impossible to be objective, then this assertion is itself subjective and open to question—unless it is merely axiomatic, in which case we need pay it no attention.

In smaller ways, however, our attempts to be value free, though wholly creditable, do trip us up. First, as Myrdal shrewdly points out, the choice of research topics is most unlikely to be value free. We look objectively into questions we have chosen in self-interest and thus preserve the general outlines of our subject. Second, the values of economic agents can and must themselves be studied, even statistically. For the proposition that "A's tend to think X, but B's tend to think Y" is an entirely empirical and objective one, open to quite ordinary statistical investigation. Myrdal is reluctant to make this point, and even other economists are very shy of admitting it, preferring to assume a single-valued *homo economicus*. But, of course, that is a quite irrational self-restriction. The objectivity of the student has no logical connection whatever with the values of the studied.

[4] As put forward in many publications. I have used Myrdal (1971).

4.5. Putting the values issue to one side, it has also been argued that the use of the ceteris paribus clause is at fault, since it imposes so high a degree of abstraction on us. But it is rightly replied that a priori reasoning and the use of ceteris paribus are due to the impossibility, or at any rate prohibitive expense, of laboratory experiment. Ceteris paribus is, of course, a logical simulation of "under laboratory conditions." And certain it is that in meteorology, astronomy, and geology we find these tactics very commonly used for the same reason, while in social psychology experimentation is cheap and some issues, at least, are disposed of in that way. In other words, the argument from expense of experiment is not confined to the social sciences, and it is surely correct; the much-admired natural sciences are not at all innocent of this same pis aller, and some social sciences are free of it. It must be much more flatly stated, however, that ceteris paribus is an inferior method. A *preference* for it is a methodological error, since all true science is as empirical as possible.

Nevertheless, ceteris paribus brings us near to the source of trouble, since it is first cousin to *abstraction*. It is not the same thing, for a ceteris paribus clause enumerates everything assumed to be constant, and much of this restriction is later relaxed, while abstraction assumes that something is not there. Thus, when we draw a demand curve, we put other prices and the incomes of the demanders expressly in the ceteris paribus clause; but in *Capital*, Book I, Marx abstracted from variations in the organic composition of capital. He did not hold c/v constant; he simply did not talk about it. Similarly, Friedman does not hold the degree of monopoly constant; he assumes it unimportant.

Without abstraction, as Friedman (and, indeed, nearly everybody) points out, one cannot handle the massive heterogeneity of economic data. But there is always a crucial level of abstraction; step above it and one's results are merely formal—too much has been left out for them to be credible or useful. Yet a high and useless level of abstraction has come to seem good in economics, and this perhaps has its root in *parsimony*, which is a misunderstanding of Occam's razor. What Occam actually said was, "entia non sunt multiplicanda *praeter necessitatem*." But this degree of necessity is a matter of human judgment, and our solutions must take account of all important facts, at whatever cost in the multiplication of premises and concepts. In particular, our ignorance or the shortage of data often leave things over-determinate: two causes are operating and neither can be ruled out. Thus, in my review of Pryor (1968) I show that although there is a reasonable correlation between defense expenditures and income within Europe as a whole, the difference between Scandinavia and the Balkans is extremely marked, for obvious historical reasons. So it must be put into any correlation, at whatever cost to "parsimony." Balkan bellicosity and Scandinavian peacefulness are not ruled out by the existence of a good fit simply for per capita income. On the contrary, since they undoubtedly exist, the relation of defense to income must be more complicated.

Parsimony is therefore false doctrine: it entails striking out alternative theories and causes, which often are quite incontestably or very probably at work, simply for the sake of—parsimony. Occam did not advocate parsimony; indeed, his razor is a rather banal statement.

Then there are *axioms* (everyone maximizes his profits; resource allocation is the only economic problem): these are not known in other sciences. An axiom (see the Appendix) is only a premise one is not allowed to question, dressed up as something grand. But it is precisely the scientist's duty to question everything! Our crime is not that we use a priori reasoning, for often we can use nothing else, but that we push a priori all the way up to the axiom. "Axiom" is, of course, a polite but impressive-sounding word for a "sacred proposition." The concept gives us the impression that it is worthwhile[5] to erect vast superstructures of deduction on virtually no fact, and this has now become a deep-rooted tradition.

Of all the crippling axioms with which we have loaded ourselves, one is so restrictive and misleading as to warrant special mention: *economic determinacy*. Economic theory must be complete and must account for every phenomenon in the theory. As many variables as possible must be endogenous—even if the insistence on endogeneity forces us to leave many out and distort the rest. This is held to be better than if the theory is incomplete, i.e., explains few phenomena in practice, while frankly

---

[5] I insist on this wording. That we *can* erect such superstructures, no one doubts. The question is, is it a scientifically fruitful ploy? Indeed, is it worth society's while? Should we be paid if we do it? For clearly, if our employment conditions are incorrectly specified, it can be worth *our* while.

leaving some problems unsolved on any level, and incorporates a large number of exogenous variables. But since custom, waste, idleness, ignorance, altruism, and desire for power play a huge role in economic affairs, the axiom of economic determinacy, which excludes them all, virtually guarantees the falsity or uselessness of most economic theories.

It is mainly by economic determinacy, or the insistence on endogeneity, that we achieve that curious self-sealingness that is the hallmark of economics.[6] Milton Friedman has been heard to observe that there are no noneconomic questions.[7] That is a fine and correct observation, but it does not mean only that economic theory should engulf more and more, such as education, childbearing, toothbrushing, and what not. For by parity of reasoning there are no purely economic questions. In particular, the prices of ordinary goods are not such a question; still less, the wages of ordinary labor (section 6). Science is indivisible.

If the new worldwide cost inflation drives us out of pure economics for the first time in order to account for wages, prices in another sector—oligopoly—have been partly noneconomic from the beginning. One man's idea of another man's reaction is of course a psychological question: pessimists will take one line, aggressive people another, paranoiacs a third. Generalizations in this regard are by definition fragments of the discipline of social psychology, and *homo economicus* will not get us very far since he is insufficiently specified for the task at hand. Oligopoly theories that depend upon him are prime examples of that merely *blackboard determinacy* which is the end result of so much of our effort.

These, then (abstractions, parsimony, axioms, economic determinacy) surely are the "Ricardian vices" to which we are all heirs; it is these that divert and corrupt our energies.

4.6. How has this peculiar corruption come about, in one science alone of them all? That it has happened, we cannot doubt. Consider, for instance, Hicks on imperfect competition:

---

[6] Economic determin*ism*, as in Marx, is both more and less ambitious. All human life hangs upon certain aspects of economics only (the relations of production). Most of what we today call economics is as much a part of the "superstructure" as theology or law.

[7] My spies report two such conversations.

It is, I believe, only possible to save anything from this wreck—and it must be remembered that the threatened wreckage is that of the greater part of general equilibrium theory—if we can assume that the markets confronting most of the firms with which we shall be dealing do not differ very greatly from perfectly competitive markets. If we can suppose that the percentages by which prices exceed marginal costs are neither very large nor very variable, and if we can suppose (what is largely a consequence of the first assumption) that *marginal* costs do generally increase with output at the point of equilibrium (diminishing marginal costs being rare), then the laws of an economic system working under perfect competition will not be appreciably varied in a system which contains widespread elements of monopoly. (1946, p. 84)

But why should anyone care about the wreckage of general equilibrium theory? We never know if an economy is, in fact, in general equilibrium; indeed, it is hardly possible to imagine how we could know. The theory is also quite useless for public policy. It suffices to know that everything has a number of consequences, which interact; we have no need to pursue them to their point of rest. Above all, if the theory cannot accommodate some fact or another, it is false, and to wreck it is a great scientific achievement.

Or consider again Stigler (1976) on *X*-efficiency, which of course he does not like. He prefers a theory explaining apparently unorthodox inefficiencies by the very orthodox costs of correcting them: information costs money quite directly; the correction of bad motivational systems leads to strikes. This seems not unreasonable until we realize that in this way all behavior is defined as maximizing behavior; no exceptions to it can even be conceived. Such a ploy destroys, not preserves, orthodox economics by rendering it a tautology instead of an interesting and refutable structure of thought and empirical knowledge. Indeed, it has been in part refuted, not least by the doctrine of *X*-efficiency. Stigler concludes:

Waste can also arise in the absence of uncertainty if the economic agent is not engaged in maximizing behavior. Unless one is prepared to take the mighty methodological leap into the unknown that a non-maximizing theory requires, waste is not a useful economic concept. Waste is error within the framework of modern economic analysis, and it will not become a useful concept until we have a theory of error.

But we don't need a theory of error: a few solid empirical generalizations will do for the meantime. Waste is already a "useful concept" because it happens empirically. A theory of waste would be fine, but the fact of it has already struck down the axiom of economic determinacy.

4.7. The corruption of a science is an event; thus, it has a history. I suggest that economics became, shortly after Adam Smith (who was an empiricist in *The Wealth of Nations*), an ideology with its appropriate protective methodology. The former was the work of the free trade movement, which promised world brotherhood and an end to war and imperialism; it undoubtedly collected about its doubtful reasonings enough political fervor and universalist rhetoric to justify the name of ideology. The methodology was the work of Ricardo (a rather tepid politician) and the combination is what we call the classical political economy. J. S. Mill and Alfred Marshall had doubts regarding both parts of the combination, but they had little effect. The Germans tried to relaunch the subject, but failed since they were even less scientific.

The marginalist revolution was a great crisis but also a great triumph. The foundation stone was changed, but the walls did not even crack; moreover, the movement could take pride in the fact that it had itself initiated and carried through this dangerous operation. The marginalists—Jevons, Menger, Walras, Pareto—believed in the ideology with greater fervor than J. S. Mill or even Ricardo. They changed the key theory (that of value) and added two unifying issues (optimal resource allocation and general equilibrium). They even introduced mathematics. But somehow all this left the axiomatic methodology untouched.

Simultaneously, however, the structure was threatened by socialism. But the latter was either purely empirical and emotional (as in Britain)[8] or out-and-out Marxist, and therefore indebted to a methodology that was not only quite clearly wrong, but also totally unfamiliar. So Western neoclassical economics (as we must now call it) pretended to itself that socialism was all about optimal resource allocation—a truly remarkable instance of the power of methodological blinkers. Having thus brought it within the pale, many practitioners voted for socialist parties. So the classical economics survived, a livable mansion, until Keynes. Like the marginalists, however, Keynes innovated (mainly) by means of the

---

[8] The Fabians, even Bernard Shaw, more or less accepted the classical methodology.

methodology, thereby saving classical economics once more and proving its continued fertility. He did, however, reject *homo economicus*.

Did not the methodology actually contribute a great deal? Both the marginal and the Keynesian analyses are great human achievements, Copernican revolutions of a sort; how then can the achievers have been unscientific? My answer is the following:

i) A bad methodology can be used well or badly. The labor theory of value and Say's law were egregious errors. They were due to this same methodology, and this must stand heavily to its discredit. Great gifts were required to correct them, but only minimal factual observation.

ii) Indeed, there was such factual observation: introspection in the case of marginal utility,[9] and the knowledge of the world slump in Keynes' case. To say that these observations are commonplace and occurred outside the laboratory is not to diminish their scientific status.

iii) Moreover, within the marginalist and Keynesian revolutions there are whole tracts of new error caused by the methodology. Consider Jevons' and Menger's denial of supply curves and of the influence of cost on price, in both cases caused by a flat refusal to consider production—only marketing counted. Nor could anything be more *a priori*—or more false—than Keynes' statement of the instantaneous multiplier (Wiles, 1969, pp. 57-58); and "saving = investment" is a classic example of an axiom, i.e., a confusion between fact and tautology—a confusion that others had to sort out with ex ante and ex post. Then, for an illegitimate abstraction, we can scarcely do better than the floating of the new macroeconomics upon a totally undefined microeconomics.

5. The status of ideology today

5.1. In this section, I shall stick very close to the restrictive definition of ideology given in section 1.1. First, do neoclassical economists, as a matter of empirical fact, behave as that definition implies? My general answer is that they have indeed the special meth-

---

[9] It appears not to be true that the laboratory observation of Ernst Weber and G. T. Fechner regarding the diminishing marginal response to cumulative stimuli inspired the Austrians (Schumpeter, 1954, p. 1058). It certainly did not inspire Jevons (1879, pp. xxix-xxxix).

odology and vocabulary that blinkers them, but no sacred propositions and, above all, no general and coherent world view. So neoclassicism is not an ideology at all but merely a stream of thought, much encumbered with a methodology that is only quasi-scientific. It has outgrown its prejudices, but has not thrown away the blinkers through which it peered during its period of tunnel vision.

Why not? Every ideology, as we noted in section 1.2, rests on a social system. But so does every methodology: *there are sacred procedures as well as sacred propositions.* Liturgy survives extremely well when theology has been refuted or abandoned. In what follows, I intend no hint of corruption or immorality and ask not to be read between the lines. Simply, the political sociology of university departments of economics has an important bearing on the crisis of our discipline.

"Human capital" does not mean intellectual resources in general, some fungible educational achievement in the abstract. Human capital is just as nonfungible (clay not putty) as physical capital; it is the quite specific things one has learned *and is therefore able to teach.* For nine centuries after the Dark Ages, when Latin had become merely the language of religion and diplomacy, it continued to be the staple of secondary education. Anglo-Saxon language and Germanic philology came in as British university subjects in the 1890s as compulsory prerequisites for English literature, partly in rivalry to Latin. As serious preparation for life in general or for the study of English literature in particular, they are clearly inferior to Latin; yet once established they have proved impossible to uproot these ninety years. The Confucian monopoly of Chinese higher education lasted two thousand years. Though admittedly it had strong political overtones, the major question in each generation was, what else can existing teachers and examiners teach and examine?

It is hardly surprising, then, that economic methods and even theories have a life of their own, independent of reality or even of political prejudice. The point is that economics is mainly a part of "Ed. Bus.," and only secondarily a tool of government. The civil service has always been pragmatic, indeed philistine and inconsistent, about its economic theory. Most civil servants, for instance, accept the importance of cost inflation, but do not feel obliged to revise the textbooks they read as undergraduates! It is in the universities that methodological conservatism is most pronounced.

After all, how human! All coherent bodies of knowledge are some-one's vested interest; elementary (and undisputed!) economic the-ory tells us that the cheapest way to get money out of obsolescent capital is to protect the market for its product. What has been learned will be taught.

In particular, academe has an appointment and promotion sys-tem that places money for juniors in the hands of senior academ-ics. As Ward (1972) has pointed out, this is not merely an intellec-tual but a social situation: the Establishment sits on the commit-tees and uses the criteria it learned when young to judge the new generation. Indeed, there is a vicious spiral here. The young, knowing what is good for them (section 1.2), have learned every-thing better, and the old are afraid of them. Nor are these commit-tees merely conservative or out to protect their own intellectual capital; there is also a large element of convenience and time-saving. For the mastery of this very advanced and demanding methodology is an extremely convenient criterion for such com-mittees. If a candidate possesses such mastery, meetings are shortened and controversy stilled. Everybody knows he has it; frauds are easily detected. This writer, on the other hand, does not have such mastery, but pleads regularly that an improved knowledge of the Polish language is an obvious priority over math-ematics in his special case—a claim invariably treated as a joke, for some reason. Consequently, people like him cannot be so easily judged. Fraud is easier. Indeed, we can only be certain of the value of such candidates after they have aged—but that ren-ders the whole academic career so uncertain that they abandon it.

Moreover, there is "publish or perish." Theoretical, especially algebraical, articles take less time to write. Their correctness—though not, of course, their value—is more easily assessed. So again those seeking promotion and those passing judgment upon them save much time. Over mediocrity and unimportance we may contest. But error we can be sure of.

5.2. The Chicago school, on the other hand, has an ideology. Its fundamental tenets are those of nineteenth-century free trade, with slightly different emphasis. The quantity theory of money and Say's law are more important, international trade less impor-tant; trade unions now exist but are denied to have any power; the public sector is studied separately and made into a *fons et origo mali*, etc. Over and above this, however, is a most interesting development into other fields. The free trade ideology only barely hinted at a theory of man as a whole. It did not encompass educational (now "human capital") or intrafamily relations (in which children have become a kind of consumer durable and love has been abolished as an interpersonal utility comparison).[10] The nineteenth century, again, knew neither cost-benefit nor cost-effectiveness, and so could not lecture to the public sector from so great a height.

But there is a voracious worm in this apple. The Chicago school shares the neoclassical methodology, of course, which acts in the required protective, blinkering manner. There are no oxen yoked to racehorses here. Indeed, this school makes far greater use of the protective effect than the neoclassicists. Stigler, quoted above, is a most striking example.

The trouble is that in the last twenty years statistical testing has become an essential element in the methodology of Western economics. Indeed, to its infinite credit the Chicago school has been in the forefront of this movement. But this is so corrosive of everything else that I venture a flat prediction: gradually the ramparts of Chicago will crumble, and the garrison will trickle out by the posterns to rejoin civilization.

5.3. Of course, erosion by statistical testing is very slow. First, we can always quarrel about the data input and the method of testing. But, second, such tests never establish the truth; they only refute certain hypotheses and establish an order of plausibility among the others actually tested. They are not in themselves explanations or theories. Indeed, at an early date the school's founder accepted nonrefutation as good enough all by itself. Neither explanation of exactly how the alleged cause produced the effect nor competition with other theories in an order of plausibility was required, and, above all, it was wrong to confront the apparently factual statements in the theory with the facts on the ground (Friedman, 1953; see the Appendix to this essay).

Much of this prescientific (or is it postscientific?) attitude remains. Thus the school never tests the hypothesis that the best correlation between national income and money supply is ob-

---

[10] See the various articles in the *Journal of Political Economy*, March-April 1973, part II. On the other hand, we must note that Malthus, whom the classics all accepted, also had an economic microtheory of the family and its reproduction.

tained by lagging money behind income. Yet in the United Kingdom (but not in the United States) the best fit is in fact of such a kind (see Hines and Nussey, 1974)—or, rather, we should say that this particular lag gives us a better fit than any other tested heretofore.

In saying that the Chicago ideology cannot survive, I am saying that, whether within or without the school, the necessary tests will eventually be made, and many Chicago hypotheses will be found —as some already have—to rank lower in plausibility than others. The commonly accepted methodology of testing can be part of an ideology only as long as tests have been improperly or insufficiently conducted. Unfavorable results will be accepted within the school—as has already on occasion been honorably demonstrated, so eventually it will disappear, leaving only those (not many, in my view) true propositions it has generated as part of our common heritage.

5.4. In this connection, it is interesting that the Austrian school (see Dolan, 1976) rejects testing outright. For a flat statement, we have to go back to von Mises (1949, p. 55):

> There are, in the field of economics, no constant relations, and consequently no measurement is possible.

But there is no doubt that "Austrians" continue to feel that way, even if in a more subdued manner.

It is a historical fact, as well as an obvious observation on a cross-sectional basis, that the Austrian and the Chicago ideologies coincide. Known individuals brought the word across the ocean, and Chicago was sired out of Austria by the correlation coefficient. But by that same token Chicago will, as we have seen, crumble away, and Austria will march onward—but with how many troops? Thus, this third school preserves for us the ideology of the classical economics as reinforced by marginalism: a passionately felt *Weltanschauung* cocooned in a protective methodology.[11]

5.5. In his great complaint against our methodology, Ward

---

[11] It is interesting that Austrian methodology began as outright Kantianism. The great praxeological axioms constitute a "categorial synthesis of phenomena" in von Mises's view: they are part of "the essential and necessary character of the human mind" (1949, p. 34); even as late as Hayek they are "part of the stuff of our thinking" (1935, p. 11). *Facta legant alii, tu felix Austria nosce.*

(1972) often quotes Kuhn, whose "paradigms" are the basic models whereby scientists try to understand their subjects at any given time.[12] Thus, the Ptolemaic paradigm put the earth at the center, with the sun, moon, and planets revolving around it. That was exactly right for the sun and the moon, but only a foundation for understanding the planets, which were revolving (on epicycles) around spots that were revolving around the earth. The Copernican paradigm put the sun at the center and used Occam's razor (correctly!) on the epicycles. Generally the new paradigm replaces the old one, says Kuhn, when an accumulation of small discrepancies makes the latter too cumbersome. But a leap of intuition in the absence of new facts, or a single great new fact, actually would do as well.

A paradigm therefore is not an axiom, though, being a community possession, it all too often becomes a sacred proposition. Indeed, it makes no methodological point at all, in any direct way except that its use is part—and not a very creditable part—of standard scientific methodology.

There are also potential paradigms, upon the proof of which much energy is expended. Einstein's general theory of relativity is such a case (Kuhn, 1970, p. 26), and in economics one thinks of the crude quantity theory of money. It would be simpler, or more interesting, if these propositions could be proved, for they would shed a great new light on everything else. But proof is difficult; meanwhile these too, alas, become sacred propositions proleptically.

In reading Kuhn and other historians or theoreticians of the natural sciences, it is well to remember that they have never studied economics. Kuhn's own paradigmatic science is physics, and his paradigmatic paradigms are physical paradigms. The situations he describes are by no means so disgraceful, and the behavior of his scientific protagonists taxes his patience and imagination but little. Consequently, Kuhn's revolutions in the natural sciences are pallid things compared with the one we need. For the supporters of the Ptolemaic system in astronomy or phlogiston in chemistry suffered only from a factual error, if a very big one. Each revolution is *only* a "paradigm change," i.e., purely conceptual, and not methodological or philosophical, let alone sociological. Kuhn is

---

[12] Kuhn, 1970, passim, but especially ch. 3. To say that Kuhn's use of his own term is very unclear is to say little more than he himself admits (1974).

too often quoted in the context of economics, for his theory is too narrow for our purposes; it is not only perfect competition that must be discarded. For economic theory is, as we have seen, "semi-Platonic." It has a complete, incorrect methodology in addition to a (partly) incorrect paradigm, and this too must be changed.

In particular, paradigms are not a good idea, but a bad habit. Basic knowledge need not (should not?) be coherent; it need only be noncontradictory. Accepted paradigms stifle basic thought. They are only a social necessity, or a crutch, or—still worse—a shibboleth, and the society of scientists should be rearranged so as to do without them. This point is of vital importance when reform is being discussed. A few people, who may be quite stupid and peripheral, see uncomfortable new facts, inconsistent with the paradigm. They have to fight inordinately hard to get the facts recognized; their careers may even suffer. Their efforts are gravely hampered, if they are stupid, by the socially accepted myth that you can only overturn one paradigm with another. This is, of course, false: you usually overturn a paradigm with a fact[13] and establish another (if you must) with several more facts. See the first epigraph.

5.6. Let us now get to the root of the neoclassical paradigm: *homo economicus*. It would be uncomfortable for humanity if its average behavior, without skewed or even very great deviation, were really that of a short-term maximizer, or even a long-term maximizer, of personal money consumption, leisure, and material fringe benefits: without regard to other people except just possibly the nuclear family, and then only in the absence of pensions and sickness insurance (since that would be to make invalid interpersonal utility comparisons); or to moral principles except for well-enforced laws (since other ethical behavior is a money-loser); or to tradition or style or sentiment or shame or malicious envy or God or even the Devil (for they are not rational); or to any saving not promising consumption to himself (i.e., no legacies); or to any nonpecuniary satisfaction from his job—and so on, for this in my self-imposed limitation of space is what I understand *homo economicus* to be.

There are a few such people, and we have a word for them: psychopaths.

[13] Copernicus overturned Ptolemy not with new facts but with Occam's razor.

6. Cost inflation

6.1. Of all the faults of neoclassical economics, its greatest recently has been its total unwillingness to theorize about, or even to discuss, incomes policy and cost inflation. What so many governments have tried (all those of the Soviet type with success) and what opinion polls show to be popular with most trade union members, let alone common citizens, can hardly be dismissed out of hand. Surely the only economists who would do so—namely, the Chicago and Austrian schools—must have an ideology with which it is incompatible. This is obvious, but what of mainline neoclassicism? Are its overt objections really the entire story? For it is very legitimate indeed to hold that permanent statutory incomes policies (by administrative fiat or by differentiated taxation) will not in fact work without communism; but the refusal to think about or publish others' articles, the reaction as if to a heresy, are in no way legitimate. After all, if impracticability were a serious ground for refusing to discuss something, most economists would lose their jobs.

6.2. A statutory incomes policy is not a politically radical notion. It arises from certain maverick economists of the center and the center-left[14] and from the mass of the people! It is certainly the polar opposite of laissez faire, but that element of classical ideology is now quite dead. Moreover, other tremendous denials of laissez faire, such as computerized linear programming and communist central planning, are perfectly acceptable subjects. Indeed, expert knowledge of them can sometimes get one tenure. To advocate an incomes policy is, as a corollary, the polar opposite of monetarism; but attacks on monetarism also lead to tenure, at least in carefully selected universities and institutes.

Other attacks on laissez faire are consummately orthodox. The externalities due to ecology are now legion, and their study is highly respectable (except in Chicago). Imperfections of competition are old hat (except in Chicago). Yet neither of these is more pervasive or more upsetting of classical orthodoxy than is cost inflation.

6.3. The incomes-policy/cost-inflation complex is not at all

---

[14] As we move to the Far Left it is rejected again, since it is incompatible with the *politique du pire* necessary for a revolution. Some on the Far Left have accordingly flirted with monetarism, but most have no methodological objections to a theory of cost inflation.

without technical interest, where "technical" means the use and extension of current methodology. Can we control prices by working through large corporations alone? If we control average prices only, by means of corporation-product-price indices, what will happen to individual prices? What will be the effect of excess demand under such circumstances? Must dividends be controlled as well as wages? If so, with what effects upon investment? These are challenging questions, worthy of the highest brow.

Moreover, the answers to these questions represent no revolution in method, no overwhelming threat to the orthodox. Thus cost-inflation theory depends absolutely on the proposition that people do not maximize their short-run profits; otherwise, they would not wait for their costs to rise before raising their prices. But there is massive orthodox warranty for the divergence between short- and long-run profit. "The literature" is replete with systematic failure to maximize profit in the short run. And the hostility toward trade unions that is the consequence of advocating an incomes policy is genuinely nothing more than the old hostility toward monopolies. Again, the union that first breaks a voluntary agreement can be convincingly analyzed along the lines of the prisoner's dilemma, and the sufferings caused to society as a whole are of course an externality. Moreover, the union itself is concentrating on short-term, not long-term, gains.

6.4 I believe that the neoclassical hang-up is nevertheless methodological: cost inflation does not merely undermine short-run *homo economicus*; it does so inconsistently. That entrepreneurs in perfect competition and non-unionized workers should be exceptions, that the public sectors should be a stronghold, is comforting. But that it should vary nationally is most distressing. Look at the list of principal sufferers: Latin Americans in the Southern Cone, Britons. . . . The whole picture is untidy and *historical*; the beautiful universality of neoclassicism and indeed Marxism is quite lost. It can no longer be argued that in practice a small percentage of human beings are not *homines economici*, or that this minority deviates from the norm in a random manner. *In some countries* the minority is bigger. When in charge of price setting it does not choose prices that vary at random about the most profitable one; it chooses *lower* prices, so that when a new wage-claim is granted the price can always be raised with impunity. Those in charge of trade unions also deviate systematically, but differently. They are aggressive for aggression's sake; they do not maximize; they are not "rational."

Here then is my offense. I believe that *homo economicus* is about 80 percent true, in some places and times more and in some less. He is "the best paradigm we've got." A better will not come along, but he is extremely misleading and untrustworthy because real people do not deviate from him in a random way. So we must learn to do without paradigms altogether and substitute empirical research in each case, to establish with what kind of human being we are dealing. This inconsistency is offensive:*cost inflation violates the axiom of economic determinacy*. We have to admit history and politics into intimate partnership, and on an issue hitherto purely economic, at that. Demand inflation is a matter for Keynes or Friedman, according to taste, but for cost inflation we must call in the labor lawyers, and indeed differentiate by countries. We must let strangers into our "defended perimeter."

History, then, has played a dirty trick on economists. There used to be no cost inflation, and deflation lowered not only output but also prices. This was a matter of monetary and fiscal policy: the economist told the government what to do. But now deflation lowers only output; nothing lowers prices, and other experts have an equal right to advise the government. We have simultaneously lost our comforting, simplifying premise, the Historical Uniformity of Man, and our monopoly of our own subject. The rate of rise of prices has become economically indeterminate.

Ecology and imperfect competition have had no such deadly effects. We invented the latter outright—long after it was due, to be sure. We have a most respectable record in regard to the former, stretching back to J. S. Mill.[15] But incomes policy and cost inflation have been a trauma. We are behind every journalist, and we should be ashamed of ourselves.

---

[15] See Mill (1848, IV/vi/2). Subsequent editions do not vary here. But although this passage fell on deaf ears, there has been continuous interest since Pigou (1920, pp. 159-63), very long before other branches of knowledge were concerned. The modern ecology movement is ordinarily dated, no doubt too arbitrarily, from Rachel Carson's *Silent Spring* (1962). But Mishan (1967) was not far behind.

APPENDIX

I. *Axioms*. For the *ageometretos* who seeks background in this subject, the articles "Axiom" and "Axiomatik" (by A. Szabo, L. Oeing Hanhoff, and H. Freudenthal) in the *Historisches Wörterbuch der Philosophie* are excellent. Euclid never uses the word *axioma*, but speaks of *koine ennoia*, a common opinion, which Proklos later rechristens *axioma*. For example, axiom no. 8 is that "the whole is greater than the part." Euclid also has "postulates," for which he uses the word *aitema*. No. 5 is the celebrated postulate that parallel lines do not meet, which is incorrectly called the axiom of parallels. But no difference is observable between the general meanings in educated ancient Greek of *aitema* and *axioma*—both mean "postulate," "assumption," or "claim." It was Proklos and Aristotle who gave the word *axioma* the special twist of "common opinion" and, further, the special sense of a "a proposition that neither can nor need be proved." The difference between Euclid's own "postulates" and "common opinions" is that the latter are more obvious; but for his purposes they might as well all be postulates.

The great *Idealtypus* of an axiom came to be, as a result of Aristotle's confusion, Euclid's fifth postulate on parallels: through a point outside a given line it is possible to draw only one line parallel to the given line. This is the perfect synthetic a priori judgment. It is not our task here to solve one of the greatest of all philosophical cruces! Enough that economics has no axiom of parallels.

There have been philosophers with a far fuller range of synthetic a priori judgments. We use this phrase in Kant's sense, of course, though philosophers before him did not do so. Pythagoras "knows" that the world is governed by harmonious numerical relationships and tries to discover some of them; nay, things themselves are generated from numbers, which are a prior sort of thing. Plato attaches each class of the phenomena of the real world (which he would call the unreal world) to an Idea. The Ideas have a logical relation to each other and to phenomena: for Plato all respectable propositions are synthetic a priori. Aquinas has many, notably the ontological argument for God's existence, but also the rather more restricted set of non-Christian arguments he took over from Aristotle (see below). More Platonic again is Hegel, whose knowledge of the habits and intentions of the World Spirit is quite absolute and whose contempt for empirical fact (and, incidentally, for merely geometrical axiom!) is notorious and open. But he did not express himself directly on the issues before us.

If these are the great exponents of the synthetic a priori, there are also great opponents who will have none of all this: Hume, Wittgenstein. I follow this party. Wittgenstein, of course, was also Viennese. But he seems to have had no interest in social science, and the contacts between the Vienna circle and the Austrian school must have been very slight.

There are also intermediate philosophers adopting various compromise positions—notably Aristotle, who is largely scientific, though certainly his doctrines of substance and teleological cause are synthetic a priori judgments.

But more relevant to economic methodology is Kant, who confronted this issue very directly and, indeed, is responsible for all of our terminology. He produced the "category," which was a necessary way of perceiving things, inseparable from the human condition. It formed the base of a few synthetic a priori judgments of a very general, nondogmatic, nonconstricting kind. Science can live with Kant, as it can with Aristotle—most of the time. Nevertheless, the "category" is in my Humean opinion an absolutely unsatisfactory doctrine, since there is neither a logical nor an empirical reason to believe that such a thing exists.

It is no accident that von Mises was actually a Kantian (section 5.4). His axioms had "categorial" status, just as the postulate of parallels did for Kant. The ghost of Kant haunts the Austrian school down through Rothbard. For Rothbard (e.g., in Dolan, 1976) makes his "primordial" facts introspective, but it was by introspection that Kant arrived at (we must not say established) the notion of a category. In fact, however, introspection is just another method of empirical observation: there is nothing "categorial" about it, and it is ordinarily fallible.

Synthetic a priori judgments are often explained as being innate, i.e., genetically determined—for example, by Plato and (effectively) by Chomsky. Modern scientific progress in explaining the brain and the gene has not ruled out such a possibility, though Chomsky has failed to deliver any element of the "deep structure of language" he inferred. Even if such elements were discovered, however, mutations obviously could alter them, and, as usual, there are philosophical problems with the genetic structure of Chomsky's own brain when he makes this assertion. Here again are large problems we need not solve! For we are concerned in economics with a satisfactorily wide range of contradictory propositions that the brains of economists and others, whatever their genetic structure, have in fact been able to conceive: the extent to which *homo economicus* is himself genetically determined is a matter of very ordinary empirical observation.

For me, then, there is no such thing as a "proposition that neither can nor need be proved" unless, of course, it is a definition. "Axiom," in the sense Aristotle gave the word, is a vicious attempt to straddle the divide between fact and definition. An economics built upon it is a house that, however handsome and commodious, is built upon the sand. It is not scientific to say, "I forbid you to argue about my assumptions."

II. *Friedman.* Friedman's (1953) methodology is a most ingenious and, I think, unprecedented accommodation of a priorism to testing. It is quite peculiar, and recognized as such by nearly all economists. So it would not have been fair to burden the text with it. Nevertheless, in its extreme mind-over-matter pathology, it is an *Idealtypus* of what I am against—though perhaps no worse than the very different views of von Mises (section 5.4). To the following selections from Friedman, I append my own notes, omitting the author's.

> In so far as a theory can be said to have "assumptions"[16] at all, and in so far as their "realism" can be judged independently of the validity of predictions, the relation between the significance of a theory and the "realism" of its "assumptions" is almost the opposite of that suggested by the view under criticism. Truly important and significant hypotheses will be found to have "assumptions" that are wildly inaccurate descriptive representations of reality, and, in general, the more significant the theory, the more unrealistic the assumptions (in this sense).[17] The reason is simple. A hypothesis is important if it "explains" much by little, that is, if it abstracts the common and crucial elements from the mass of complex and detailed circumstances surrounding the phenomena to be explained and permits valid predictions on the basis of them alone. To be important, therefore, a hypothesis must be descriptively false[18] in its assumptions; it takes account of, and accounts for, none of the many other attendant circumstances, since its very success[19] shows them to be irrelevant to the phenomena to be explained. (pp. 14-15)
>
> The theory of monopolistic and imperfect competition is one example of the neglect in economic theory of these propositions. The development of this analysis was explicitly motivated, and its wide acceptance and approval largely explained, by the belief that the assumptions of "perfect competition" or "perfect monopoly" said to underlie neoclassical economic theory are a false image of reality. And this belief was itself based almost entirely on the directly perceived descriptive inaccuracy of the assumptions rather than on any recognized contradiction of predictions derived from neoclassical economic theory. (p. 15)[20]
>
> The basic confusion between descriptive accuracy and analytical relevance that underlies most criticisms of economic theory on the grounds that its assumptions are unrealistic as well as the plausibility of the views that lead to this confusion are both strikingly illustrated by a seemingly innocuous remark in an article on business-cycle theory that "economic phenomena are varied and complex, so any comprehensive theory of the

---

[16] Note all the quotation marks, implying that realism is not real but assumptions are.

[17] No examples are given: I think this claim is false.

[18] "False" is wrong; "abstract" is the correct word, in the sense of section 4.4. Descriptive falsehood is always a handicap.

[19] This begs the question of what is meant by success. A theory based on the "other attendant circumstances" might, if tested, prove to be better. For instance, trade union militancy is such a circumstance in monetarist theory, but it has great explanatory power in cost-inflation.

[20] Cost inflation is such a contradiction, and it depends altogether on imperfect competition.

business cycle that can apply closely to reality must be very complicated."[21] A fundamental hypothesis of science is that appearances are deceptive[22] and that there is a way of looking at or interpreting or organizing the evidence that will reveal superficially disconnected and diverse phenomena to be manifestations of a more fundamental and relatively simple structure. And the test of this hypothesis, as of any other, is its fruits—a test that science has so far met with dramatic success. (pp. 33-34)[23]

One confusion that has been particularly rife and has done much damage is confusion about the role of "assumptions" in economic analysis. A meaningful scientific hypothesis or theory typically asserts that certain forces are, and other forces are not, important in understanding a particular class of phenomena. It is frequently convenient to present such a hypothesis by stating that the phenomena it is desired to predict behave in the world of observation *as if* they occurred in a hypothetical and highly simplified world containing only the forces that the hypothesis asserts to be important. In general, there is more than one way to formulate such a description—more than one set of "assumptions" in terms of which the theory can be presented. The choice among such alternative assumptions is made on the grounds of the resulting economy,[24] clarity, and precision in presenting the hypothesis; their capacity to bring indirect evidence to bear on the validity of the hypothesis by suggesting some of its implications[25] that can be readily checked with observation or by bringing out its connection with other hypotheses dealing with related phenomena; and similar considerations.

Such a theory cannot be tested by comparing its "assumptions" directly with "reality." Indeed, there is no meaningful way in which this can be done. (pp. 40-41)[26]

---

[21] But the quotation is borne out by the total failure of any business cycle theory to gain acceptance!

[22] There is no such hypothesis.

[23] Science has very often had no such success. Subatomic particles and cosmological theories multiply like rabbits. The chemistry of the gene is a great discovery, but in no way simple. Meteorology and geology have revealed no "fundamental and relatively simple structure." This kind of success (in accounting for a diversity of *facts*) occurs only now and again. It is very desirable, of course, but economics has never known it. It has experienced only the replacement of a diversity of *theories* by a single one.

[24] This is the parsimony fallacy. Clarity and precision are, of course, compatible with a massive injection of disparate facts.

[25] Note again the curious notion that we must test a theory's implications against fact, but not its assumptions.

[26] This astounding statement is directly untrue. For instance, one can ask businessmen how they fix their prices.

REFERENCES

Carson, Rachel L. *Silent Spring*. Boston, 1962.

Dolan, Edwin G. (ed.). *The Foundations of Modern Austrian Economics*. Mission, Kan., 1976.

Dow, Sheila C. *Journal of Post Keynesian Economics*, Spring 1981, Vol. 3, No. 3, pp. 325-340.

Engels, Friedrich. *Anti-Dühring*.

Friedman, Milton. "The Methodology of Positive Economics." In *Essays in Positive Economics*. Chicago, 1953.

Granick, David. *Managerial Comparisons of Four Developed Countries*, MIT 1972.

Gueullette, Roger. *Chirurgie de l'Estomac*. Paris, Masson, 1956.

Hayek, Friedrich, (ed.). *Collectivist Economic Planning*. New York, 1935. (Introduction by the author.)

Haynes, Renee. *Encounter*, Aug.-Sept. 1980.

Hicks, John R. *Value and Capital*. Oxford, 1946.

Hines, A. G., and Nussey, C. *The International Monetarist Theory of Inflation*. London, Birkbeck College, April 1974.

Jevons, William S. Preface to *Theory of Political Economy*. 2nd. ed. London, 1879.

Kuhn, Thomas S. *The Structure of Scientific Revolutions*. 2nd ed. Chicago, 1970.

_____. "Second Thought on Paradigms." In *The Structure of Scientific Theories*, ed. by Frederick Suppe. Urbana, Ill., 1974.

Lange, Oskar. *Political Economy*. Vol. I. New York, 1963.

Marx, Karl. *Die Deutsche Ideologie*.

_____. *Kapital*. Vols. I and III.

Medawar, Peter. Review of B. A. Farrell, *The Standing of Psychoanalysis*, Oxford, 1980, in the *Sunday Times*, 12 April 1981.

Mill, John Stuart. *Principles of Political Economy*. London, 1848.

Mishan, Ezra J. *The Cost of Economic Growth*. New York, 1967.

Myrdal, Gunnar. Gordon Allport Memorial Lecture. Harvard, 1971.

Pryor, Frederick L. *Public Expenditures in Communist and Capitalist Nations*. Homewood, Ill., 1968.

Pigou, Arthur C. *The Economics of Welfare*. London, 1920.

Ritter, Joachim (ed.). *Historisches Wörterbuch der Philosophie*. Darmstadt, 1971.

Rousseas, Stephen. *Journal of Post Keynesian Economics*, Spring 1981, Vol. 3, No. 3, pp. 340-351.

Schumpeter, Joseph A. *History of Economic Analysis*. Oxford, 1954.

Stigler, George J. "The Xistence of *X*-efficiency." In *American Economic Review*, March 1976.

Von Mises, L. *Human Action*. London, 1949.

Ward, Benjamin. *What's Wrong with Economics?* New York, 1972.

Wiles, Peter J. D. *Price, Cost and Output.* 1st ed. Oxford, 1956.

_____ . Review of Frederick L. Pryor, *Public Expenditures in Communist and Capitalist Nations, Weltwirtschaflitches Archiv*, 1969.

_____ . "Ideology, Methodology and Neoclassical Economics," *Journal of Post Keynesian Economics*, Winter 1979-80, Vol. 2, No. 2, pp. 155-180.

_____ . *Journal of Post Keynesian Economics*, Spring 1981, Vol. 3, No. 3, pp. 352-358.

Williamson, O. E. (1975), *Markets and Hierarchies: Analysis and Antitrust Implications.* New York, Free Press.

Wilson, T., and Andrews, P. W. S. (ed.) (1951), *Oxford Studies in the Price Mechanism.* Oxford, Oxford University Press.

Peter E. Earl

5

A BEHAVIORAL THEORY
OF ECONOMISTS' BEHAVIOR

‖‖‖‖‖‖‖‖‖‖‖‖‖‖‖‖‖‖‖‖‖‖‖‖‖‖‖‖‖‖‖‖‖‖‖‖‖‖‖

1. Introduction

This essay uses elements from a behavioral/post-Keynesian analysis of choice (developed at length in Earl, 1983a, 1983b) to explain why a behavioral—or indeed some other, more realistic alternative to the dominant neoclassical theory—has not been adopted by more than a small minority of economists. It arrives at conclusions which support, particularly within the context of economics, Feyerabend's (1975) anarchistic view of scientific behavior. The main point is that ideas find academic acceptance not necessarily because of their intrinsic scientific worth—for there is no unambiguous way of specifying what this means in a world of partial knowledge—but rather because they are salable as tools which enable their users more easily to reach their goals.

A neoclassical reader will find it difficult to accept what follows without placing herself in something of a quandary and giving herself cause for anxiety with regard to the adequacy of her normal theory of choice. Owing to its lack of concern with the complications caused by complexity and ignorance, neoclassical theory cannot justifiably be used to model the behavior of scientists, and

The author's indebtedness to Brian Loasby for inspiration should be obvious to anyone familiar with his work. He should also like to acknowledge helpful discussions and/or correspondence with A. W. Coats, G. S. Harcourt, T. W. Hutchison, J. Irving. S. J. Latsis, F. S. Lee, W. Samuels, P. Tompkinson, and two anonymous referees. However, he alone is responsible for any errors and for the views contained in the paper.

then explain its own success and the relative neglect of behavioral economics. To avoid inconsistency, a neoclassical theorist must either reject her theory in favor of an alternative with such reflexive properties, or exclude the workplace choices of people such as herself from her area of inquiry. To use a behavioral theory of choice to understand the academic's choice of techniques and areas of specialization, and neoclassical theory to explain all other choices, would be to embrace two habitually incompatible frames of reference.

During the course of investigating the neglect of behavioral economics we shall not refer only to the American organizational theorists, such as Cyert and March, Simon, and Williamson. We shall also devote considerable attention to a group of English economists who have been concerned more with the theory of the firm in its market context, but who share a similar subjectivist, disequilibrium view. The inclusion of this group seems particularly necessary since the American behavioralists have rather played down the market contexts in which organizations function. The English group's perspective on the nature of markets and the process of building up sales seems applicable, furthermore, to explaining why some ideas are more salable than others. This group of English disequilibrium economists comprises P. W. S. Andrews, J. Downie, E. T. Penrose, and G. B. Richardson. As a shorthand we shall often refer to them as the post-Marshallian school, since they draw their inspiration in large measure from the nonmarginalist, disequilibrium elements in Alfred Marshall's work.

With the exception of Downie, all of these economists, both American and English, figure prominently in Loasby's (1976) inquiry into the problem of choice in a world of ignorance and complexity, and how that problem has been treated by equilibrium theorists. All of them have had little influence on the way most academic economists view the world. Loasby's book also makes much of the neglect in mainstream economics of Shackle's (1973) perspective on Keynes's macroeconomic ideas. For reasons of space we shall leave out of the arguments in this paper an analysis of the fate of this view of macroeconomics, even though, as Loasby's work shows, it is very much within the behavioral spirit. A discussion of the history of monetary economics, using the same analysis as the present paper, is to be found in Dow and Earl (1981, 1982, especially Chapter 13 of the latter).

The rest of this essay is structured as follows. In section 2 the goals of the academic scientist are examined in the context of a lexicographic theory of choice. Section 3 considers scientific research strategies in a world of relativistic knowledge. Parallels are drawn between the behavioral approach and the well-known work on scientific research programs by Lakatos. Section 4 illustrates with case studies the kinds of failures to meet aspirations which provoke the search for new ideas. Section 5 explains how potential aids to the solution of problems may be screened by the academic economist and shows why some of the authors cited in this Introduction are likely to be filtered out long before they are fully understood and perceived to meet the needs of their readers. Section 6 is concerned with the final screen, the choice between ideas felt to be equally well understood. Finally, section 7 is a brief summary and conclusion.

2. The goals of the economic scientist

A behavioral theory of the activities of academic economists does not presume their sole interest is in understanding real-world economic affairs and being able to offer policy solutions to economic problems. It assumes instead that the academic scientist's position is analogous with that of managers in business enterprises as outlined by Scitovsky (1943, pp. 57-60) and Williamson (1964). Scitovsky pointed out that even owner-managers must choose between their leisure activities and the pursuit of profit, despite the threat posed by market competition to those insufficiently diligent in the search for profit. Williamson suggested that, even while working, managers might be interested in things other than profits, such as sales volume (since larger sales would justify a larger department and salary) or pet projects, the quality of the work environment, an expense account, and on-the-job leisure.

In deciding what to do to suit herself the manager has to bear in mind the feedback effects of her choices on the longer-term position of her company, if, of course, she plans to stay there in the longer term. Similarly, an economic scientist may be concerned with the long-term credibility of her discipline insofar as this affects her future earnings and ability to justify her position to others who are not economists. Andrews (1958, pp. 28-31) has emphasized that managers need to be seen to be performing at least as well as those by whom they could be replaced, for the same basic cost, by higher level managers or shareholders. Academics will have similar concerns, particularly those who are attempting to secure tenure or, having achieved this, promotion. But it is in the very nature of specialist jobs that they should be associated with what Williamson (1975, p. 31) has labeled "information impactedness"—that is to say, individual departments, or workers within departments, may be able to carve pleasant niches for themselves because the higher authorities who allocate resources and promotion lack the idiosyncratic knowledge that comes with experience as a particular kind of specialist. Information impactedness permits opportunism and the earning of payments, pecuniary and otherwise, in excess of transfer fees.

In the light of the above discussion we suggest that academic economists may be trying to achieve a variety of goals in the course of their work, just as Williamson's managers have utility functions which contain a variety of arguments. However, while Williamson models the utility functions of his managers in strangely neoclassical terms, we suggest that academics should be seen as choosing their activities according to certain priorities among their goals rather than by trading off the characteristics of activities against each other. In behavioral theory it is recognized that lexicographic forms of choice are more plausible than compensatory models because they make lower demands on the information processing capabilities of boundedly rational decision takers (see Fishburn, 1974, Bettman, 1975, and, for a more detailed treatment with extensions to cover the budgeting of resources, Earl, 1983b).

Thus we assume that academics set targets for the characteristics in which they are interested, ranking the characteristics in order of priority. They then avoid considering trade-offs and attempt independently to pursue as many of the targets as possible. The priority ranking acts as a conflict resolving and filtering tool until only one of the competing plans of action remains. (There is no reason why Williamson's managerial theory cannot be rewritten along such lines so that it occupies less of a no-man's-land between neoclassical and behavioral economics.) We bear the behavioral analysis of choice in mind as we move on to consider the likely working goals to which an academic will aspire and look at some of the problems she will encounter on the way toward meeting them.

The following goals seem likely to be among those that an academic economist will rank highly, though they will not necessarily be ranked in the order shown:

(1) to acquire, at a particular rate, the ability to predict and control aspects of the economic environment (scientific aspiration);

(2) to achieve a particular level of fame and a place as an originative thinker in the history of economic thought ("self-image" aspiration);

(3) to obtain, at least, a particular configuration of consumption activities (life-style aspiration);

(4) to obtain particular target levels of attainment in her social, natural, and teaching environments, which conform with her image of how a university ought to be (environmental aspiration(s);

(5) to expend no more than a particular amount of effort while seeking knowledge and income (indolence aspiration);

(6) to keep situations of unfamiliarity within particular tolerable bounds (anxiety-avoidance aspiration).

Since it is not clear, in a world of partial knowledge, which is ultimately going to be the best approach to solving economic problems (see further, section 3) and since there are many economic problems to be solved, an economist should, in principle, have scope for much discretion as she goes about attempting to meet her goals. There is no single scientific rule necessarily requiring all academic economists to adopt the same practices, any more than it is necessary for managers to attempt to maximize profits when it is not clear how to do so. Academic economists may rank their goals differently, have different endowments of human capital, and exhibit different degrees of interest in particular areas of the subject. However, in the present competitive academic environment it is easy to see that, if such an economist wishes to achieve a high rate of published contributions to knowledge, high prestige, and high income, it will be rational for her to attempt to be an orthodox neoclassical theorist or econometrician. Furthermore, sunk costs of investments in such behavior militate against subsequent changes of a dramatic kind.

In order to acquire fame in her discipline, an economist will need to turn out works that the *profession* ranks highly, whether or not she believes her contributions to knowledge take her very far toward reaching her own scientific aspirations. Life-style aspirations will also be more easily attained by producing works that receive the professional seal of approval. A famous economist will be able to obtain positions in prestigious institutions, as well as consultancy and government-sponsored research work. Teaching loads may be lighter in more prestigious universities, which will mean there is more time for research and consultancy, leading to more fame, and so on. High-status institutions may also enable environmental aspirations more easily to be met, since they will attract better students, famous colleagues, and donations of private funds to improve their stocks of already elegant buildings.

If the majority of economists are orthodox neoclassical theorists, then, in order to obtain prestige or, even, for the young, relatively unknown economist, *any* kind of academic position at all, the wisest strategy may be to be a neoclassical economist too and carry out research along similar lines. It will certainly be the most anxiety-free career strategy, quite apart from a neoclassical economist's being able to feel comfort in the fact that she is not alone in her views. Conformity with the orthodox viewpoint, which will enable contributions to knowledge to receive the profession's seal of approval, is particularly advantageous in career terms, since an information impactedness situation typically exists in academic promotion and appointment committees where some members are not economists. If neoclassical economists, who usually comprise the majority of economics representatives on such committees, assert that work of a similar kind to their own is of the highest merit, noneconomists are not in a position to disagree. Candidates whose research implies that their potential colleagues and superiors are misguided fools are inevitably going to face hostility from them. The economist who does not conform with mainstream economists' images of an economic scientist is in great danger of being swept aside as one whose values are rubbish, and may find herself unemployed as a result. A previous appointment as an unconventional economist at a university full of similar eccentrics is a doubly unfavorable background for the academic attempting to move elsewhere, since even those writing letters of references may not be taken seriously.

Once an employment contract has been obtained, uncertainties and potential trade-offs abound with regard to the most fruitful way of achieving tenure or promotion. Information has to be sought from colleagues about the past decisions and supposed preferences of superiors before decisions can be taken on how best to budget time between teaching, administration, and research activities.

It is then necessary, in this hierarchy of choices, to decide upon the nature and target rate of publications to be aimed for, given the planned allocation of time to research. The problem is more complex than a mere calculation of how to maximize the length of the list of publications. The academic has to aim for, and achieve, a *curriculum vitae* the sum of whose component contributions comprises a bundle of characteristics which will survive most stages in the filtering processes of senior staff members on academic development and staffing committees.

Such concerns will be on the academic's mind when a piece she has submitted for publication has been rejected despite its not being exposed as nonsense. She has to decide on the relative merits of investing further time and effort in rewriting it; submitting it to a less prestigious outlet; or simply abandoning attempts to get it published, turning instead to other schemes. From time to time learned journals publish analyses of successful and rejected submissions, and of the time lags between submission and publication, to aid such choices. However, these can only make a limited contribution to removing the economist's anxiety in such a situation, unless the contribution in question conforms pretty much with some conventional mold. With idiosyncratic new ideas, all notions of a "probability of acceptance" are meaningless; anyone considering devoting effort to writing unorthodox papers must have a high tolerance of anxiety and be willing to risk a failure to obtain professional approval.

As is evident from the work of Hawkins et al. (1973) and Eagly (1975), the journals that command the highest prestige and are most frequently cited are concerned with the areas of research to which the *profession* accords the highest status. They do not necessarily need to offer much direct relevance to understanding everyday economic affairs. According to Ward (1972, p. 10) the lowest ranking of the dozen compartments into which economics is usually divided are the history of economic thought, economic development, and comparative economic systems. Next come labor, industrial organization, and economic history. The second-ranking specialties Ward considers to include international trade, public finance, and money and banking. Pride of place goes to micro and macro theory, along with econometrics. Thus it is that the study of the problems of the Third World comes to contribute less to academic advancement than abstract theorizing about Walrasian contingent commodity systems that do not exist.

Bounded rationality clearly prevents most economists from attempting to be among the leaders in more than a few narrow fields, but academics have a strong propensity to compete with each other at the top end of the ranking of subdisciplines. Self-supporting "snob effects" will have a part to play in this, since the economist who can shine in the most prestigious and highly competitive areas will be thought to be particularly outstanding. The academic who desires to maintain a self-image as a leader in her profession, rather than as a worker who is less in control and gets her hands dirty, will find her self-assertive tendencies most fully catered for in the highest status fields, even if their immediate practical contribution is small. This is because they "define the nature of acceptable research problems in economics and the appropriate procedures to use in solving them" (Ward, 1972, p. 10). The fact that many economists choose to concentrate their talents in top-ranking areas does not mean that there is a lack of demand from journals for their contributions. To judge from the proliferation of new journals and the increasing formalism of new ones, Say's law (i.e., supply creates its own demand) appears to be operating fairly well in the market for contributions to knowledge that display technical virtuosity.

The neoclassical style of research also happens to be much more economical in terms of effort than that which characterizes the group of economists with whose neglect we are concerned. The essence of the behavioral approach is stated by Cyert and March (1963, p. 1) at the beginning of their book, where they "propose to make detailed observations of the procedures by which firms make decisions and use these observations for a theory of decision making within organizations." Andrews (1951, p. 172), in urging the abandonment of the concept of static equilibrium, observes, likewise, that the alternative patterns of analysis "will have to be built up out of empirical studies, just as Marshallian concepts were largely informed by their founder's studies of historical processes. No amount of spinning out logical chains of analysis based upon static concepts will help in this task." As is evident in, for example, Andrews (1949), Andrews and Brunner (1950, 1952, 1975), Cyert and March (1963), Penrose (1971), Richardson and Leyland (1964), and Williamson (1964), the behavioralists have certainly been willing to engage in the highly time-consuming activity of going out into the field and talking to managers, in order to be able to construct more realistic theories by an approach verging on induction.

This kind of behavior is most unpopular with positivist neoclassical econometricians, or even purveyors of untestable hypotheses who promise to produce, in the long run, work susceptible to econometric analysis. They allege that case study work is biased due to the nature of the questions asked and suggest that sample sizes are too small. Criticisms of the latter kind seem particularly hypocritical given that neoclassical theorists are usually quite prepared to use a statistical (probabilistic) approach to the analysis of crucial decisions.

Econometricians can produce articles much more rapidly than those who engage in case studies. It is thus to be expected that economists who believe themselves to be of a high enough technical caliber will aspire to the easy approach to hypothesis testing. Such economists are able very easily to generate respectable publications by noting where, say, U.K. data are deficient and then virtually plagiarizing articles based on U.S. data the moment U.K. figures become available. Reekie (1980) has argued that this has been how a number of important U.K. articles on the economics of advertising have originated. By constructing new regression equations the authors of such papers have clearly "contributed to knowledge." But even econometric work may seem arduous when compared with pure theory. The mathematical economist who, as Hahn often puts it, "likes and can do theory" can generate contributions very rapidly with very little need to read lengthy monographs if she has a measure of creative luck or a new theorem to apply. Furthermore, if theory papers are quick to write, the cost of rejection is also low in terms of time wasted.

In seeking to keep her exertions below some tolerable level the economist will also attempt to avoid, as far as possible, revolutionary shifts in her frame of reference or usual working practices. In doing so she escapes the need for an investment in reading about and understanding new concepts. Because of the investments already sunk in a previous area of research it will often seem worth searching nearby for solutions to patch up perceived holes in the existing approach. Ideas representing or requiring incremental adjustments, which have been proposed by other economists, will be welcomed; those that call for a discontinuous change will be met with outright hostility or simply ignored (cf. Kuhn, 1970).

The outputs of the behavioral and post-Marshallian economists involve little use of high-grade mathematics, often wander outside the accepted boundaries of the discipline, and make frequent use of case studies. As a result, they have acquired little prestige, yet require a great deal of effort to digest. On these grounds alone we should not be surprised that they have failed to generate much research or come to be taught as core components of the discipline, despite their attempts to achieve realism and the absence of clear-cut refutations of their theories. However, as the next three sections show, there are other, more complex, obstacles which hinder their acceptance. That these works have been published at all, or that their authors have achieved significant academic appointments (even, in H. A. Simon's case, the Nobel Prize), is indicative of the presence of imperfections or a segmented market for academic contributions. Just as, in the work of Richardson (1960) and Hirschman (1970), slack allows financial and product markets to function in a relatively orderly manner conducive to risk taking, so slack in the academic "market" permits the survival, at least for a time, of maverick thinkers fascinated by particular ideas from which ultimately progress may come.

3. Scientific research strategies

In the course of their research, economists are continually faced with the twin problems of bounded rationality and the nonavailability of relevant information. To cope with these facts of life they need to choose a set of procedural rules comprising a search strategy for their chosen areas of specialization. Specialization of any kind is possible only if it can be assumed reasonably safe to disregard, or take for granted, certain features of the world and thus escape information overloads. It is necessary to be able to presume that the theories thus constructed are unlikely to go wrong due to a failure to perceive a close coupling of their components with those of interest to other scientists. But the researcher can never know in advance whether or not her chosen strategy will lead her astray.

The economist's entire academic upbringing will have provided her with evidence that most of the time it is safe to take a large amount on trust and apply simple procedural rules to search for new hypotheses and information, in order to overcome anomalies in her area of interest. She will have learned the subject layer by layer, gradually adding definition to detailed aspects of subdisciplines after starting with such fundamental tenets as "there's no such thing as a free lunch" (which is common to behavioral as well as neoclassical economics) and, if she is being brought up in the "vulgar" neoclassical mold, "stable Pareto efficient equilibrium conditions can be defined for any and all markets relevant to economic research and analysis" (Remenyi, 1979, p. 59). She will have seen effective ways of dealing with criticisms and anomalies and will have noted that attempts to propose theories at odds with fundamental postulates are usually met with extreme hostility, sometimes culminating in an institutional response whereby dissidents are ostracized with a refusal to appoint them or publish their work. She will also have been able to infer the successful procedural rules that such dissidents use, such as: "if publications are refused, set up a specialist journal with like-minded dissidents" (cf., *The Cambridge Journal of Economics, The Journal of Post Keynesian Economics*).

If the process of learning determines in large measure how an academic will behave once she has served her apprenticeship we should not be surprised to find that most academic economists turn out to be neoclassical equilibrium theorists. It is rare for students to be schooled in Marxian and behavioral/post-Keynesian theory simultaneously with general equilibrium analysis. Most concentrate almost entirely on the orthodox paradigm and are then required to come to grips with modern techniques upon beginning graduate work. They are then encouraged to use their technical expertise, particularly their skills as econometricians, in doctoral work. (Econometric work is favored in this context because it is much more assured of *some* kind of results than research in pure theory; it is much less resource intensive or dependent on the cooperation of external bodies than questionnaire-based case study work; and it is felt easier to pronounce upon as a novel contribution to knowledge.)

Economists with such upbringings will look for equilibrating forces and equilibrium configurations in everything they analyze. They will be well equipped to find these equilibrium features if they have grasped by some kind of inferential learning process (cf. Chomsky, 1959) the procedural rules of the game for frequently successful decision taking—not only this, but, as we argued in the previous section, they will tend to be attracted by the leisure or promotion advantages that come from practicing as a technically competent equilibrium theorist rather than attempting to swim against the tide as, say, a behavioral economist. In order to be able to continue to push back the frontiers of their economic knowledge, academics will usually shut their eyes to the Popperian problem that a framework may one day suddenly begin to seem defective because conditions have changed, even though it has performed well in the past. It may then appear inferior to a rival approach or, if it lacks a rival, its heuristic powers might simply degenerate, leaving anomalies resoluble only by the addition of increasingly ad hoc assumptions.

To summarize, the academic makes headway by ignoring as far as possible the interdependencies between theories and the partial nature of her theories, by making the least change necessary to "resolve" inconsistencies, and by avoiding getting bogged down in methodological arguments about basic principles. In Simon's (1962) terms, she assumes that the world is "decomposable" and that she has decomposed it in the appropriate way. She can then look at a portion of it at a time and build models involving only a limited number of relationships on the assumption that all others are of trivial importance to the problem at hand. If an anomaly is discovered, information overloads are avoided by not asking difficult questions. A limited rule-guided search will usually provide a way of coping with a difficulty without challenging fundamental assumptions even though, in the long run, the procedural rules may cease to deliver the goods. The procedural rules employed by the scientist will be very much the result of her upbringing. As long as they seem to be working and the scientist is able to meet her aspirations she will have no obvious reason to question them: only with the benefit of hindsight can they be shown to be incorrect and even this is not always possible.

This discussion of the nature and use of scientific research strategies on the way toward meeting the economist's overall goals has some features in common with the work on Scientific Research Programmes (SRP) associated with Lakatos (1970) and, more recently, Latsis (1976) and Remenyi (1979). Lakatos calls the set of background presumptions that scientists take without question when building auxiliary hypotheses the "hard core" of the SRP. The sets of procedural rules—the "dos and don'ts" of the SRP—he calls the "positive and negative heuristics." If anomalies are discovered when auxiliary hypotheses are being tested, this is taken to indicate that something is wrong with the hypothesis in question, or the test procedure, not with the hard core.

But this similarity between our behavioral analysis and the Lakatosian view of the evolution of ideas is only partial. The SRP approach is excessively rationalistic and neglects the role played by scientists' personal motivations in determining the popularity of ideas. Lakatos (1970, p. 55) suggests that scientists have an objective criterion by which they can decide whether to switch between competing research programs. This is the ability of a rival SRP to offer excess empirical content while explaining how the past successes of the dominant SRP came about. The problem with this criterion is that theoretical structures may not be commensurable *even if* they do yield testable hypotheses. Furthermore, test results may be interpreted in different ways or test methods queried (see section 4b below). In a world of partial models all knowledge is relativistic and current test results can never be claimed to be unambiguous or definitive. In part, knowledge must always be accepted because of faith. If such a criterion could be applied it would be hard to explain why anyone would trouble to pursue new ideas until they had generated empirical results: *someone* has to adopt a rival SRP before Lakatos's criterion can be confronted with any new set of results.

The lack of a clear-cut dividing line between progressive and degenerating research programs enables scientists whose SRPs have different logics of appraisal to apply different choice criteria and different justifications for their practices. For this reason, economists' justifications of their continuing adherence to a particular SRP, or for switching to a rival SRP, need to be examined carefully. If the potential of any given SRP is ambiguous, there is, in principle, no reason why an economist may not concoct a justification for her behavior that enables her to conceal her "real" motivations, which may have more to do with her desire to preserve her self-image and not look a fool or with anxiety avoidance, indolence, or absolute careerism.

The arguments in the previous paragraph, and the discussion of economists' effort outputs in section 2, may seem to imply that we believe economists are willing to embrace dishonesty if it generates "contributions to knowledge" that advance their careers. We believe that such extreme careerist behavior is really rather rare: few economists will *consciously* ignore the truth if the effort needed to debunk heretical suggestions is judged too high. But to say this does not preclude the possibility that the choices of many economists are unconsciously shaped by a fear of the sacrifices that their opportunity costs might entail. An economist may, for example, rank the preservation of her own self-image more highly than her desire to make genuine contributions to economic analysis. If a switch to a new SRP would have no positive career payoff, yet would involve an admission that she believes she has hitherto been foolishly wasting her time, the economist may carry on as before, despite attacks from "minority theorists," and claim that in the long run her SRP will provide the answers (cf. Hahn's 1972 statement of faith in the promise of general equilibrium theory).

The economist who behaves in such a way may indeed *believe* she is telling the truth and see herself as a humble seeker after truth rather than a careerist. However, there is a wealth of evidence from the work of cognitive psychologists which suggests that in situations of ambiguity a person's cognitive processes will shape her perceptions so that what she sees fits in with her view of the world and herself (cf. Steinbruner, 1974, Chapter 4). Hence the cognitive processes of any economist who is not a self-confessed opportunist will ensure that her perceptions of her own scientific endeavors are molded so that she *sees* her subsequent career development as a fortuitous complementary development and her choice of SRP as offering the greatest prospect for obtaining economic knowledge.

A second failing of the SRP approach to the history of science is that it appears tacitly to assume that scientists are aware of all the presently discovered anomalies in their fields and all the attempts of scientists who have used other techniques for investigating the problems of interest and have suggested solutions. In a world of bounded rationality this is an unreasoanble assumption to make. In the next three sections we shall attempt to show how ideas forming a coherent SRP may fail to take hold because they are not perceived as forming a coherent program, are not perceived as necessary because the scientist is unaware of difficulties with her work, or are simply not perceived at all, even by the scientist who is not a careerist but a humble seeker after truth.

4. The failure to meet aspirations

Inquisitive activity is a process alien to a state of equilibrium. The successful construction of a new theory, or satisfactory completion of empirical work, enables the scientist to begin to search for solutions to knowledge puzzles which previously she had not found sufficiently worthy of attention. If she thinks she is failing to meet her target rate for contributing to knowledge, the scientist must step up her search activity, following her usual procedural rules, or, if something more fundamental appears to be wrong, look for an altogether new strategy. There are four kinds of inadequate attainment, in addition to the obvious one of a research program's having run out of puzzles to solve, which are particularly likely to make an academic economist amenable to new ideas, should she come to discover them in the process of search. We shall illustrate them with case study examples.

(a) An inability to cope with growing technical demands

Economists may fail to achieve the publication rates to which they aspire if they cannot keep abreast of the mathematical developments that will lend greater rigor and formalism to their work. Few economists could act as Hicks did in his early sixties when, while writing his (1965) book, *Capital and Growth*, he realized that it was necessary to use mathematical techniques that were new to him and, with some assistance from Professor Morishima, successfully managed to come to grips with them. Lesser economists, in analogous situations, will be forced to retreat from work at the frontiers of their SRP, or consider the possibility of switching to alternative SRP, or even to another profession.

(b) The discovery of important empirical anomalies

Initially such anomalies will be approached as if they represent merely the result of using inadequate auxiliary hypotheses. They will thus be tackled as a part of the business of normal science using the procedures of the positive heuristic. A neat example of this is Baumol's (1958) attempt to construct a theory of the firm in which managers were assumed to wish to maximize sales revenue rather than profits. While acting as a consultant he noticed that managers of large corporations did not seem to treat changes in fixed costs or profits taxes as the existing theory predicted (i.e., they attempted to pass them forward into higher prices). The managers also claimed to be more interested in the value of sales than the level of profits. Baumol produced a model consistent with these observations which kept the core neoclassical assumptions that individuals engage in profit-behavior and that firms know their cost and demand constraints. Managers maximized their utility by maximizing sales revenue subject to a minimum profit constraint, which was more demanding the less imperfect the workings of the stock market control mechanism. Profit maximization was allowed in this model as a special case.

Where minor adjustments do not resolve anomalies without additional ad hoc fudges' being necessary, a more wide-ranging search may be carried out. Where anomalies are discovered not by econometric investigation but by fieldwork, the findings may sometimes seem instantly to provide a new hard core, permitting an approach to theory formation that is not far removed from induction. As Andrews (1951, p. 140) explains, his (1949) disequilibrium theory of the competitive oligopoly firm came about as a result of his discussions with managers in the U.K. textile and footwear industries. These discussions made him aware of the importance that was attached to goodwill, and of fears that the charging of excessively high prices or the failure to provide adequate deliveries of an adequate product to regular customers would result in the permanent loss of hard-won markets. Such factors, absent from the marginalist equilibrium model, became central to his new theory. Andrews's theory, it must be added, provided an alternative solution to Baumol's anomaly even before Baumol perceived the problem, since it showed that long-run profit maximization and sales revenue maximization amounted to the same thing in a disequilibrium framework. Andrews's closely related, nonmarginalist theory of investment came about similarly, as a result of a lengthy business history investigation carried out with Elizabeth Brunner (Andrews and Brunner, 1952).

But it should be stressed that one person's empirical anomaly is often another's supportive evidence in a world of partial and interdependent models. An obvious example of this is the debate about whether firms set their prices according to marginalist rules or in the light of normal costs. Case study investigations by Hall and Hitch (1939), Saxton (1942), and Barback (1946)—the last of which was greatly influenced by Andrews's work—have been accused of containing conclusions that can be interpreted to be consistent with both views and that are based on small sample sizes with biased questionnaires. Economic investigations conducted more recently have failed to settle the dispute to the satisfaction of participants on both sides. Laidler and Parkin (1975) alleged that the antimarginalist conclusions drawn by Godley and Nordhaus (1972) from a battery of regression equations were the reverse of what the data really implied. The reply of Coutts, Godley, and Nordhaus (1978) has received very mixed reactions. The debate thus continues, with the possibility that the normal cost view might be correct, posing a severe threat to the monetarist theory of inflation (see Dow and Earl, 1982, Chapter 15).

(c) The discovery of a fundamental logical flaw

The demi-core of macroeconomics emerged as a result of Keynes's well-publicized discovery that previous theories attempting to relate changes in unemployment and money wages were beset by a fallacy of composition. But the removal of this logical flaw led to the discovery of another. When followers of Keynes attempted to extend his ideas into the realm of growth theory they discovered that the definition of an essential feature of the neoclassical theory of aggregate income distribution, namely, the marginal productivity of capital, rested on a circular argument. The ensuing "Cambridge Controversies in the Theory of Capital," which Harcourt (1972) has documented, greatly stimulated the development of an alternative post-Keynesian SRP based on the demi-core of Keynes's macroeconomics.

The controversies provide a nice demonstration of the sequential search processes and defense mechanisms of the neoclassical SRP. Eventually, Samuelson and his neoclassical colleagues conceded that there was no way round the logical flaw.[1] But this did

---

[1] See the essay by Chase in this volume.

not lead them to abandon their SRP. Instead they seem to have adopted an ultra-positivist stance, for they now argue that they will treat their logically defective theory as an "as if" model until someone demonstrates to their satisfaction the real-world existence of aggregate production functions that exhibit reswitching or capital reversing. They seem utterly oblivious to the objection that post-Keynesian economists have set against their approach, namely, that such a demonstration will never be possible. Such an impossibility does not arise because the production function perversities that attracted the bulk of the attention during the controversies are only problems of pure theory. The real problem, as Joan Robinson (1975) emphasizes, is that the "given" production functions of neoclassical theory cannot exist in the irreversible real world of technical change and historical time. If capital is not some malleable, putty-like substance, and if the book of blueprints keeps adding new pages, it is meaningless to speak of given production *functions* along which it is possible to move in *any* manner, well behaved or otherwise, as conditions change in factor markets.

(d) The discovery that assumptions may no longer be realistic

When criticized for extreme "as if" theorizing, the neoclassical economist displays herself as an ardent positivist. Beneath this outward appearance there actually lies a more reluctant follower of Friedman's methodology. As Latsis (1976, p. 22) notes, part of the positive heuristic of the neoclassical SRP consists in the procedural rule that, once it has been set up to yield a determinate solution, attempts should be made to refine a model to incorporate more realistic assumptions. This reluctant positivism means that even neoclassical theorists will be seeking to amend their models as conditions change, so long as they can preserve the notion of equilibrium. Behavioral theorists aim for realistic assumptions at the outset, even if this means that their models lack determinacy and are often ill suited to econometric testing. Therefore, when there is a change in what constitutes a realistic assumption, the attainments of neoclassical and behavioral SRPs will be affected. If this causes assumptions to become insufficiently realistic we should expect there to be a search for ways of incorporating the new environmental features in theories explaining how components of the world fit together.

Changing patterns of ownership and control in companies over the past century have repeatedly threatened economists' aspirations with regard to assumptive realism, forcing them to develop new theories of the firm. In the early editions of his *Principles*, Marshall depicted individual firms as family businesses which always died off in the long run because the quality of their owner-dominated management declined through time. A firm never lived long enough to obtain a monopoly hold on its market by undercutting its rivals and exploiting economies of scale. However, joint stock companies could hire superior management from outside and might never die off, so the question of what stopped monopolies from emerging was once more in need of a solution. Joan Robinson's (1933) *Economics of Imperfect Competition*—which followed Sraffa's (1926) suggestion that the growth of firms was restricted by the difficulties of expanding sales without bidding prices down and encountering negative marginal revenues—was one solution. Less well known is the work of Andrews (1951) and Downie (1958), which amends Marshall's disequilibrium analysis to incorporate the possibility of corporate longevity by allowing firms to jostle for industrial leadership. Central to this work is an abandonment of the neoclassical assumption that firms produce given products, always at minimum cost, with some objectively given production function. This leaves firms with scope to fight back against the transfer of their markets to firms currently enjoying superior competitive positions, by innovation and the discovery of hidden potential. In many ways this rejection of static analysis for a post-Marshallian approach anticipates, but does not appear to have inspired, Cyert and March's (1963) views on the emergence and uptake of slack.

The rise of joint stock companies also led to attempts to decide whether firms continue to be controlled by shareholders as the total number and value of shares grows, or whether they become dominated by managers keen to pursue interests of their own which conflict with shareholder welfare. Attempts to establish precisely what constitutes a realistic assumption about patterns of ownership and control are still in progress after almost fifty years of controversy, during which time the rise of institutional shareholders such as insurance companies and pension funds has given rise to concern as to whether or not the pendulum is, so to speak, swinging back whence it came. The associated debate over the relative performance characteristics of "owner"- and "manager"-controlled companies also has yet to be resolved.

5. The screening of contributions to knowledge

When the economist's aspirations exceed her attainments she will be most receptive to novel ideas. However, such contributions will make the impact intended by their authors only if they are discovered and comprehended as containing what their authors believe them to contain, and if, once understood, they seem to fit the economist's image of an acceptable theory. In a world of bounded rationality there is no guarantee that a work will reach the attention of its latent market of potentially receptive economists, quite apart from the profession in general. It is not possible for an individual to know everything about which economists have written in the past, or are working on at present, even within a fairly narrow specialty.

Before a contribution can become part of normal science it has to pass through a series of screens, just as does any consumer good before it is selected for purchase. The screening process may filter it out of a scientist's attention long before it is even appreciated as a work that perhaps *ought* to affect the way in which she views the world, even if ultimately its characteristics fail to conform with her image of what is acceptable.

(a) The publication screen

Unless they spread by personal contact, ideas will have the potential to influence the conduct of a discipline only if they are actually published or receive widespread circulation as discussion documents. If referees are insufficiently diligent or perceptive, incorrect contributions may get into print and lead others astray until their deficiencies are discovered. Similarly, novel ideas may be wrongly condemned, sometimes with traumatic results: Phelps Brown (1980, p. 9) recalls, for example, how Harrod suffered a nervous breakdown after his paper on what is now known as the marginal revenue curve was rejected on its first submission to the *Economic Journal*. There are four particularly unsatisfactory features which must be mentioned as affecting the way in which this screen works.

First, as Feige (1975) has pointed out, there is a tendency for econometric contributions to be accepted only if they contain strong results. This being known, careerist economists have a strong incentive to tailor their submissions so as to leave out any discussion of related, but "inconclusive," work. Such tailoring may take the form of adjusting the sample source, size, or time period, until impressive relationships are shown, or of the failure to include work with slightly different specifications whose weak results would cast doubt on allegedly impressive discoveries. The result may be that other academics waste a lot of time duplicating the "weak" results and, because these fail to achieve publication, the process continues. Feige suggested to the editors of the *Journal of Political Economy* that they should accept such articles prior to calculations' being made from specified data samples. It was a suggestion to which a distinctly cool reception was accorded (see also Cooley and LeRoy, 1981).

Second, work by Crane (1967) seems to suggest that the evaluation of scientific articles is affected to some degree by nonscientific factors. Journals were found to contain a disproportionate number of papers by people with the same backgrounds as their editors. She proposed two possible explanations of the role played by nonscientific elements (1967, p. 200):

(1) As a result of academic training, editorial readers respond to certain aspects of methodology, theoretical orientation, and mode of expression in the writings of those who have received similar training;

(2) Doctoral training and academic affiliations influence personal ties between scientists, which in turn influence their evaluation of scientific work. Since most scientific writing is terse, knowledge of details not usually contained in journal presentations may influence the reader's repsonse to an article.

She was proposing, in effect, that the bias may arise either because academics with similar backgrounds have in mind a similar image of what constitutes a contribution to knowledge as they prepare or referee a paper, or because when referees know the background of an author they will be more tolerant of particular omissions or shortcuts that have been taken. A statistical investigation of these interpretations, in which she attempted to find out whether a journal that did not get articles refereed anonymously was any more prone to bias (she used the *American Economic Review* as an example, but it must be added that since 1974 it has stopped the practice), led Crane to conclude that the first, rather than the second, was the most likely explanation. Matters are not, therefore, *quite* as bad as they might be: an academic does not have to be a protégée of members of an editorial board to find a place for her work, but she will increase its possibility of acceptance if she construes correctly what referees are looking for by studying the characteristics of their work and then forces what she submits into the appropriate mold.

The third factor which makes this screen particularly hard to penetrate is the tendency for journals to include a disproportionate volume of contributions by members of their own editorial boards. This is hardly surprising given that, as we noted earlier, many journals are set up by academics who have been unable to get their ideas accepted in mainstream publications (either because they did not appreciate the importance of making them appear to fit in the usual mold, or because they were inherently incompatible). But this is little consolation for the young academic who lacks the prestige required to achieve an editorial position. This factor becomes particularly important if an academic wishes to write a critique of a piece by a member of an editorial board which has appeared in her own journal. Eminent academics do not easily accept images as incompetent researchers who should know better and, since the conventional practice is to send a copy of the critique to the victim in the first instance, they are particularly well placed to suppress threatening work if they enjoy editorial powers.

Finally, we note that the practice of sending pieces to referees judged to have expertise in the same field, while it ought to result in greater critical insight being applied, is not without its disadvantages. In such situations it is not really the editor who acts as the final gatekeeper, for she is not sufficiently competent to judge the accuracy of what referees' reports say. Information impactedness allows opportunistic behavior by careerist referees who can see that a piece of work is complementary or competitive with their own. This problem is particularly acute with drafts or synopses of academic books, since publishers (unlike most journal boards) pay referees and the cost of doing so means that the convention is not to appoint more than one referee unless the first report is ambiguous—either this, or the second referee is asked merely to comment on the general impression given by the work.

(b) The agenda screen

If a work has achieved publication there is no guarantee that a scientist will read it, however relevant it may be for the problem she is trying to solve. She must first discover it and perceive that it might be useful. But she must search selectively and cannot know in advance whether she is casting her net unnecessarily wide or even whether she has, in the event, cast it wide enough. Literature search strategies thus involve an element of faith, just as do the more fundamental strategic decisions the scientist has to make about which concepts to allow into the hard core of her SRP, which we discussed in section 3.

Political, parochial, and technical considerations will be the main agenda restriction factors employed in routine scanning (e.g., neoclassical choice theorists will not normally read *The Journal of Consumer Research* even if their economics library happens to stock the journal, but will read *Econometrica*; Chicago monetarists will not normally read the *Cambridge Journal of Economics* or *Capital and Class*; and so on). Insofar as works are cross-referenced their titles and author reputations (about which we shall have more to say in the next part of this section) will be crucial, along with the sequence in which they are read, insofar as related works make only partial reference to each other. Publications such as *Contents of Recent Economics Journals*, the fact that libraries usually display new acquisitions in a separate, conspicuous section, and the tendency for authors to cite their previous works (which makes their discovery much easier) all help to ensure a concentration of routine scanning attention on recent publications.

Agenda restriction means that potentially important ideas placed in obscure journals, or even hitherto ignored ideas in old issues of mainstream journals, or ideas in books no longer in print and thus not listed in publishers' catalogues may go unnoticed for long periods. The rate of growth of knowledge is thus slowed down and effort is wasted on reinventing ideas. In economics, a good example of the consequences of inefficient screening techniques is the (re)discovery of the problem of investment coordination and the attainment of equilibrium in economies which operate without future markets. This problem deserves to be known as the Richardson Problem after the post-Marshallian theorist G. B. Richardson, who spent most of his academic life investigating and unsuccessfully trying to persuade his fellow economists to take it seriously.

The essence of the Richardson Problem is that, in any market which is not naturally destined always to be occupied by a vertically integrated monopoly producer, the profitability of the investments of any single firm will depend not only on aggregate investment and consumer choices but also on the amount of competitive and complementary investment undertaken by other firms. Unless there are fairly narrow bounds on who else might see a market opening and be able to act upon it, a firm will have no way, short of collusion or espionage, of forming conjectures about the demand price for its output, *even if* it has accurate knowledge of consumer preferences. Furthermore, it cannot know the future supply price of its inputs or whether it will be worth investing in vertical integration unless it knows who else is planning to invest in future supply capacity.

Richardson was not, in fact, the first person to discover the difficulty. That honor seems to rest with Morgenstern, who aired his concerns about the prospects of attaining economic equilibrium without perfect foresight in papers published in German in 1929 and 1935, some time before he began to work seriously on *The Theory of Games*, with its related prisoners' dilemma problem. Useful discussions of these papers are to be found in the contribution of Borch to Hicks and Weber (eds.) (1973, pp. 67-68). Dobb (1937) and Joan Robinson (1954) raised the same kind of question and, writing from a left-wing viewpoint, presented the coordination problem as an inherent defect in capitalism. However, they provided no evidence to show how serious were its consequences. More open-minded treatments were offered by Williams (1949) and Richardson himself (1956, 1959). Richardson then went on in his (1960) book and subsequent (1967, 1971, 1972) articles to consider how serious a problem it had to be and whether or not planning might necessarily be better.

Eventually a formal mathematical discussion was provided by Radner (1968), who was at pains to emphasize that most economists devote attention to only the first of the following two types of uncertainty that affect economic transactions: (1) that uncertainty due to states of nature not being known in advance (which affects a good's value in use), and (2) that uncertainty caused by people not knowing what other traders are going to do (which affects value in exchange). It was, as Loasby (1977) has pointed out, rather unfortunate for Richardson that Debreu's (1959) axiomatic attempt to "handle uncertainty" within a general equilibrium framework, which deals only with "state-of-the-world" uncertainty in a highly implausible institutional context, appeared at the same time as his own less formal work. It must have been a major distraction. Now that Radner has set out the nature of the Problem in the language of the general equilibrium theorists they should have less reason to neglect it (and a similar point can be made with respect to behavioral theories of the firm now that Radner, 1975, has attempted to model satisficing behavior by managers in formal terms).

However, the problem is that, while one can set up the Problem in the language of general equilibrium theory, it is not possible to "solve" it except by making assumptions that are utterly unrealistic, in the manner of Debreu. Thus, the common practice of those who are aware of Radner's paper is to cite and then assume there is an auctioneer or a recontracting process whereby equilibrium prices may be generated in all markets (including a complete set of futures markets) prior to production's taking place. General equilibrium theorists remain unaware of Richardson's disequilibrium analysis, in which the scale of the Problem was limited by the existence of knowledge imperfections about profit opportunities; by forms of implicit or explicit collusion (possible only in a situation of competition between small numbers of firms); by the existence of goodwill and other "institutional" ties between buyers and sellers of inputs; and by barriers to entry (which might include limit pricing of the kind suggested by Andrews). All of these factors are, in any case, at odds with the formal perfectly competitive system of general equilibrium analysis.

The example of the Richardson Problem illustrates particularly well the effects of the agenda screen (and perhaps the tendency for people to filter out ideas at odds with their core beliefs), since there is a complete absence of cross-referencing between those who discovered it. Furthermore, apart from Morgenstern's original contributions, none of the articles appeared in obscure journals, while Joan Robinson's paper figures in a well-known collection.

(c) The novelty screen and the role of reviews

The fact that an economist has discovered a work which seems a possible aid to the solution of puzzles in her area of interest does not guarantee she will actually read it for herself in its original form. When trying to decide whether or not to examine a work, and in what detail, the economist is in a position entirely analogous to that of managers in Kay's (1979) behavioral theory of the allocation of resources to corporate research and development (R & D). If a manager knew what the result of R & D expenditure was going to be she would have no need to undertake it, but how can she know whether it is worth making if she has little idea of what the result could be? Once more, the inquisitive person is driven to choose a set of rules for choice which experience suggests will provide an adequate way, so to speak, of separating the wheat from the chaff, a way of distinguishing helpful schemes from those, now on her agenda of possibles, which it might be a waste of time to read.

Academic rules for the selection of works worth serious study are just specialized forms of the cybernetic decision rules we use to simplify the process of shopping in a supermarket. The works of authors with established reputations for innovative flair or expertise in a particular area are more likely to be picked from library shelves than works by those who are unknown or who are known to repeat the same ideas over and again. At this stage in the screening process vital roles will usually be played by the precise wording of titles and the clarity of abstracts, along with the reports of colleagues and reviewers. Mathematical equilibrium theorists may very rapidly shut a book if a brief examination indicates low mathematical content, while disequilibrium theorists, whose methodological perpectives often rule out mathematical expositions, will look only at books with a high enough ratio of words to notation to conform with their image of economics. Furthermore, books may be selected only if they are stocked.

Clearly, then, authors of new contributions to knowledge are in the same position as sales managers in Andrew's theory of the firm, desperately trying by nonprice means to attract goodwill from people who will usually look to offerings from suppliers of consumer and industrial products with established reputations. Like such managers, unknown academics may find it easier to acquire reputations via product differentiation, so long as they do not confuse potential readers or lead them to believe that their work will destroy existing understandings and replace them with anxiety. Just as critics' reactions can often make or break a Broadway show on its opening night, so academic reviewers may affect beliefs about a contribution to economics depending on how they distinguish a work from related contributions, assess how logical are its arguments, and delimit its favorable or unfortunate characteristics.

(d) The comprehension screen

After a scientist has decided to explore the contents of a particular piece of work she has continually to ask herself whether she has devoted sufficient attention to it. If it is not easy to understand and requires several readings before it can be grasped fully, the impression may begin to develop that the arguments contained in it are misconceived. The comprehension screen is a communications barrier that any product, be it a scientific theory or a traded commodity, *must* overcome in order to demonstrate that it *is* superior. Academics will not lightly allow their time to be wasted and will bring further procedural rules of appraisal into operation to prevent this from happening. If their personal strategies have hitherto seemed to be working adequately there is no clear reason why they should choose to use any new rules of appraisal to decide whether they have got enough out of a particular contribution to knowledge. A work which is in some doubt and does not conform to economists' typical images as laid down by their rules of appraisal will lose their attention.

The works of Andrews, Penrose (1959), and Williamson (1975) are particularly good examples of contributions presented in ways which may cause a mainstream reader's attention to be removed too soon, even supposing they actually survive earlier screens and get read at all. The heuristics of the neoclassical SRP demand rigor, and the technically competent practitioner of this SRP is used to dealing with compactly presented models in which she can check, say, the general structure and first- and second-order conditions rapidly to complete her understanding. This is perhaps the reason that reviewers of Andrews's work, despite supposedly being captive audiences, often came to the conclusion that it was only a description of what firms might do, set out for managers, rather than a set of interwoven arguments that exposed the problems that confront firms in disequilibrium, oligopolistic markets and then deduced the kinds of business policies that would lead to long-run viability (see Irving, 1978).

6. Choice between alternative bodies of thought

There is no guarantee that an attempted contribution to knowledge will survive all of the screens discussed in the previous section. But, if someone chooses to publish it, if academics choose strategies comprising procedural rules that lead them to discover it and deem it worthy of detailed attention, and if their cognitive processes cause them to understand it as something not obviously logically defective or at odds with reality, it still has to survive competition with the academic's existing body of ideas before she will adopt it. This is so even if her existing ideas presently seem inadequate as tools for enabling her to meet her aspirations. We have come back, after our discussion of aspirational failures, search, and the screening of ideas, to the difficult area of choice exposed in section 3 in our critique of Lakatos's objective criterion for choosing between competing research programs, as well as in section 4. In this section we reiterate the main thrust of the arguments behind that critique, boldly state our view of the nature of the choice between ideas that get this far in the screening process, and consider a factor, which we have hitherto neglected, that seems to play an important part in determining the fate of a body of work.

The essential difficulty with Lakatos's view of the reasons why scientists switch between sets of theories is that in a world of partial models all knowledge is relativistic and current test results can never be claimed to be unambiguous or definitive. Unless research is controlled by some form of dictatorship, then, there is no necessary reason why scientists should agree on the merits of competing theoretical explanations of particular phenomena, on the value of entire research programs, or even on the choice of which problems are worthy of investigation. Ambiguity is antithetical to the idea that there should be a generally accepted logic of appraisal. If test results are ambiguous, adherence to positivism must rest on faith and the fact that, as a way of proceeding in research, it fits in with its user's world view and priority system. The fact that there can be many theories to explain the same phenomenon, none of which can be a complete model, likewise means that those who criticize positivism have no obviously more secure basis for maintaining that a particular model that they accept on a priori grounds for its assumptive realism will not lead them astray.

Each theoretical framework will have a particular set of perceived characteristics, just as will competing investment or consumption schemes outside the realm of academic work. Since there is no obviously acceptable logic of appraisal to use when choosing between rival theories, just as there is no obviously best

investment or consumption scheme, choice between theories ultimately rests on personal preferences and perceptions, shaped as
they are by predispositions, by upbringing in a social/academic/
economic context, and by the selectivity of cognitive processes.
Economists can do no more than assert what they believe to be
the appropriate priority rankings for economic scientists to have
over the characteristics that rival theories might be construed to
contain, and then make their choices accordingly.

It is rare for a novel way of thinking to be able to provide all its
potential users with a means of meeting some of their goals without preventing them from meeting others that it seems possible to
attain if they adhere to their existing frameworks. In order to
catch on widely, new ideas may therefore need to be marketed in
a way which makes it seem that they offer a bundle of characteristics which will survive better than their rivals the filtering processes
of the bulk of their potential users. If they cannot be made to appear in such an image, and if it is not possible to persuade potential users to change their aspirations and priority rankings to form
a mold which they will fit, they will be restricted in appeal to only
a small segment of the academic world. As an example of how not
to sell a body of ideas even to a potentially receptive minor segment we shall consider once more the case of Andrews's work. But,
before we do so, we should note that we have so far failed to discuss one particular characteristic which scientists seem to rank highly when deciding whether or not a body of thought is acceptable.

Skinner (1979) has shown that a characteristic scientists frequently demand from a contribution to knowledge is that it
should be able to account for as many features from as few principles as possible. Skinner demonstrates that Adam Smith, Popper,
and Shackle have strikingly similar views on the need for economy
and universality in theoretical approaches to science. He quotes
Adam Smith as saying ". . . it gives us pleasure to see the phenomena which we reckoned the unaccountable all deduced from the
same principle (commonly a well-known one) and all united in one
chain." When a scientist has a simple theory which seems to explain many things she has less need to be a specialist and restrict
the scope of her inquiry. Furthermore, since any theory is but a
partial model which can be treated only in a restricted way, al-
lusions to general applicability, illustrated with the aid of diverse
case studies and analogies, help reduce anxiety when one uses it.

Andrews's contributions to economics, unlike, say, Keynes's (1936) *General Theory*, were launched completely without regard to their ability to satisfy economists' aspirations for generality. The features which disadvantage them in this respect also hinder them with regard to other characteristics in which theorists seem to be interested. His contributions dispense with marginalism, emphasize the characteristics of aggregates, are not reductionist (unlike neoclassical theories), and concentrate on disequilibrium processes. Each of these features violates the conditions required to define states of Pareto optimality, without offering any obvious alternative criteria for making judgments about changes in welfare. As a result, only a specialized industrial economist is likely to be very receptive to his work. But, even within the narrow area of industrial economics, Andrews made two blunders, the effect of which was to make his work seem less general than it was. First, he made the mistake of attacking potential allies such as Cyert and March, and Penrose, failing to see that their ideas were actually compatible with his own. He also published his ideas in stages over a long period, in an inconvenient order, and never integrated them as a single volume (see Andrews, 1949, 1950, 1951, 1958, 1964, Andrews and Brunner, 1952, 1975, and Andrews and Friday, 1960).

7. Conclusion

In this essay we have attempted to use a synthesis of behavioral ideas, with a strong marketing perspective, as a novel way of approaching the history of economic thought. This seems to represent an important expansion of the generality of behavioral analyses of choice. Philosophers of science characteristically do not consider the motivations and decision-taking process of scientists. We have used our proposed theory of economists' behavior to criticize Lakatosian SRP analysis, but our arguments are entirely consistent with Feyerabend's (1975) anarchic extension of the (1970) work of Kuhn and help to explain the behavior patterns these authors have observed in the physical sciences. To illustrate how the new theory works we have made a case study of the failure of earlier attempts to write disequilibrium economics (to which this paper is complementary) to affect more than a small minority of academic economists.

We have taken the position that an academic worker is not fundamentally different from any other workers, since the products of academic labor are both monetary and psychic income, while the incumbent of an academic job inevitably faces anxiety as to whether she is going about it the right way and as to how her peers will view what she does. Whether or not academics are aware of the possibility, there is much scope for personal anxieties to shape their perceptions about the nature of the contributions they are making. This scope exists because, in a world of partial models, it can never be shown unambiguously that one model is, or will be, superior to another in terms of its empirical performance or even the realism of its assumptions. Thus, although each academic research program will have some logic of appraisal there is no reason for a universal set of choice criteria to be applied when theories are being evaluated.

Contributions to knowledge have been treated as if they are not fundamentally different from consumer products or investment goods, about whose merits nonacademics have to argue in the ordinary business of everyday life. As in everyday life, there is no guarantee that the economic scientist will be aware of a pressing need to consider trying out something new as an aid to understanding economic events. She may be blissfully ignorant, even, of high-level difficulties in her framework of analysis. If these are pointed out by someone else she may remain "justifiably" convinced that it will be possible to resolve them without abandoning the framework. This will especially be the case if the framework has hitherto been very helpful and is not under attack from all directions. There is no guarantee that she will be aware of alternative theories or, if she discovers them, will take the trouble to ensure that she has understood them in the ways intended by their authors before she rejects them. The greater the time pressure and volume of potentially useful ideas, the more selective her search processes have to be to ensure she escapes information overloads and makes enough tangible contributions to knowledge.

It will be rare for a body of thought to be perceived as dominating over its rivals in all of its characteristics. Because of this, the academic's own priority ranking, rather than any unanimously agreed logic of appraisal, has the final say in determining which theories she will accept. Feelings of anxiety may cause cognitive processes to shape perceptions of the merits of contributions to knowledge in regard to lower priority characteristics in situations where inconsistencies would otherwise be implied by a particular choice of analytical tool. Thus, whatever choice the academic makes, she will feel that she is making an honest selection, except in rare cases of careerist behavior by charlatans. Such cases are entirely possible in a world of incomplete and impacted information. It is not easy to draw the line between the charlatan and the seeker after truth whose perceptions have been shaped by the selectivity of her cognitive processes and reading.

The pressures of the modern academic life-style make it particularly hard for a scientist to take a detached view of why she is doing what she is doing. Other academics pass judgment on the soundness of this and, during her upbringing as an economist, shape her expectational environment. The signals most economists receive are that mathematical tractability is to be rated above realism of assumptions, or "presently available" testable predictions. The economist who writes disequilibrium theories of words restricts both the prestige and number of potential outlets for her work and may be subjected to hostile taunts to the effect that, say, what she is doing is mere "economic poetry" because it lacks mathematical rigor. Such an economist also has to read lengthy monographs or undertake time-consuming case studies instead of being able merely to inspect formal constructions and engage in "number crunching" with published data.

Our analysis leads to two connected ways of explaining the dominance of neoclassical economics. One is that it is safer and more rewarding to be an equilibrium theorist of the conventional kind. The other is that upbringings affect the constructions young economists form of what it is that economists do and they then act in conformity with this image unless given an exceedingly strong cause to behave otherwise. Kuhn's (1970) suggestion that a scientific revolution will not succeed until older scientists have died off seems entirely reasonable from a behavioral standpoint. If a mature scientist is to undergo a personal scientific revolution she will have largely to dispense with a well-formed world view. Since the choice will not usually be clear-cut, such a transition, if made, would entail a period during which she suffered nothing short of a scientific nervous breakdown.

But it has not been the intention of this essay to suggest that we should never see a radical, nonequilibrium economist, or perceive mainstream economists as members of a mutual admiration society which the public at large lacks the qualifications to criticize. The market for ideas is sufficiently segmented, and contains enough slack, to permit some economists with different upbringings, perception tendencies, and past reading to be able to follow unorthodox schools of thought if they wish to do so. For such economists, slack in the economic system provides hope. A given body of thought (such as, at the subdiscipline level, Keynesian macroeconomics) can initially win favor only later to be replaced by a resurgence of the originally supported research program (cf. Dow and Earl, 1982, Chapters 13 and 18). It can itself come back to the fore, so long as some academic mavericks take an interest in it, in a way rather akin to Downie's (1958) depiction of the competitive struggle between firms. A permanent transfer can occur only if there is no entry by a new body of thought or if there is an inadequate innovative response from what most would presently judge to be an outclassed approach.

REFERENCES

Andrews, P. W. S. *Manufacturing Business*. Macmillan (London), 1949.

_____. "Some Aspects of Competition in Retail Trade." *Oxford Economic Papers* No. 2 (New Series), 1950.

_____. "Industrial Analysis in Economics." In *Oxford Studies in the Price Mechanism*, edited by T. Wilson and P. W. S. Andrews. Oxford University Press, 1951.

_____. "Competition in the Modern Economy." Reprinted from *Competitive Aspects of Oil Operations*, edited by G. Sell. Institute of Petroleum (London), 1958.

_____. *On Competition in Economic Theory*. Macmillan (London), 1964.

Andrews, P. W. S., and E. Brunner. "Productivity and the Businessman." *Oxford Economic Papers* No. 2 (New Series), 1950.

_____. *Capital Development in Steel*. Basil Blackwell, 1952.

_____. *Studies in Pricing*. Macmillan (London), 1975.

Andrews, P. W. S., and F. A. Friday. *Fair Trade: Resale Price Maintenance Re-examined*. Macmillan (London), 1960.

Barback, R. H. *The Pricing of Manufactures*. Macmillan (London), 1964.

Baumol. W. J. "On the Theory of Oligopoly." *Economica* No. 25 (New Series), 1958.

Bettman, J. R. "Issues in Designing Consumer Information Environments." *Journal of Consumer Research* No. 2, December 1975.

Chomsky, N. "B. F. Skinner's *Verbal Behaviour*: A Review." *Language* No. 35, January 1959.

Cooley, Thomas S., and Stephen F. LeRoy. "Identification and Estimation of Money Demand," *American Economic Review*, December 1981, pp. 825-844.

Coutts, K. J., W. A. H. Godley, and W. D. Nordhaus. *Industrial Pricing in the United Kingdom*. Cambridge University Press, 1978.

Crane, D. "The Gatekeepers of Science: Some Factors Affecting the Selection of Articles for Scientific Journals." *American Sociologist* No. 2, November 1967.

Cyert, R. M., and J. G. March. *A Behavioral Theory of the Firm*. Prentice-Hall (Englewood Cliffs, N.J.), 1963.

Debreu, G. *Theory of Value*. Wiley, 1959.

Dobb, M. H. *Political Economy and Capitalism*. Routledge, 1937.

Dow, S. C., and P. E. Earl. "Methodology and Orthodox Monetary Policy." Paper presented at Cambridge Journal of Economics Conference on The New Orthodoxy in Economics, Sidney Sussex College, Cambridge, 22-25 June, 1981.

_____. *Money Matters: A Keynesian Approach to Monetary Economics*. Martin Robertson, 1982.

Downie, J. *The Competitive Process*. Duckworth, 1958.

Eagly, R. V. "Economics Journals as a Communications Network." *Journal of Economic Literature* No. 8, September 1975.

Earl, P. E. "The Consumer in His/Her Social Setting: A Subjectivist View." In *Beyond Positive Economics*? edited by J. Wiseman. Macmillan (London), 1983a.

_____. *The Economic Imagination: Towards a Behavioural Analysis of Choice*. Wheatsheaf Books/M.E. Sharpe, Inc., 1983b.

Feige, E. L. "The Consequences of Journal Editorial Policies and a Suggestion for Revision." *Journal of Political Economy* No. 83, December 1975.

Feyerabend, P. K. *Against Method: Outline of an Anarchistic Theory of Knowledge*. New Left Books, 1975.

Fishburn, P. O. "Lexicographic Orders, Utilities and Decision Rules: A Survey." *Management Science* No. 20, July 1974.

Friedman, M. "The Methodology of Positive Economics." In M. Friedman *Essays in Positive Economics*. University of Chicago Press, 1953.

Godley, W. A. H., and W. D. Nordhaus. "Pricing in the Trade Cycle." *Economic Journal* No. 82, September 1972.

Hahn, F. H. "Notes on Vulgar Economy." University of Cambridge (mimeographed), 1972.

Hall, R. L., and C. J. Hitch. "Price Theory and Business Behaviour." *Oxford Economics Papers* No. 2, 1939.

Harcourt, G. C. *Some Cambridge Controversies in the Theory of Capital*. Cambridge University Press, 1972.

Hawkins, R. G., L. S. Ritter, and I. Walter. "What Economists Think of Their Journals." *Journal of Political Economy* No. 81, September 1973.

Hicks, J. R. *Capital and Growth*. Oxford University Press, 1965.

Hicks, J. R., and W. Weber (eds.). *Carl Menger and the Austrian School of Economics*. Oxford University Press, 1973.

Hirschman, A. O. *Exit, Voice and Loyalty*. Harvard University Press, 1970.

Irving, J. "P. W. S. Andrews and the Unsuccessful Revolution." Unpublished Ph. D. thesis. Wollongong University, 1978.

Kay, N. M. *The Innovating Firm: A Behavioural Theory of Corporate R and D*. Macmillan (London), 1979.

Keynes, J. M. *The General Theory of Employment, Interest and Money*. Macmillan (London), 1936.

Kuhn, T. S. *The Structure of Scientific Revolutions* (2nd edition). University of Chicago Press, 1970.

Laidler, D. E. W., and M. Parkin. "Inflation: A Survey." *Economic Journal* No. 85, December 1975.

Lakatos, I. "Falsification and the Methodology of Scientific Research Programmes." In I. Lakatos and A. Musgrave, *Criticism and the Growth of Knowledge.* Cambridge University Press, 1970.

Latsis, S. J. "A Research Programme in Economics." In *Method and Appraisal in Economics*, edited by S. J. Latsis. Cambridge University Press, 1976.

Loasby, B. J. *Choice, Complexity and Ignorance.* Cambridge University Press, 1976.

_____. "On Imperfections and Adjustments." University of Stirling Discussion Papers in Economics, Finance and Investment No. 50, 1977.

Marshall, A. *Principles of Economics* (8th edition). Macmillan (London) 1920.

Penrose, E. T. *The Theory of The Growth of The Firm.* Basil Blackwell, 1959 (2nd edition, 1980).

_____. *The Growth of Firms, Middle East Oil and Other Essays.* Frank Cass, 1971.

Phelps Brown, E. H. "Sir Roy Harrod: A Biographical Memoir." *Economic Journal* No. 90, March 1980.

Radner, R. "Competitive Equilibrium Under Uncertainty." *Econometrica* No. 36, 1968.

_____. "A Behavioural Model of Cost Reduction." *Bell Journal of Economics* No. 6, Spring 1975.

Reekie, W. D. "Advertising and Profitability." Lecture given to University of Stirling Staff Seminar, April 1980.

Remenyi, J. V. "Core Demi-Core Interaction: Toward a General Theory of Disciplinary and Subdisciplinary Growth." *History of Political Economy* No. 11, Spring 1979.

Richardson, G. B. "Demand and Supply Reconsidered." *Oxford Economic Papers* No. 8 (New Series), June 1956.

_____. "Equilibrium, Expectations and Information." *Economic Journal* No. 69, June 1959.

_____. *Information and Investment.* Oxford University Press, 1960.

_____. "Price Notification Schemes." *Oxford Economic Papers* No. 19 (New Series), November 1967.

_____. "Planning Versus Competition." *Soviet Studies* No. 22, January 1971.

_____. "The Organization of Industry." *Economic Journal* No. 82, September 1972.

Richardson, G. B., and N. H. Leyland. "The Growth of Firms." *Oxford Economic Papers* No. 16 (New Series), March 1964.

Robinson, J. V. *The Economics of Imperfect Competition.* Macmillan (London), 1933 (2nd edition, 1969).

_____. "The Impossibility of Profits." In *Monopoly and Competition and Their Regulation*, edited by E. H. Chamberlin. Macmillan (London), 1954.

_____. "The Unimportance of Reswitching." *Quarterly Journal of Economics* No. 89, February 1975.

Saxton, C. C. *The Economics of Price Determination.* Oxford University Press, 1942.

Scitovsky, T. "A Note on Profit Maximization and Its Implications." *Review of Economic Studies* No. 11, 1943.

Shackle, G. L. S. *Epistemics and Economics*. Cambridge University Press, 1973.

Simon, H. A. "The Architecture of Complexity." *Proceedings of the American Philosophical Society* No. 106, December 1962.

Skinner, A. S. "Adam Smith: An Aspect of Modern Economics?" *Scottish Journal of Political Economy* No. 26, June 1979.

Sraffa, P. "The Laws of Returns under Competitive Conditions." *Economic Journal* No. 36, December 1926.

Steinbruner, J. D. *The Cybernetic Theory of Decision*. Princeton University Press, 1974.

Ward, B. *What's Wrong With Economics?* Macmillan (London), 1972.

Williams, B. R. "Types of Competition and the Theory of Employment." *Oxford Economic Papers* No. 1 (New Series), January 1949.

Williamson, O. E. *The Economics of Discretionary Behavior: Managerial Objectives in the Theory of the Firm*. Prentice-Hall (Englewood Cliffs, N.J.), 1964.

_____. *Markets and Hierarchies: Analysis and Antitrust Implications*. The Free Press, 1975.

Richard X. Chase

6

THE DEVELOPMENT OF CONTEMPORARY MAINSTREAM MACROECONOMICS: VISION, IDEOLOGY, AND THEORY

‖ ‖

I. Introduction

In the early pages of *The Economic Consequences of the Peace*, published in 1919, one finds a clear statement of Keynes's perception of the destabilized capitalism that was emergent in the aftermath of the First World War.[1] Joseph Schumpeter saw in this the seeds that were to develop into *The General Theory of Employment, Interest and Money* some seventeen years later.[2]

To Schumpeter, Keynes's 1919 perception evidenced a gestalt-like "vision" that was the necessary prerequisite for the latter's subsequent scientific, i.e., analytic, endeavors on the structure and function of the mature capitalist economy. The essential purpose of this largely intuitive vision was to give Keynes (the ideologue) something for Keynes (the scientist) to be scientific about.[3] Within this context Schumpeter then sees *The Tract on Monetary Reform* (1923) and *The Treatise on Money* (1930) as the most important of Keynes's subsequent struggles to develop and articulate his earlier prescience.[4]

Revista Internazionale di Scienze Economiche e Commerciali, 1981, No. 6.

[1] J. M. Keynes, *Collected Works*, Vol. 2, Chapter 2, especially pp. 7-16.

[2] Joseph Schumpeter, *History of Economic Analysis* (New York: Oxford University Press, 1954), p. 42 and also p. 1171.

[3] Schumpeter develops this theme in his Presidential Address to The American Economic Association, "Science and Ideology," *American Economic Review*, March 1949, especially pp. 345-52.

[4] Schumpeter, *History of Economic Analysis*, p. 1171.

The Treatise on Money—Keynes's most serious academic endeavor prior to *The General Theory*—failed to express his vision adequately. As a result, according to Schumpeter, "with admirable resoluteness, he [Keynes] determined to throw away the impeding pieces of apparatus, and bent to the task of framing an analytic system that would express his fundamental idea *and nothing else*."[5] In support of Schumpeter's thesis, there is Keynes's own expression of his self-conscious purpose in writing *The General Theory*. In a letter to George Bernard Shaw in 1935, he wrote that

> ... I believe myself to be writing a book on economic theory that will largely revolutionise ... the way the world thinks about economic problems. When my new theory has been duly assimilated and mixed with politics and feelings and passions I can't predict what the final upshot will be in its effect on action and affairs. But there will be a great change ...[6]

And what did indeed follow in the wake of *The General Theory* was the upheaval that Keynes foresaw.[7]

But revolutions are not events; they are processes. The development of the Keynesian revolution would be no exception to this rule, and, as Keynes himself points out in the above quotation, he expected nothing else.

A primary endeavor of this essay will be to outline the basic course taken by the mainstream of the so-called Keynesian revolution as it articulated both the theory and the underlying vision of the modern market economy, particularly as such relate to the United States. The theoretical and visionary schema that unfolds

[5] Ibid., pp. 1171-1172 (emphasis in the original).

[6] Keynes, *Collected Works*, Vol. 13, pp. 492-493.

[7] In writings published prior to *The General Theory*—e.g., *Let Lloyd George Do It* (1929) and *The Means to Prosperity* (1933)—Keynes not only put forth his insight about stimulating effective demand via public loan expenditure; he even offered a program for achieving the desired ends. However, very little theory was offered in support of the insight and the corollary program.

On this matter of theory, Dudley Dillard has pointed out, "What remained in order to create a revolution was to construct a system of analysis that would elaborate the insight and justify the program." (See Dillard, "Revolutions in Economic Theory," *Southern Economic Journal*, April 1978, p. 712.) And, as is well known, Keynes addressed *The General Theory* not to policymakers or "men of affairs" but rather to his "fellow economists."

Also, as J. Ronnie Davies documents, pre-*General Theory* policy proposals aimed at fiscal stimulation of the economy were quite common in the United States, "conservative" Jacob Viner being one outstanding example. See Davies, *The New Economics and the Old Economists* (Ames, Iowa: The Iowa University Press, 1971.)

will be useful as a point of reference for interpreting and understanding the import and meaning of what might, at first blush, appear to be arcane and/or highly specialized trivia in the development of economic theory. In seeking our insights, we will bring attention to bear on particular developments in general equilibrium theory and in capital theory, and on the relationship that these developments had in establishing the groundwork for what is now coming to be seen as economics in a *post* Keynesian era.

II. Identifying the Keynesian revolution in economic theory

Keynes's intuitive vision of an unstable capitalism was confirmed during the interwar years and the processes of the theory–policy revolution in economic science that bear his name gathered momentum. Sidestepping the logical and semantical difficulties of the term "revolution,"[8] we find that the pertinent question for our purposes at this point is: what is it that distinguishes and separates the *theoretical* aspects of that *historical* episode, launched by Keynes and loosely known as the "Keynesian Revolution" from whatever it was that proceeded it?

Basic to understanding Keynes's theoretically revolutionary sally in *The General Theory* is the recollection of that period's dichotomization of economics into the theory of value and distribution of *real* resources on the one hand and the theory of *money* on the other. Keynes felt that this split was an improper one for analyzing the structure and function of the market economy of his age, and he spoke quite directly to the point in *The General Theory*:

> The division of Economics between the Theory of Value and Distribution on the one hand and the Theory of Money on the other hand is, I think, a false division. The right dichotomy is, I suggest, between the Theory of the Industry or Firm and of the rewards and the distribution between different uses of a given quantity of resources on the one hand, and the Theory of Output and Employment as a whole on the other hand.[9]

[8] For example, whether the historical watershed called the Keynesian revolution is best interpreted as the discontinuity (and nonrationality) of a Kuhnian paradigm switch or as the accretive (and rational) change from a "degenerating" scientific research program (SRP) to a "progressive" one, à la Imre Lakatos, is not at issue here. (Some further reference is made to this issue in Section 6 and footnote 45 below.)

[9] Keynes, *Collected Works*, Vol. 7, p. 293.

This realignment of the subdivisions of economic analysis is important in that it establishes the basic aggregate or macroeconomic stage on which Keynes was to choreograph the more specific elements of his revolution in economic theory. And, focusing on this aggregate or macroeconomic aspect of Keynes's dichotomization of economic theory, James Meade, in addressing the question of the particular nature of Keynes's theoretical revolution, offered the graphic observation that

> Keynes's intellectual revolution was to shift economists from thinking normally in terms of a model of reality in which a dog called *savings* wagged his tail labeled *investment* to thinking in terms of a model in which a dog called *investment* wagged his tail labeled *savings*.[10]

But this basic causative process—starting from investment and running to savings (via the multiplier effect on income)—that Meade identifies as the heart of the Keynesian revolution is also a process that is both unstable and noncalculable. For behind the neat diagrammatic exposition that runs from liquidity preference to the marginal efficiency of capital—the latter being the key determinants of the rate of interest and thence the level of investment—lies what G. L. S. Shackle has called "the horrid void of indeterminacy and nonrationality."[11] For the smoothly drawn schedules of liquidity preference and the marginal efficiency of capital both rest on such foundations as mood and confidence and animal spirits concerning the future; and nothing can be more subject to nonprobabilistic uncertainty than the future. And, indeed, to Keynes the historically given probabilities of the Benthamite calculus which guided the variables of "classical" theory were an illusion.[12] Such calculations are to be considered more as palliatives to distract and put to rest the disquieting sense of risk and jeopardy that must be incurred in the real world of actions and affairs where the frequency occurrence of past experience cannot in fact be taken as applying to the future. This is to say that the

[10] James Meade, "The Keynesian Revolution," Milo Keynes (ed.), *Essays on John Maynard Keynes* (London and New York: Cambridge University Press, 1975), p. 82.

[11] G. L. S. Shackle, "Keynes and Today's Establishment in Economic Theory: A View," *Journal of Economic Literature*, Fall 1973, p. 517.

[12] Keynes explicitly stresses this point in his clarifying article, "The General Theory of Employment," *The Quarterly Journal of Economics*, pp. 212 ff and also p. 222.

probability calculations properly applicable to the replicable games of *chance* of the casino are not so applicable to the various "games" of *risk* in the (nonreplicable) future-oriented marketplace.

For reasons such as these, Joan Robinson sees the basic hallmark of Keynes's revolution as the placing of the processes of the market-guided economic system within the context of historical time, i.e., within the realm of "real" (as opposed to "logical") time that moves only one way: from a past that can't be changed to a future that can't be known. Thus what we imagine as happening in the here and now may likely be betrayed by the processes of history, and the "rules of thumb" (as Keynes once called them) that guide the pragmatic decisions of daily life may be shown as the illusions that they in fact are, when the present has moved from the beginning to the end of some time interval. In Mrs. Robinson's words: "On the plane of theory, [Keynes's] revolution lay in the change from the conception of equilibrium to the conception of history; from the principles of rational choice to the problem of decisions based on guesswork or on convention."[13]

The position taken herein is that both these perspectives of *the* essential feature of Keynes's revolution—i.e., Meade's emphasis on causal reversal and the Robinson/Shackle stress on noncalculable uncertainty—represent interrelated aspects or facets of the basic theory system of *The General Theory* and that, when these are placed within the context of Keynes's suggested micro—macroeconomic theoretical dichotomy, the effect was to substantially alter the commonly held "image" or "knowledge structure"[14] of economic reality.

In short, then, the position taken here is that the Meade—Robinson/Shackle views are both consistent and complementary with one another, and that, when they are placed within the theoretical (micro—macro) context that Keynes saw, there is defined a clear point of departure identifying the onset of the Keynesian revolution in economic *theory*. Keynes's macro—micro split is fundamental to this view of his revolution in economic theory since it

[13] This theme crops up at frequest intervals in Mrs. Robinson's writings. This particular quotation comes from her article "What has Become of the Keynesian Revolution?" *Challenge*, January-February 1974, pp. 7-8.

[14] These are Kenneth Boulding's terms. See his book *The Image* (Ann Arbor: The University of Michigan Press, 1956).

was this dichotomy that objectified and delineated the particular (macroeconomic) corpus which was to serve as the vehicle for his path-breaking attempt at merging the real and the financial sectors of economic theory.

III. Developing the revolution: the internal logic of the static system

A primary criterion for scientific theory is that its internal logic be valid and correct on its own assumptive grounds. And it soon became apparent that Keynes's *analytical* system was logically flawed as to both its internal consistency and its completeness.

In this section we shall examine the problem of the lack of *internal consistency* in Keynes's static (and comparative static) analysis and, even more importantly, the results of dealing with this problem. (In the following section we shall deal with issues, connected with *completing* Keynes's system in the sense of articulating its inherent dynamic properties.)

As is well known, Hicks was the first to point out that the basic Marshallian "*process* analysis"[15] that Keynes developed was indeterminate, and was so even with the appropriate ceteris paribus assumptions concerning expectations, technology, and other "exogenous" factors. This indeterminacy resulted essentially because the determination of the liquidity preference schedule—which was necessary in order to find the interest rate and consequently the levels of investment and of output and employment—will itself be affected by the level of aggregate output (= income) through the transactions demand for money. The point, of course, is that one needed to know aggregate income (and thereby output and employment) in order to find out what one wanted to know in the first place (national output and thereby employment and income).

---

[15] The term "process analysis" in this context has been attributed to Alex Leijonhufvud and has been put forth as being more accurately descriptive of Marshall's method than is the more familiar term "equilibrium analysis." (On this see Robert Clower, "Reflections on the Keynesian Perplex," *Zeitschaift für National Okonomie*, 35 (1975), p. 4 and footnote 14.)

The distinction, Clower argues, is useful to clearly differentiate the Marshallian step-by-step methodological approach to an ongoing economy from the Walrasian approach of simultaneous solution—the latter being more broadly and appropriately described as *equilibrium* analysis.

Hicks, of course, neatly solved this analytically logical difficulty in his famous 1937 *Econometrica* article, "Mr. Keynes and the Classics: A Suggested Interpretation," where he put forth the now commonplace IS/LM mechanism for *simultaneously* solving for generalized systemic levels of the interest rate and of output. Hicks's solution solved the logical problem of internal consistency, but at a cost of burying Keynes's *process* analysis of an ongoing economy, with its uncertainty, "animal spirits," and other nonrational elements, under two seemingly deterministic "lines"; and mere lines is what they were, for IS and LM are not behavioral or functional schedules in any sense. Rather they are the tracings of loci of various (partial) equilibria in goods (IS) and money (LM) markets.

But Hicks's essential point was *logically* correct, at least as far as it went, and Keynes was quick to accept the latter's argument.[16] Also, Hicks's generalization has the further and great scientific appeal of taking two apparently alternative theoretical explanations —Keynes's and the "Classics"—and of combining them into a single construct where each becomes a special or limiting case of a more broadly generalized theory system.

Furthermore, this statical "synthesis" by Hicks was not only supportive of, but also apparently compatible with, his own analytical approach in *Value and Capital*, on which he was then working and in which he was attempting to develop the conceptual groundwork for a macroeconomic analysis built upon the microeconomic foundations of a well-specified elaboration of a (neo-) Walrasian general equilibrium system.[17]

The logical impossibility of combining Keynes's Marshallian *process* analysis (where shifts in expectations and knowledge could be held in abeyance under self-conscious ceteris paribus assumptions, and where money and liquidity served as a link between the present and an unknown future and thereby as a measure of "our disquietude") with a simultaneously determined Walrasian general *equilibrium* system (where there is perfect knowledge and foresight and where money is only a here-and-now medium of exchange) was not then recognized. The key point for our purposes

[16] John Hicks, "Recollections and Documents," *Economica*, February 1973, pp. 2-11.

[17] On this see E. Roy Weintraub, *Microfoundations* (London, New York, and Melbourne: Cambridge University Press, 1979), pp. 55 ff.

is that there was then no compelling reason *not* to envision the IS/
LM generalization as essentially another mode for expressing a
Walrasian-like interrelated system of output and resource markets;
and, furthermore, there was also no apparent reason *not* to envision this as a system wherein parameters relating to particular
"equilibrium" levels of macroeconomic activity could be affected
from outside the market or private sector by the self-conscious
policies of a public sector. And Hicks, convinced at that time of
the essential "rightness" of the general equilibrium vision expressed
in his *Value and Capital*, apparently saw his IS/LM construct in
terms of such a (neo-) Walrasian extension of Keynes.[18]

As is now well known, the assumed compatibility between
Keynes's (Marshallian) process approach to market interaction and
Walrasian simultaneous determination is simply incorrect. The
crucial flaw lies with what Robert Clower has called the "logistics
of exchange."[19] That is to say, there is no logically rigorous explanation that can reconcile an ongoing process of the *execution*
of exchanges in a Keynesian-type monetized system with the
point-in-time *scheduling* of commodity exchanges by a central co-
ordinator or auctioneer in a Walrasian-type system where money is
merely a "numeraire" and has no store of value function.[20] And
Keynes, instinctively, but not with rigorous or mathematical precision, raised various objections to Hicks's 1936 review of *The
General Theory* in *The Economic Journal*, where Hicks interpreted
Keynes *not* as a generalization of a Marshallian process analysis of
an ongoing market system, but rather as a special case of the neo-
Walrasian general equilibrium analysis that he (Hicks) was then
working out in *Value and Capital*.[21] And even earlier, in a 1934
letter to Hicks concerning aspects of Walrasian analysis, Keynes
wrote ". . . I shall hope to convince you some day that Walras's
theory and all the others along those lines are little better than
nonsense!"[22] As Clower puts it, "Keynes did not view the analysis
of *The General Theory* as 'Variations on a theme of Walras.' "[23]

[18] Clower, "Reflections on the Keynesian Perplex," op. cit., p. 6.

[19] Ibid., p. 13.

[20] Ibid.

[21] Keynes, *Collected Works*, Vol. 14, pp. 71-77 and 203-204.

[22] Quoted from Clower, "Reflections on the Keynesian Perplex," op. cit.
p.5.

[23] Ibid., p. 4.

Yet the generalized "Keynesian" analysis incorporated into the IS/LM construct of "Mr. Keynes and the Classics" was indeed *seen* as consistent with, and as an alternative expression of, the neo-Walrasian analysis emanating from *Value and Capital*. And it was not until the middle of the 1950s and on into the decade of the 1960s that the utter (analytical) incompatibility between the two approaches became clearly recognized, at least by a respectable number of general equilibrium theorists engaged in "puzzle solving" on the frontiers of their esoteric subdiscipline.[24] But by this time the fundamental (static) "Keynesian" vision of a market interrelated (circular) flow that was subject to manipulation by consciously determined public policies affecting the level of aggregate demand had become firmly established as expressive of the fundamental structure and function of what came to be called the "mixed economy."

In short, the important point of *Keynes's* revolution concerning inherent systemic instability due to not being able to know the unknowable was both hidden and/or muddled by theoretical "elegance" *and* confusion that were erroneously supportive of a vision of the efficacy of rational and foresightful public management of the economy via aggregative policy actions.

But rather than viewing Keynes's *General Theory* as being "general" in the sense of a "carelessly executed version of a few-commodity Walrasian model," as did Hicks,[25] it would seem more appropriate to see the *generality* of *The General Theory* in Keynes's attempt to integrate the real and financial sectors of the economy within one (aggregative or macroeconomic) theoretical framework.[26] And, of course, such a real financial sectoral integration is not only quite consistent with, but is, as already noted, dependent upon, Keynes's "revolutionary" shift in the dichotomization of economic theory away *from* the "real" (value and distribution) versus monetary split which marked the theoretical orthodoxy of his day and to the now familiar macro—micro

[24] Ibid., p. 12. In documenting this observation, Clower calls special attention to the following theorists: Hicks in 1957, himself in 1965, Hahn in 1965, Barro and Grossman in 1971, and Leijonhufvud in 1969. (For reference details, see Clower, pp. 19 ff.)

[25] The point of view and language are Clower's, ibid., p. 5, footnote 17.

[26] This point is developed by the Dutch scholar, A. Nentjes, in *Van Keynes Tot Keynes* (Groningen, The Netherlands: Wolters-Noordhof, 1977), pages 348 to 350 of the English summary appended to the Dutch text.

split.[27] For in Keynes's macro analysis the monetary sector (via liquidity preference) and the real sector (via m.e.c.) clearly interact with one another, if only that uncertainty and changes in business expectations could be expected to act on *both* schedules, causing them both to shift. For example, in depression, liquidity preference would tend to shift upward or increase, thereby requiring a higher rate of interest all along the schedule so as to induce *any* degree of substitution of (financial) investment for liquidity, i.e., for the holding of cash. Furthermore, and at the same time, there would *of necessity* be an inward shift in the marginal efficiency of capital schedule. This would result not only because pessimism would likely deleteriously affect expectations concerning the flow of future returns on real capital, but also because the rate of discount necessary to equate *any* expected flow of returns with the now higher interest rate *must* also rise. This latter change in the rate of discount would, of course, decrease expected present values from investment and would indicate that at any rate of interest there would be less (real) investment.

Thus in Keynes's macroeconomics the real and financial sectors were inextricably intertwined both with one another and with the uncertainties of real time—while in the Hicksian schema, on the other hand, there was a subtle but distinct return to the *pre*-Keynes-theory dichotomy in that the real (IS) and the monetary (LM) sectors were depicted as independent of one another. Furthermore, the role of the uncertainties of real time is much less apparent and important in Hicks than in Keynes, and the rate of interest is more of a determined (equilibrium) variable than a determining (and disequilibrating) one as it is in Keynes.

IV. Developing the revolution: from statics to dynamics

Soon after the problem of the logical inconsistency of the static Keynesian system was grappled with, attention came to be focused on the fact that the theoretical analysis was incomplete in the

[27] Emphasis on Keynes's efforts to integrate the real and financial sectors is at the root of the recent work of Hyman Minsky. See his *John Maynard Keynes* (New York: Columbia University Press, 1975). For a good summary of Minsky's argument, see his essay "The Financial Instability Hypothesis: An Interpretation of Keynes and an Alternative to 'Standard' Theory," *Challenge*, March/April 1977, pp. 20-27.

sense that, if the strategic Keynesian variable, investment spending, was larger (or smaller) than capital replacement needs (and divergence was the most likely case), a dynamic and self-reinforcing (and, most likely, a self-reversing) cyclical process would be set in motion.[28]

The essential point here, of course, refers to the insights of Roy Harrod in England and Evesy Domar in the United States that net investment creates not only additional demand, but also additional capacity that need be absorbed by further increases in demand. This insight turned on the notion that any changes in investment spending would marry the Keynesian multiplier effect to the volatile "kicker" of the acceleration principle—the latter, of course, involving the basic notion that if investment, or capital formation, brings about some change in output (and thus income) there must be an additional increase in the capital stock (financed by further investment spending), since the (incremental) capital–output ratio is larger than 1. If one assumes, as did Harrod and Domar, fixity in the capital-output ratio (i.e., equality of the average with the incremental capital–output ratios), a bit of reflection indicates that the *direction* of accelerator forces will be positive as long as the initiating change in investment spending (capital formation) is increasing. If net investment (capital formation), even though high, remains at a constant level, or increases at a decreasing rate, the acceleration effect on induced investment will fall. Further, the effect of this induced fall on income and employment will be accentuated by a multiplier process thrown into reverse. Thus, with a fixed capital–output ratio, changes in the course of investment spending will tend to have both volatile and cumulative effects on income and employment. And if, in this now familiar process, one also assumes (along with fixity in the capital–output ratio) that the amount saved out of income is constant, one arrives at what Joan Robinson called the "simple piece of arithmetic" that:

> When a constant proportion of income is added to capital every year and capital bears a constant ratio to income, then income expands continuously at a constant proportional rate. Thus, when 10 percent of net income is invested every year and the stock of capital is five years purchase

[28] The basic source explaining the mathematical and technical properties of this cyclical phenomenon is, of course, Paul Samuelson, "Interaction Between the Multiplier and the Principle of Acceleration," *Review of Economics and Statistics*, May 1939.

of net income, then the stock of capital, the rate of investment per annum and net income per annum all expand cumulatively at 2 percent per annum.[29]

The 2 percent per annum noted above is what Harrod called the actual growth rate. And, as is easily seen, it would only be accidental for this actual growth rate to be equal to what Harrod defined as the natural growth rate—i.e., that ("full employment") growth rate that would absorb increases in the labor force adjusted for increases in productivity. And it would be a most unlikely accident for the actual or natural growth rates to be equal to what Harrod termed the warranted rate of growth—the latter being that growth rate wherein (ex ante and thus uncertain) entrepreneural *expectations* concerning investment decisions are met (ex post), i.e., wherein the amount of capacity created (by entrepreneural "real" investment ventures) is just offset by the increase in the (money) demand created via their (multiplicative) investment spending. A disappointment of such expectations would tend to bring about changes in entrepreneural investment decisions that would call forth highly magnified changes (through the multiplier—accelerator interaction) in the actual rate of change in income and thereby in employment.

Thus, Keynes's basic static model of aggregated systemic processes had been extended into a dynamic theory of the business cycle that was *directionally* descriptive of an unstable capitalist system moving through time. Only an improbable balancing act along a "knife-edge" of sustainable and "balanced" growth would keep the system from generating self-perpetuating cycles, or, more to the point policy-wise, from cumulatively falling away to depression and unemployment or soaring off into an inflationary spiral.

Such Harrod—Domar, multiplier—accelerator models were Keynes-like in that volatile and uncertain investment spending was the prime mover which would set in motion *processes* that would change the level of economic activity, and thereby incomes and consumption spending. In this process, the necessary increase in savings to match the initiating increase in investment spending would come about passively, as a residual from unspent income.

However, the perplexing problem that now arose was that real-world economic systems were not so explosively unstable as the

[29] Joan Robinson, "The Model of an Expanding Economy," *Economic Journal*, March 1952, p. 42.

simple mechanical multiplier—accelerator formulations of the Harrod—Domar type would indicate for any reasonable values of the capital—output ratio (i.e., the accelerator) and of the savings ratio (i.e., the multiplier).[30] Thus, the theory's consistency with the "facts" was still deficient.

In short, the internal logic and/or relationships within the dynamic Harrod—Domar extension of Keynes's static theory either did not fully explain, or perhaps did not even incorporate, the pertinent economic factors in the real world. Other or more subtle forces than those subsumed within the Harrod—Domar type formulations must be at work so to dampen and stabilize the processes of economic adjustment.

Given what we might term a scientific imperative for theory refinement and articulation, one reasonable if not an obvious place to begin (or rather, to continue) this process would be with the assumptions of fixity in the capital—output and savings ratios of the Harrod—Domar formulations.[31] With the assumption of variable (incremental) capital—output and savings ratios, the sources of the extreme instability of the Harrod—Domar models would be mitigated since, obviously, it is these ratios that determine the strength and nature of the accelerator and multiplier interaction of the models. But the elaboration of such "variable ratio" models would, as we shall see, lead to the final repudiation of Keynes's

---

[30] The Samuelson article, "Interaction between the Multiplier and the Principle of Acceleration," op. cit., is pertinent here.

[31] J. R. Hicks, of course, was among the first to attempt to ameliorate the overly explosive mechanism of the simple multiplier—accelerator interaction inherent in the Harrod—Domar formulations. The approach he took in his *Contribution to the Theory of the Trade Cycle* (Oxford: Oxford University Press, 1950) was embodied in a model in which explosive cumulative movement was constrained to oscillate between "floors" and "ceilings" determined respectively by rates of disinvestment and bottlenecks to labor force expansion.

This attempt by Hicks, it could be argued, was inherently less satisfying than the approach of relaxing of the assumptions of fixity in the capital—output and savings ratios of the Harrod—Domar formulations. This follows from Occam's Razor in that Hicks was "ad hoc—ing" external (and "complicating") constraints onto the theory structure, whereas relaxing the a priori assumptions of fixity in the two relevant ratios would be an internal (and "simplifying") refinement to the body of the theory structure itself. (For various reasons Hicks himself has recently expressed serious misgivings with the model of his *Trade Cycle*: "I don't now think much of the book. . . ." See J. R. Hicks, "On Coddington's Interpretation: A Reply," *Journal of Economic Literature*, September 1979, p. 989. Of even more note, however, is Hicks's repudiation of his seminal *Value and Capital*. See Section 7 below.)

revolution via the development of a once-hailed "Grand Neo-classical Synthesis," along with the latter's (uncertain) relative, neoclassical growth theory.

V. The neoclassical synthesis and growth theory: the dynamic statements of the general system in the short and long run

In economists' coming to grips with the above discussed problems of a dynamic Keynesian system, there emerged that hybrid model which came to be known as the neoclassical synthesis. This synthesized construct was eventually to be cast into the two time frames of the short and the long runs. In the former, the spotlight was on questions of cyclical stabilization, while with the latter—the long run—the focus of attention was on intertemporal paths of systemic growth. It is the relationship to these two time frames to which we now turn our attention.

(a) The short run

The key ideas behind the theory models of the short-run neoclassical synthetic genre are: (1) that Harrod–Domar assumptions of fixity in the savings and of the capital–output ratios (with marginal = average) be relaxed, (2) that capital and labor be taken as substitutes and (3) that such substitutability, or variation in the capital–labor ratio, be engendered by the relative price signals of an interconnected market system, and (4) that interest rates be one of these (relative) prices and be responsive to monetary policy.

Concerning the above ideas, Paul Samuelson, under the heading "The Neoclassical Synthesis," wrote in a 1963 paper:

> All this can be found in all but the first two editions of my elementary text book, in Tobin's *Journal of Political Economy* article of [April] 1955, in T. Swan's *Economic Review* article [November] 1956 and in Solow's *Quarterly Journal of Economics* article of [February] 1956. . . . [T]hese involved departures from the special "depression version" of the Keynesian system in which making credit cheaper and more available could have no substantial effect on investment spending because of either a liquidity trap on interest due to liquidity preference or a virtual inelastic schedule of the marginal efficiency of investment.[32]

[32] Paul Samuelson, "A Brief Survey of Post-Keynesian Developments" (1963), *Collected Papers*, Vol. 2, p. 1534.

The result of all this was what Samuelson once called in his influential textbook a "Grand Neoclassical Synthesis," i.e.:

> ... by means of appropriately reinforcing monetary and fiscal policies, our mixed-enterprise system can avoid the excesses of boom and slump and can look forward to healthy progressive growth.
>
> This fundamental being understood, the paradoxes that robbed the older classical principles dealing with small-scale "microeconomics" of much of their relevance and validity—these paradoxes will now lose their sting. In short, mastery of the modern analysis of income determination genuinely validates the basic classical pricing principles; and—perhaps for the first time—the economist is justified in saying that the broad cleavage between microeconomics and macroeconomics has been closed.[33]

The above quotation is from Samuelson's seminal, although long superceded, third edition (1955). The *term* "neoclassical synthesis" appeared for the last time in the seventh (1967) edition of the text; however, the basic statement above-quoted continues to appear in all subsequent editions, albeit with qualifications via references to such contemporary problems of the real world as cost-push inflation and stagflation.[34] *But the concept itself lingers on.*

In the tenth (1976) edition of his text, immediately following the (nonlabeled) expression of the neoclassical synthesis, duly qualified by reference to the "unsolved dilemma of stagflation in the mixed economy," Samuelson (still) writes:

> With good conscience we turn to the analysis in Part Three of how the great social aggregates of national income and employment *get determined in their detailed parts* and to Part Four's analysis of income distribution.[35]

Thus the key ideas inherent in the neoclassical synthesis stay with us, along with their crucial implications that, within the context of conscious macroeconomic management, capital and labor are rationally substitutable in accordance with market price signals. This implies further that there exists on the *macroeconomic*

---

[33] Paul Samuelson, *Economics* (New York: McGraw-Hill, Inc., 1955), 3rd ed., p. 360.

[34] The eighth (1970) edition drops the term "neoclassical synthesis"; the ninth (1973) edition qualifies the statement by reference to cost-push factors; and the current, at this writing, tenth edition takes note of stagflation.

[35] Ibid., 10th ed., p. 373 (emphasis in original).

level the "principle of derived demand," which in turn implies that the so-called "factors of production"—particularly capital and thereby capital formation or investment[36] —are, "functionally" speaking, *supply*-side phenomena. This is to say that these factors are taken as "independent" variables within the framework of an *aggregated* (neoclassical) production function of the general form $O = F(L,K)$—the latter being a simple *causal* statement abstracted from and expressive of an interrelated (circular flow) market-price system. Such aggregation, despite its many difficulties, is a simplification that is necessary in order to make such a system in its Walrasian or general equilibrium form empirically or otherwise operationally useful.[37]

This neoclassical synthetic model is concerned with *short-run* macroeconomic matters, as was Keynes, in that it is placed within the context of a given technology and resource supply limits, and its policy focus is on cyclical stability.

But the macrodynamics of this short-run model represent a very significant turn away from Keynes's revolution. The latter's primary emphasis on macroeconomic *income* effects and *quantity* adjustments activated from an uncertain and unstable *demand* side is substantively diluted by reintroducing the fundamental importance of consciously and rationally manipulable *price* and *substitution* effects, principally those inherent in the *supply* side (as represented by the "independent"—i.e., the direct and immediate operational—variables of an aggregate neoclassical production function).[38] Even monetary policy, reintroduced into the system as a "tool" of demand management, is seen primarily as working *through* its price effects on changes in interest rates (the supply price of "capital") and is thus consistent with the basic idea of the role of substitution effects via relative price changes. (It is princi-

[36] The obvious stock-flow confusion between "capital" and "capital formation" here is discussed further in Section 7 below.

[37] Mark Blaug, *Economic Theory in Retrospect* (London: Cambridge University Press, 3rd ed., 1978), p. 494. The problems and limitations of such aggregation, of which Blaug is keenly aware, are discussed further in Section 7 below.

[38] Alfred Eichner calls specific attention to the relative importance of income and quantity effects in Keynes's and in contemporary post-Keynesian analysis as opposed to the emphasis on price-substitution effects in orthodox neoclassical theory. On this see *A Guide to Post-Keynesian Economics*, Alfred S. Eichner (ed.) (White Plains, N.Y.: M. E. Sharpe, Inc., 1979), pp. 12 and 168-171.

pally in this way that "money matters *too*," as James Tobin somewhere expressed it.)

In short, in the process of short-run economic adjustment, the neoclassical synthetic model, while not totally ignoring the income and quantity effects of aggregate demand, subtly, but definitely, reintroduces a major emphasis on the systemic equilibrating effects of market price changes, especially as these relate to supply-side factors. In the model, these price-substitution effects are *indirectly* induced and guided via the *rational* management of aggregate demand (and its consequent income and quantity effects) via the manipulation of fiscal and monetary tools. Also, the market incentives and effects expressed in the marginal productivity analysis of value and distribution are not only implied in and consistent with this model, but are crucial to it in that they provide the "logical" coherence that binds together the market processes of the system as a whole. This is, in essence, the model that Joan Robinson has labeled "Bastard Keynesianism"—the illegitimate heir of Keynes.[39]

(b) The long run

Once it is recognized that an economy can be conceived of as being cyclically stabilized via the policy manipulations of the (short-run) neoclassical synthetic model, it is but one short step to see that economy as being tracked, at least in theory, along a continuum of "short runs" that, by definition, become one and the same with some "long-run" path of growth. But with such a vision, even the "illegitimate" ties of a lineage to Keynes are severed. For since successful aggregate management in the short run would by definition imply no problem of uncertain and volatile macroeconomic demand, the *only* adjustment factors pertinent to the *secular* trend of economic growth would of necessity be from the supply side. And Keynes's initial vision of an inherently unstable capitalist economy, existent in a real world with an unknown and unknowable future, would have been, for all intents and purposes, obliterated. Thus, Keynes's economics is returned to the "Classics," i.e., to the probabilistic world of a "Benthamite Calculus." In a word, mainstream "Keynesianism" has very little if anything at all to do with Keynes and his revolution.

[39] Joan Robinson, "What Has Become of the Keynesian Revolution?" op. cit.

Focusing now on formally defined (long-run) neoclassical growth theory, we note that its basic thrust is directed at such questions as how various (assumed) types of technical change—e.g., whether a technical change is capital saving, labor saving, or neutral as to its potential impact on the capital–labor ratio—affects the productivity of some (assumed) changed (or changing) labor supply, and how this would in turn relate to various paths of growth given other assumptions made about consumption and savings and investment patterns. And the primary operational or policy interest of these (aggregated) models is the explanatory light that they may throw on such things as the role that technical change and the growth of knowledge play in economic growth, how increased thrift may affect growth and consumption, and the like.

In fact, however, such neoclassical growth models "explain" nothing, since the deux ex machina resides in factors that are exogenous to the models along with the particular assumptions made about those factors and with the technical specification of the particular model. The "theory" thus degenerates essentially to mathematical exercises aimed at solving various "puzzles" about the growth paths *implicit* in the model's assumptions—e.g., whether some path "exists," is stable or sustainable, etc. Thus, from this aspect, formal neoclassical growth theory has to do mainly with assumptions and mathematics, and very little, if anything at all, with economic processes in a real world moving through real or historical time.

Thus, it is quite clear that the entire corpus of neoclassical growth theory—i.e., *both* the short- and long-run macrodynamic systems—has little if anything to do with Keynes and his revolution. *It is not so immediately clear, however, that these two strands of neoclassical growth theory have nothing whatsoever to do with one another.* And traditional methodological technique and modes of thought can serve to make a relationship between the dynamic short runs of neoclassical synthetic growth theory and the long run of more formal neoclassical growth theory appear to be almost so obvious as to be not worth the trouble of much further thought and inquiry. For example, the simple and indeed useful technique of relaxing ceteris paribus assumptions—thereby allowing the exogenous factors of technical change and population to affect the supply-side arguments of the aggregate production function—provides a familiar methodological mode for slipping, almost unconsciously, into the notion of an underlying relationship between the secular continuum of short runs of the neoclassical synthesis and the defined long run of neoclassical growth theory.

(c) Theory error once again

But not only do the secular continuum of short runs of neoclassical stabilization theory (Bastard Keynesianism, so-called) and the long run of neoclassical growth theory have little if anything to do with Keynes's revolution, they have, as already alluded to, nothing whatsoever to do with one another. In fact, they are inconsistent with one another.

As the idea was developed in Section 3, the growth economics of the neoclassical synthesis initially evolved out of Hicks's (Marshallian general *process*) IS/LM analysis of "Mr. Keynes and the Classics," while long-run neoclassical growth theory has developed out of his (Walrasian general *equilibrium*) analysis in *Value and Capital*. And, as has been shown, the two strands are incompatible with one another due to their differing "logistics of exchange," recalling Clower's phrase. What has been called the "Keynesian Counterrevolution," with its IS/LM roots and its neoclassical synthesis, on the one hand, simply does not mix with the "neo-Walrasian Revolution" of general equilibrium analysis and neoclassical growth theory on the other hand. What is most important here relative to orthodox theory, and thus to whatever policy guidance that it may purport to have, is *that even in pure theory* a successfully cyclically stabilized (neoclassical) economy cannot meaningfully be seen as some moving continuum of "short-run" points along some possible "long-run" neoclassical growth path. As far as mainstream economic theory is concerned, one neoclassical growth model can offer no analytical insight into the other. (And one can only be reminded here of Keynes's famous quip about mortality rates in the long run, for it is in this time frame that his revolution finally perished.)

(d) The off-the-wall vision

Thus the facts are that the two major strands of contemporary economics theory purporting to "explain" the macrodynamic nature of our economy are inconsistent with one another. But the fact also is that this has not had much effect on changing the essential mainstream vision of the structure and function of the so-called mixed economy. Figure 1 is a fair two-dimensional theoretical representation of the paradigmatic vision in its static (and closed) form. See that representation in three-dimensional "dynamic" form—i.e., moving through time in some sense, or, as Joan Robinson once put it in a lecture, "coming off the blackboard"—and you have a fair representation of the essential paradigmatic view of mainstream economics in the United States.[40]

The *aggregate* production function linking output and factor markets that is made explicit in Figure 1 is of *central* importance and is quite in order. As already noted, such aggregation is fundamental to the empirical work necessary to operationally articulate and/or test the various implications of general equilibrium theory, which of itself is empirically useless.[41] It is also appropriate to insert explicitly into Figure 1 the crosshatched area between the public and private sectors. This is to indicate that the theory linkages between these two sectors have not been established and, Samuelson notwithstanding, the "broad cleavage between microeconomics and macroeconomics" has *not* in fact been closed. There are serious and seemingly irreconcilable theoretic difficulties that inhibit the bridging of this gap .

VI. The "tenacity of theory"

But the contemporary vision of the so-called mixed economy continues to be held onto ("tenacity of theory")[42] despite the various technical and logical difficulties of its analytical corpus, not to mention its current problems with operational policy significance. But, much theoretical work is in process which is aimed at bridging the problems of the neoclassical theoretical description of the

[40] On the question of the "fairness" of Figure 1 in depicting the basic framework of current mainstream economic science: check the basic textbooks, as Thomas Kuhn would suggest. For it is there that one finds the currently accepted "statement" of the (exemplary) paradigm of a science. (The exemplary paradigm is the delimiting framework within which so-called "normal science" takes place.) See Thomas Kuhn, *The Structure of Scientific Revolutions* (Chicago: University of Chicago Press, 2nd ed., 1970), especially pp. 136-138 on the "Invisibility of Revolutions." For the paradigm as exemplar, see pp. 187 ff.

[41] Blaug, *Economic Theory in Retrospect.*

[42] The term is from A. W. Coat's "Is There a Structure of Scientific Revolutions in Economics?" *Kyklos,* 1969 (2), pp. 289-297.

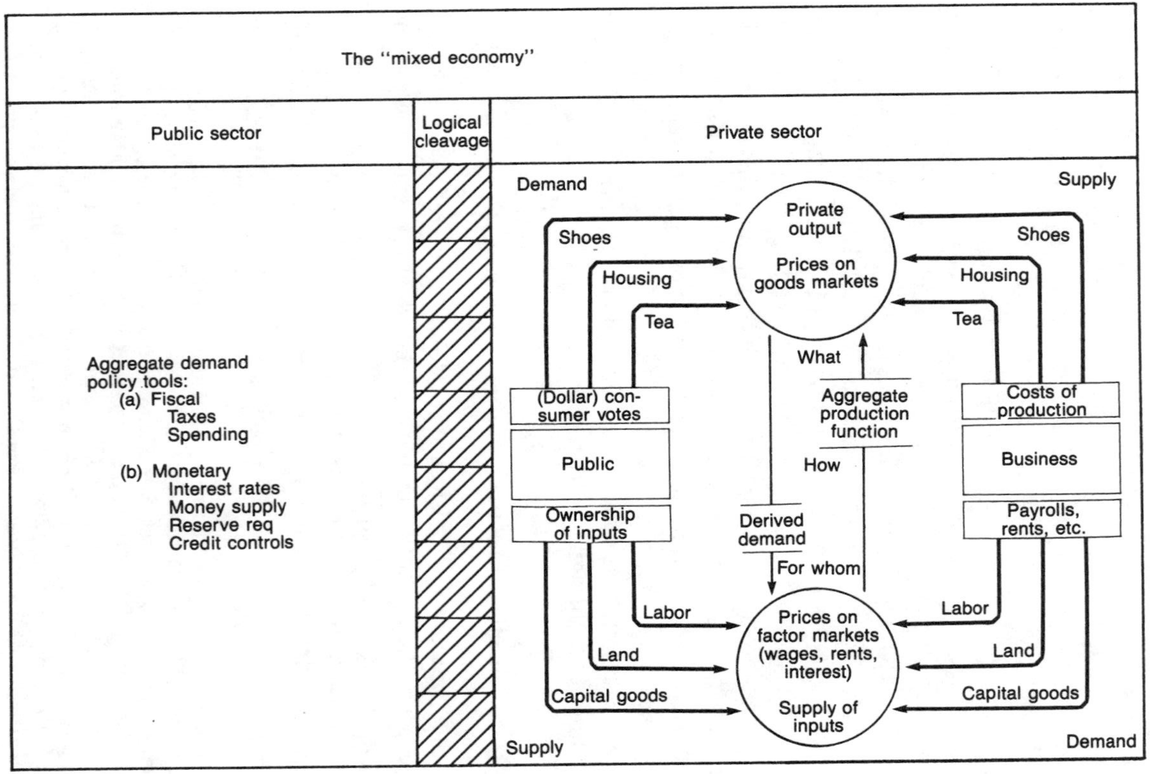

The "mixed economy"

Public sector | Logical cleavage | Private sector

Demand   Supply

Private output / Prices on goods markets

Shoes
Housing
Tea

Costs of production

Business

Payrolls, rents, etc.

Land
Labor
Capital goods

What — Aggregate production function — How

Derived demand — For whom

Prices on factor markets (wages, rents, interest) / Supply of inputs

Shoes
Housing
Tea

(Dollar) consumer votes

Public

Ownership of inputs

Labor
Land
Capital goods

Demand   Supply

Aggregate demand policy tools:
(a) Fiscal
    Taxes
    Spending

(b) Monetary
    Interest rates
    Money supply
    Reserve req
    Credit controls

Figure 1

Source: Paul Samuelson, *Economics* 11th ed., McGraw-Hill, Inc., copyright 1980.

envisioned mixed economy,[43] perhaps now more appropriately referred to as the "dichotomized economy." Strong and deeply entrenched scientific forces (not even to mention ideological and habitual ones) are at work to encourage efforts toward such reconciliation. The obstensible end purpose, of course, is to gain more effective operational policy insight into the real-world system.

For example, Samuelson, an important contributor to, and certainly the most influential disseminator of, the current neoclassical theory system, began his path-breaking *Foundations of Economic Analysis* with a telling quotation from the mathematician E. H. More:

> The existence of analogies between central features of various theories implies the existence of a general theory which underlies and unifies them with respect to those central features.[44]

And in the *Foundations* Samuelson attempts to work out the implications of this "principle of generalization by abstraction," for *both* theoretical and applied economics.[45] This "principle of generalization" can be seen as the expression of a logical (scientific) imperative that fuels a continuing search for an integrative theoretical generalization—analogous to an Einsteinian-like "unified field

---

[43] For example, see Clower's article ("Reflections on the Keynesian Perplex," op. cit., pp. 13-19) for a brief statement of one current line of analysis concerning the problem of the *processes* of exchange (in the absence of a Walrasian auctioneer) in the *general* system. Here Clower describes a *Marshallian*-type approach to the problem by postulating the existence of a class of middlemen—traders who hold stocks and who are thereby able to react to market signals in the theoretically troublesome problem area of inadequate (i.e., "ineffective") systemic demand.

Also, see E. Roy Weintraub, *Microfoundations*, for succinct surveys of other recent approaches for dealing with issues of general systemic equilibrium and disequilibrium problems within both Walrasian and Edgeworthian frameworks.

The continued lack of success in these endeavors is perhaps the major theme of a recent conference suggested by John Hicks and sponsored by the International Economic Association. The papers and proceedings of this conference have been published under the title of *The Microeconomic Foundations of Macroeconomics*, Geoffrey Harcourt (ed.) (Boulder, Colorado: Westview Press, 1977).

It is interesting to note that the basic issue on this "frontier" of economic science deals with the basic question raised by Adam Smith long ago concerning the "invisible hand" and how and if it works in society.

[44] Paul A. Samuelson, *The Foundations of Economic Analysis*, Harvard Economic Studies, Vol. 80 (Cambridge: Harvard University Press, 1947) p. 3.

[45] Ibid. and Samuelson, *Foundations*, Preface.

theory"—that harmonizes disparate explanations of basic interactive processes of the envisioned modern (mixed) economy.

Furthermore, there is no obvious or "objective" reason to dis-
courage this search—or rather the searchers—from attempting to
span the existing gaps and dichotomies in contemporary neoclassical theory. As already noted, abstract theory can be viewed as an
articulatable expression of an enculturated vision, and such a vision, being preanalytic, is by definition metaphysical and non-
testable. But such a vision, though ideologically laden and ephem-
eral, is, as pointed out above, necessary so as to give the scientist
something to be scientific about. Or to put the issue within the
structure of contemporary philosophy of science: the acceptance
of a clearly delineated and nonquestioned paradigmatic framework
allows the scientist to devote his full attention and energy to the
(scientifically) productive puzzle-solving activities of normal
science (à la Thomas Kuhn), or, to say much the same thing (in
this instance), to enable him to single-mindedly pursue what is
thought to be a viable, i.e., a still "progressive," Scientific Research Program (SRP) (à la Imre Lakatos).[46]

Thus the "tenacity of theory" is not necessarily an irrational,
much less a bad, thing—at least until there is a more promising alternative available to fill the (scientifically existential) void that
would be created by the abandonment of the existing paradigm
(Kuhn), or until the new directions and directives of an emergent
and truly "progressive" SRP became manifest out of the continuing research efforts (Lakatos).

---

[46] The references to Kuhn and Lakatos refer, of course, to the debate on the
nature of scientific progress. Kuhn talks in terms of the discontinuous, revolutionary, and largely nonrational change of "paradigm shifts." Lakatos, on
the other hand, develops the alternative thesis that science evolves rationally
and smoothly from a "deteriorating" scientific research program (i.e., one
that ceases to yield novel facts, solutions, and predictions and which becomes
increasingly protected by a layering of ex post and ad hoc "explanations") to
a "progressive SRP" (which is, essentially, one having characteristics opposite
to a deteriorating one). On this see Thomas Kuhn, *The Structure of Scientific
Revolutions* (Chicago: University of Chicago Press, 2nd ed. 1970); and Imre
Lakatos, *Criticism and the Methodology of Scientific Research Programmes*,
Proceedings of the Aristotelian Society (69), pp. 149-186.

The two theses, though proffered as alternatives to one another, do have
points in common as indicated by their justapositioning in the text above.
Indeed Kuhn has argued that Lakatos's thesis is quite consistent with his own.

An excellent series of essays dealing with aspects of the Kuhn and Lakatos
theses as they pertain to economics may be found in *Method and Appraisal in
Economics*, S. J. Latsis (ed.) (London: Cambridge University Press, 1976); see
especially the essays by Leijonhufvud and Blaug.

Sidestepping the details and subtleties of the paradigm–SRP debate, we allow the discussion above to provide us with a useful basis for understanding the nature and importance of the now famous capital controversies which spanned the decade from the mid-1950s to the mid-1960s. These decade-long, arcane, and often acrimonious fulminations over what might be seen as abstract theoretical trivia can be more usefully viewed as a process of "creative destruction," to employ another lively Schumpeterian concept. This is to say that this attack on neoclassical economics can be interpreted in terms of its "bankrupting effects" on fundamental aspects of the theory system expressing a dated or otherwise misleading orthodox vision of the mixed economy. Such a bankruptcy would serve to clear the field for the development and acceptance of an alternative system of theory— one giving form to a more accurate vision of the structure and function of the contemporary market-directed capitalist economy.

VII. Creative destruction: the significance of the Capital Controversies

(a) Capital and the theory of the aggregate production function

It is of interest that the theoretical statement of the current mainstream vision of the mixed economy reached its fullest form in Cambridge USA and, further, that the first and most significant theoretical attack on this theory structure emanated from Cambridge UK—the birthplace of Keynes's originating "revolution."

The beginnings of this attack can be conveniently dated with the publication of Joan Robinson's well-known paper "The Production Function and the Theory of Capital" in 1954.[47] This was the first major sally in the theoretical wars which extended into the mid-1960s and which have come to be known as the Cambridge Controversies.[48]

From the tactical point of view, the various and particular ar-

[47] Joan Robinson, "The Production Function and the Theory of Capital," *Review of Economic Studies*, 1953-53(2), pp. 81-86.

[48] The substantive end of this debate can be dated with the November 1966 issue of the *Quarterly Journal of Economics*, which was entirely devoted to a Symposium on Capital Theory. In this issue, Paul Samuelson's paper, "A Summing Up" (pp. 568-583), acknowledged the correctness of the theoretical arguments taken by the proponents of the Cambridge UK position.

guments put forth by the participants in this debate were highly abstract, esoteric, and technically complex. From the broader, strategic point of view, however, the identification and understanding of the essential objectives of the Cambridge UK attack was clear and straightforward, and is easily explicated via the simple schema of Figure 1.

Figure 1 is intended to present the basic theoretical structure expressing the orthodox (Cambridge USA) vision of the (static) Walrasian private sector of an interrelated market system and to show how this private sector is related to the "public sector" so as to form the basic orthodox view of the "mixed economy." Dynamic neoclassical theory, both long and short run, moves this structure, as we have already noted, off the page into the third-dimensional dynamics of time (in some sense of that latter term).

We have also noted that implicit in the schema of the private economy is the principle of derived demand at the *macroeconomic* level and its corollary, the idea of generalized or *aggregate* production function, of the basic (neoclassical) form $O = F(L,C)$. It has also been observed that such aggregation is necessary in order to develop an operational *systemic* explanation of the fundamental neoclassical theories of value and distribution and of growth. For without such aggregation, as Mark Blaug has pointed out, we are left with the empirically useless idea of a Walrasian circular flow mechanism of market interconnection, wherein everything depends on everything else.

Thus, it has been the supremely important ideas of the ordered existence of, and a consistent logic for, this *aggregate* production function that have been the focal points for attack in these Cambridge intellectual wars. With the serious undermining of this lynchpin, the aggregate production function, and thereby the derivative theories of value distribution and growth, the basis for the neoclassical rationale explaining the coherence and systematic ordering of general systemic market process has been placed in severe jeopardy, if not actually destroyed—at least from the standpoint of its scientifically theoretical and analytic validity.

The analytical or theoretical success of the Cambridge UK attack on this (aggregate) neoclassical production function has turned on, most importantly, its ability to call into question the orthodox concept concerning the nature and meaning of the (functional) "argument," capital.

The thrust of the attack is straightforward. The neoclassical theories of value, distribution, and growth depend upon the possibility of the theoretical existence of the idea of competitive pricing and thus substitution of factor inputs in accordance with the logic of the marginal productivity analysis. (No one, of course, ever argues that such a situation actually exists in the real world— merely that, at a high enough level of abstraction, the theory is logically and technically viable and thus able to serve as a valid basis or first approximation for further investigation of less restrictive and less abstract analyses of real-world economic processes.)

As noted, for the purpose of general systemic or macroeconomic analysis, the articulation of the marginal productivity theory requires the existence of an aggregated production function which, in turn, obviously requires the ability, at least in theory, to aggregate the "arguments" of that function.

The aggregation of "labor" as such presents no theoretical difficulty, since this factor can be reduced to homogeneous units stated in its own terms, e.g., man-hours of particular grades of work. However, this is not the case with capital. Here we have, simply put, the well-worn apples and oranges problem in that "capital" is made manifest in the form of a stock of heterogeneous plant and equipment. And to aggregate such a stock we must find a common denominator, which is to say we must reduce it to value terms. But to value, or "capitalize" a stock of heterogeneous plant and equipment we need to know its yields; i.e., we need to know the rate of interest. But this means that the "production function" thereby derived cannot be used to determine the rate of interest as the marginal product of that capital. The problem is obviously one of circularity (or of tautology, depending on how one sees the issue).

However, to rescue the situation, it may be argued, as does Mark Blaug, that the value of the capital *stock* itself is not really the problem, since this variable serves in actuality only as a convenient proxy for the *flow* of factor services, and measurement of this flow does not require knowledge of the rate of interest.[49] Thus, as an alternative approach to the problem, Blaug suggests that we begin with the various *micro* production functions—since the concept of a "production function" is theoretically viable at

---

[49] Mark Blaug, *The Cambridge Revolution: Success or Failure* (London: Institute for Economic Affairs, 1974), p. 5.

the micro level—and add them so as to arrive at a *macro* function for the economy.

But, this additive approach is in fact no solution at all and only begs the basic question. This is so since the crucial problem of product exhaustion between or among factor inputs requires the existence of a so-called "well-behaved" production function, i.e., one that has the property of constant returns to scale, along with the property that, if one of the inputs is zero, output is zero. (Technically, this describes the so-called linear homogeneous production function of degree one.) But production functions with such characteristics are *logarithmatic* in form, and logarithmatic functions simply are not additive.[50] The summing up of exponents is in mathematical fact a multiplicative process.

Thus such an "aggregated" production function would have no useful or clear economic meaning relative to the analytical problems at hand. Blaug recognizes this summing-up problem but brushes it aside with the comment that the Cambridge UK position is right, but for the wrong reasons, in that the essence of the problem is not the valuing of capital, but the achieving of economically meaningful and consistent aggregation of the various *micro* functions—the latter concept of the production function being a theoretically viable one.[51]

But since properly specified (logarithmic) functions cannot be additive, we are thrown back on the use of the value of the *stock* of capital as a proxy for the (more properly specified) *flow* variable. Thus Blaug, in attempting to defend the logic of the marginal productivity theory on the aggregate level of analysis from the charge of specious circularity, actually compounds the difficulty by saddling the theoretical construct of the aggregate production function with an additional technical difficulty that undercuts its raison d'être in the first instance. This is to say, the case for aggregation of production functions, which Blaug has argued is necessary for empirically operational economic theory as opposed to the empirically useless concept of the Walrasian concept of general equilibrium, is on the horns of the dilemma of being either logi-

---

[50] Cobb–Douglas and Constant Elasticity of Substitution (CES) production functions are the best known particular types of such logarithmic functions, the former embodying the property of *unity* (as opposed to constant) elasticity of factor substitution.

[51] Blaug, *The Cambridge Revolution*, pp. 6-10.

cally circular or mathematically and empirically impossible.[52]

(b) The reswitching anomaly: the consistency and coherence of systemic processes in pure theory

The situation may now seem to have become sufficiently muddled so that one might find a sufficient presumption of doubt to allow for the metaphysics of what Paul Samuelson has termed the "neoclassical parables." And as Samuelson once noted, "until the laws of thermodynamics are repealed, I shall continue to relate outputs to inputs—i.e., to believe in [aggregate] production functions."[53]

To put Samuelson's position in the strongest light, let us perform the mental experiement of imagining a distinction between actual (heterogeneous) capital goods and "capital" as an "abiding entity," as J. B. Clark once put it, that resides in a continuum as does water in a waterfall. Further, let us assume that this capital is totally malleable—call it, as some have, "putty," "jelly," "leets," or "meccano sets." Still, as we shall see, the basic neoclassical theory explaining a vision of a consistently ordered and rational market system breaks down on its own grounds, i.e., on purely theoretical terms.

But to continue with the laws of thermodynamics, let us relate inputs to outputs and do so on the basis of the strongest case. This is to say, let us arbitrarily assume the existence of an aggregate production function with totally malleable capital (à la J. B. Clark), so that this capital may be freely substituted for labor on the basis of (assumed) diminishing marginal productivities to both

---

[52] Adolph Lowe argues that, at a high enough level of abstraction, it is quite possible to find a common denominator for different types of real capital without entering the value dimension and thus exposing oneself to circular reasoning. Lowe argues for the circular nature of capital formation itself and points to the double function of "machine tools." The latter, Lowe notes, produce not only all other types of real capital but also themselves. From this it follows that, in principle, every specific type of real capital can be "measured" by the quantity of machine tools and labor that enter into its production. (The substance of this note is based on personal correspondence with Professor Lowe, letter dated October 4, 1979.) More details on the nature and implications of Lowe's concept of capital and capital formation are contained in his book *The Path of Economic Growth* (London and New York: Cambridge University Press, 1976), pp. 9-10 and Chapter 3.

[53] Paul A. Samuelson, "Rejoinder, Agreements, Disagreements, Doubts and the Case of the Induced Harrod-Neutral Technical Change," *Review of Economics and Statistics*, November 1966, p. 444.

factors, within the context of constant returns to scale. That is, let us assume the orthodox aggregate production function that is linear and homogeneous to degree one, so that, given competition, we can postulate that both capital and labor would receive the value of their marginal products and that in so doing total product would be exhausted.

Systemic coherence and order in the theoretical logic of this neoclassical theory statement of the market-interrelated economy would require that, as relative prices of factor inputs changed, there be substitution of more of the (relatively) cheaper factor for less of the (relatively) more expensive.

That such "rational" substitution within this neoclassical production function—the latter representing a purely theoretical but operational statement indicative of the ordered and consistent circular flows of a market-interrelated economy—is not necessarily to be expected is the essential point of the so-called reswitching phenomenon which gained some prominence as a result of the capital controversies.

Broadly put, reswitching (or double-switching as it is sometimes called) relates to economic incentives that favor a *particular* production technique, or capital–labor ratio, *at more than one level of relative factor prices*, with other techniques being desirable at intermediate levels.[54] A useful illustration of this, originally alluded to by Piero Sraffa,[55] is wine making, where capital intensity is relatively low in the very beginning of the production process

[54] The following generalization on reswitching follows my article, "The Ruth Cohen Anomaly and Production Theory," *Challenge*, November/December 1978, p. 33 ff. This article has been reprinted under the abbreviated title of "Production Theory" in Eichner (ed.) *A Guide to Post-Keynesian Economics*.

[55] Piero Sraffa, *Production of Commodities by Commodities* (Cambridge: Cambridge University Press, 1960), pp. 81-88. This is a generalized statement of the phenomenon. Joan Robinson, among a few others, had also taken note of this "anomaly." At first Mrs. Robinson tended to regard it in the narrower terms of a technical problem in capital theory. On this basis, she labeled the phenomenon, almost whimsically, 'The Ruth Cohen Curiosum,' after the Cambridge associate who observed it and called it to Mrs. Robinson's specific attention. See her book *The Accumulation of Capital* (London: Macmillan, 1956), pp. 109-110.

Mrs. Robinson was, however, the first to recognize the more general nature and implications of Sraffa's critique and presentation, and that by it the whole structure of conventional economic theory was being called into question. On this, see her "Prelude to a Critique of Economic Theory," *Oxford Economic Papers*, Vol. 13, 1961, pp. 7-14.

(picking and sorting), but very high for the remainder of the process as the wine is held to maturity (via capital goods)—five years, it seems, being a minimum period for a merely palatable wine. (Sraffa contrasts this instance to the "old oak made into the chest" situation where the reverse labor–capital intensity is the case, in that cutting and processing timber is more capital-intensive than the subsequent carpentering and finishing.)

In wine making, an increase in the rate of interest would have strong effects on the costs of production, particularly felt through the highly capital-intensive aging phase of the process. Thus, an increase in interest costs would probably tend to induce producers to economize by shortening the aging stage closer to its limits, given the acceptable quality standards for the wine. Such a "switch," of course, would tend to lower the capital intensity of the process as a whole (conversely raising its labor intensity) and would be in accord with what neoclassical theory would predict in light of the increase in interest costs. However, further increases in the rate of interest would, at a point, raise the costs of holding wine so much that producers would find it advantageous to switch to some technique of higher capital intensity that would speed up, that is shorten, the production process. This *latter* switch would be perverse according to orthodox theory and its "law" of substitution—this, of course, calling for higher labor intensity and lesser capital intensity as the cost of capital rises. But how does one transform the foregoing, which is largely a "parable" of assertions, into a parable of *significant* and *general* economic importance?

The key to the transformation noted above lies with time and the resulting *compounding effects* of interest rate changes on the comparative cost of the capital and labor inputs. For example, the compounded effects of an interest rate increase on such long-term processes as wine producing would be quite significant, particularly when capital intensity becomes quite high early in the production process (when the aging stage commences). Thus, as interest costs rise, it may pay at first to cut capital intensity by, say, cutting the term of the aging stage; but if interest costs rise further, the exponential compounding of interest charges will give rise to a situation where it will pay to switch and to use *more* capital—particularly if applied toward the end of the production process where the results of compounding will be relatively slight—

so as to shorten the time required in the process of production. Thus, the switching of technique back to a more capital-intensive method can also have the effect of changing the types of capital used in production. And so it is not merely the degree of capital intensity that is altered, but also what form "capital" takes in the production process and thus the duration and the very nature of that process itself. The foregoing factors are of importance in that they affect the time period over which compounding takes place and thus the points of desirable switching and reswitching. *And this is the cutting edge*: in light of the foregoing argument, it can reasonably be expected that changes in the relative costs of labor and capital—real wages and interest or profit rates—will work to induce *rational* substitutions of capital for labor, and labor for capital, that lack the consistency and ordered coherence postulated by neoclassical capital and production theory *even in its purest form*. Such a situation, of course, would strike at the very essence of the neoclassical view of how production is ordered and coordinated in a market system.[56]

The key point here, of course, is that the traditional theory that expresses the vision of a market-coordinated production system (together with derivative—longer term—growth and distribution theories) is invalidated, even when taken on its own terms and on the strongest possible assumptive grounds.[57]

[56] A relatively minor point relating to the pure logic of the reswitching controversy is that, under the stationary conditions which the neoclassical "parables" assume, the supply of labor is fixed. This precludes switching from a capital-intensive to a labor-intensive technique since such a switch assumes an elastic labor supply. Hicks was the first (and apparently only) one to take specific note of this argument in his *Capital and Growth* (Oxford: Oxford University Press, 1965), p. 138. (I am indebted to Adolph Lowe for pointing this out to me in correspondence dated October 4, 1979.)

[57] Nor should this be a particularly surprising result when one reflects on the fact that neoclassical growth theory *assumes* competition, so that the rewards to the *endogenous* factors, labor and capital, are equal to their marginal products by assumption and not by "explanation." Then, to compound matters, what is not "explained" by assumption, the famous residual, is then arbitrarily attributed to exogenous factors, most importantly, the effects of technical change. At best, this residual is more accurately described as a measure, if not a tacit admission, of ignorance.

Concerning the ability of Cobb-Douglas and CES production functions to successfully "predict" the *distributive shares* of labor and capital: relatively recent technical research has shown that this "ability" is inherent in the mathematical properties of these functions as specified when combined with

(c) Beyond reswitching

To make the case against neoclassical orthodoxy even stronger, recent work by John Hicks and others has demonstrated that reswitching, though sufficient, is not even a necessary condition for undermining the theoretical validity of neoclassical production theory. This is to say that, irrespective of changes in relative prices, it is a simple technological fact that, because of the nature of "capital" itself, there are structures of production where substitution is irreversible and thus for which the neoclassical relation between the sphere of production and the market simply does not hold.[58] As a result, Hicks has been led to explicitly repudiate the idea of an aggregate production function and of rational neoclassical substitution within this construct.[59] And what is even more, he has been led to the repudiation of neoclassical economics itself, inclusive of his own *Value and Capital*, from which, as noted above, a major strand of today's orthodoxy has been developed. His words:

> Clearly I need to change my name. Let it be understood that *Value and Capital* (1939) was the work of J. R. Hicks, a "neoclassical" economist now deceased; *Capital & Time* (1973)—and *A Theory of Economic History* (1969)—are the works of John Hicks, a non-neoclassic who is quite disrespectful toward his uncle.[60]

In short, the upshot of the controversies over the nature and meaning of "capital," and of the aggregate production function, is that the "invisible hand" simply does not work along the lines envisioned by contemporary neoclassical theory to coordinate and rationalize the processes of today's market-oriented economic system.

---

stability of the data on income shares. That is, shares will be successfully "predicted" by these functions as long as actual shares remain roughly constant over the time period from which the data is drawn. On this see F. M. Fisher, "Aggregate Production Functions," *Econometrica*, Vol. 37, October 1971.

[58] On this see John Hicks, *Capital and Growth*, and also Murray Brown, "Substitution-Composition Effects, Capital Intensity Uniqueness and Growth," Discussion Paper No. 2, Economic Research Group, State University of New York at Buffalo, 1967.

[59] See Hicks's Nobel Prize Lecture, "The Mainspring of Economic Growth," *Les Prix Nobel*, 1972 (Stockholm: Imprinerie Royale, F. A. Norstedt, 1973), pp. 232-246.

[60] John Hicks, "Revival of Political Economy: The Old and the New," *The Economic Record*, September 1975, p. 365.

(d) Some policy implications

The importance of the foregoing not only for economic theory, but also for policy, is that the neoclassical vision of an inherently equilibrating circular flow (existent in real time) provides much of the metaphysical foundation for the shorter term theory system made manifest via the currently embattled version of "Keynesian" management of the "mixed economy"—that is, the placing of major policy emphasis on the indirect tools of fiscal and monetary policies so as to purposively affect, through microeconomic market responses, various key macroeconomic objectives, such as production and employment and the price level (and the balance in external payments in an opened system). And as for long-run neoclassical growth theory, not only do the operational validity and meaning of, for example, the various "explanations" of the nature and sources of economic growth become suspect in and of themselves; they also become ambiguous if not outrightly meaningless as to how these explanations and estimates relate, if at all, to the secular continuum of short runs of neoclassical stabilization theory, for, as we have seen, these two strands of neoclassical macrodynamic theory are analytically inconsistent and nonaccommodative with one another.

It is one thing to say that the theoretical neoclassical explanation of how the economy is structured and how it functions is not consistent with experience because of the existence of such real-world problems or "imperfections" as bottlenecks, power, premature inflation, inflationary expectations, random shocks, ratchet and spillover effects, and the like. In such situations, an economically coherent and consistent market-based system of production and distribution and growth can still be assumed to exist, even though it is overlaid with and inhibited by political, institutional, and psychological factors that affect actual economic adjustment and performance. The basic strategy, in this case, would be to maintain the general neoclassical macrodynamic emphases on fiscal and monetary management (with perhaps somewhat greater stress on the monetary tool, if the monetarists were to have their way and to supplement these tools with finely targeted direct and specific devices—for example, stricter antitrust enforcement, more sharply focused incentive (and disincentive) taxes, expanded job training and subsidization programs, and more emphasis on the gathering and dissemination of information and knowledge. The objective here would be, of course, to allow and encourage the effective functioning of the envisioned market system.

It is quite another thing, however, to argue that the interrelationships among markets in the system (notably those in the resource or input sector) and that key linkages in the system (such as linkages between output markets and resource markets, as well as those between the "public" and the "private" sectors) do not possess the fundamental economic characteristics necessary to the orderly systematic functioning that is postulated by the macrodynamic theories of mainstream economics. In this case, the entire theory system of mainstream neoclassical economics loses its unifying consistency and coherence. And, as a consequence, the paradigmatic vision underlying the corpus of neoclassical economic theory becomes open to serious question as to its reliability and usefulness as an "image" or "knowledge structure" of how the economic system in reality is structured, how it functions, and how and why it progresses through time.

VIII. The current state of economic theory and the basis of a post-Keynesian vision

Thus the implications of the capital controversies are profound. And they may reasonably be viewed as a stage of "creative destruction" in the paradigmatic development of contemporary economic theory which also calls into serious question the validity of the *underlying vision* of the (mixed) economy that mainstream theory purports to explain. None of this, of course, means that contemporary economic theory, and the policy implications implicit in that theory, are soon to be overthrown. Recalling the (not unuseful) "tenacity of theory," we understand that the Cambridge criticisms, along with those of the modern general equilibrium theorists, may be viewed (in Kuhnian terms) as anomalies, i.e., as puzzles for "normal science" to set about to solve. The scientific research program (to use the Lakatosian concept) of current orthodox economic theory may be a degenerating one, but a "progressive" replacement has as yet not been widely recognized, much less accepted.

The primary protective strategy of orthodox neoclassical economics at this point appears to be a rearguard holding action, in the sense that the major tack has been to shift the whole problem to the arena of econometric testing. As the late Charles Ferguson once put it in his influential text on neoclassical production and distribution theory:

> The question that confronts us is not whether the Cambridge Criticism is theoretically valid. It is. Rather, the question is an empirical or an econometric one: is there sufficient substitutability within the system to establish the neoclassical results?[61]

As all who have reached this juncture well know, econometric hypothesis testing, based on the falsification criteria of the logical positivistic methodology, even under the most favorable circumstances, seldom if ever yields unambiguous results.

But the current situation in economic theory goes far deeper in that the essential question relates to the very core of neoclassical economics as a *scientific* theory system capable of supporting the activities of "normal science" or of a "progressive scientific research program." *And this question cannot even be asked, much less (scientifically) tested*, for the crucial issue—which Ferguson clearly identifies—of systemic factor substitutability can be posed only within the framework of an aggregate production function— and as we have seen this framework does not even exist outside the realm of metaphysics. No matter how rarified the theory or elegant the mathematics, the aggregate production function does not and cannot have any empirical validity or analytical meaning. Thus, the fact is that the neoclassical vision cannot be objectified in that the theoretician cannot give the econometrician anything to be scientific about. And Mark Blaug, who as we have seen is no proponent of the Cambridge UK school, has given voice to what is perhaps the most fundamental of *scientific* criticism concerning the current attempt to rescue or preserve the neoclassical paradigm by labeling it "measurement without theory."[62]

Thus, it would seem to be no overstatement to conclude that the current state of mainstream neoclassical economic theory has simply come down to a matter of faith. And, in light of the results and implications of the capital controversies, Ferguson himself

---

[61] Charles Ferguson, *The Neoclassical Theory of Production and Distribution* (London: Cambridge University Press, 1969), pp. 265-266.

[62] Blaug, *The Cambridge Revolution*, p. 80.

noted that ". . . placing reliance upon neoclassical economic theory is a matter of faith. I personally have the faith," he continues, "but at present the best I can do to convince others is to invoke the weight of Samuelson's authority as represented by [his belief in the laws of thermodynamics and their relationship to production functions]."[63]

But, as noted, mainstream neoclassical economic theory is the explication of a vision of an underlying reality of how the economy is structured and how it functions. And thus it follows that this underlying vision must also be opened to thoughtful question and reconsideration. For in the words of another textbook writer (the King James edition), "Now faith is the substance of things hoped for, the evidence of things not seen." Concerning the neoclassical vision, no valid substance *can* be hoped for; no scientific evidence *can ever* be seen.

As for what the future holds in store for economic theory, it would not only be beyond the scope of this essay, but it would also be premature to attempt to outline in any detail the theory structure specifying some *generally* accepted school of thought relevant to a post-Keynesian era.[64] The germs of the present will become clear only in the light of a future sensitive to its past. However, it seems quite in order, even at this point, to venture that not only will this emerging theory system be based on a different vision of the modern postindustrial economy, but that fundamental to this vision will be a radically changed view of the nature and function of the basic institution of capitalism, *the market and the market system.*

No longer will the market be seen à la Lionel Robbins, merely as a mechanism for allocating resources toward alternative ends, primarily through the substitution effects of relative price changes, thereby answering the "whats," "hows," and "whos" of society. Rather, it seems reasonable that, in the economics of a post-Keynesian era, the emerging theoretical structure will most likely

---

[63] Ferguson, *The Neoclassical Theory of Production and Distribution*, p. XVII and flyleaf.

[64] A recent general survey of one set of views on the subject of post-Keynesian economics is the series of essays appearing in Eichner (ed.), *A Guide to Post-Keynesian Economics.* For a survey essay in a similar vein that aims to outline the main features of a post-Keynesian paradigm, see Alfred S. Eichner and Jan A. Kregel, "An Essay on Post-Keynesian Theory," *Journal of Economic Literature*, December 1975.

be based on a vision of the market and the market system as a *social* device that transfers, i.e., (re-)distributes, primarily via income effects, suprasubsistence resources (call this "discretionary expenditure" or the social surplus) from one social-functional category (call it labor or wage receivers) to other social-functional categories (call these capital, or the "non-wage-receivers" of "residual income," both private and public).[65] In this view, the essential purpose of the market system is to accomplish the various and particular tasks relative to what Adolph Lowe has called societal "provisioning"[66]—e.g., for capital accumulation and growth or for consumption, for armament, for social services and other redistributive purposes, etc. Objectifying and delineating such goals means, of course, that the corollary economic theory will be developed in a context that takes account of political and economic power and the problems and issues of conflict resolution inherent therein.[67] And it is useful to note at this point that the whole

[65] The enquoted terminology is from Eichner and Kregel, "An Essay in Post-Keynesian Theory."

Also, it need be noted, if only in passing, that the above view of the market is inherent in the macrodynamics of the theory system developed by Michal Kalecki. As is well known, Kalecki's macroeconomic explanation of the fundamental *modus operandi* of the market-oriented economy is essentially similar to, as well as consistent with, Keynes's and was developed by Kalecki independently of Keynes and, in some respects, even prior to Keynes. On this see Kalecki's essays, written (in Polish) between 1933 and 1935 and published in English under the title *Selected Essays on the Dynamics of the Capitalist Economy* (Cambridge, London: Cambridge University Press, 1971).

Although Kalecki's theory system was not as developed in some respects as was Keynes's in the *General Theory*, the Cambridge UK school of thought, particularly as represented by Mrs. Robinson, has come to prefer Kalecki to Keynes as a theoretical starting point. The primary reason for this switch of allegiance appears to be the basic view (vision) of the market and the market economy that is inherent in the Kaleckian model. Also, Kalecki's basic theory system is free of the various problems and issues, both theoretical and ideological, that have been layered onto Keynes's basic system as the latter has been developed and linked to neoclassical market theory and its underlying vision. (Kalecki, a Pole, was trained in Marxian economics and his basic model serves as the theoretical bridge to the Marxian orientation of the Cambridge UK school.)

[66] See Adolph Lowe, *On Economic Knowledge* (New York: Harper & Row, 1965).

[67] The well-known work of J. K. Galbraith hardly needs mention in this context, except perhaps to point out that he is his own best summarizer in *Economics and the Public Purpose* (Boston: Houghton Mifflin Company, 1973).

Alfred Eichner calls attention to this issue in *A Guide to Post-Keynesian*

problem area of the wage–price issue—i.e., of anti-inflationary incomes policy—implicitly if nothing else subsumes this redistributive interpretation of the market place.

The foregoing does not necessarily mean, however, that neoclassical technique and tools must be abandoned with such a change in vision. Rather, and more likely, neoclassical analysis will provide important means and techniques relevant to the *description* of goals and end states consciously sought after, and also "instrumentalities" useful in a monitoring process concerning progress in achieving and maintaining these stated objectives. Adolph Lowe has long and cogently argued for such an approach to economics under the rubric of what he terms the end → means regressive analysis of "Political Economics." This is to say that, rather than assuming, as does conventional economics, certain behavioral cause → effect relationships and then attempting to *predict* likely outcomes or directions of change (given ceteris paribus assumptions), Lowe argues for a (reversed) end → means approach that involves the political determination of consciously determined goals —i.e., some desired or "planned for" (internally consistent and feasible) end state—and then the use of "efficiency" or "scarcity" analysis to find and maintain the best way or some feasible way of getting there. The latter is "backward looking" in the sense that it "regresses" from an unrealized goal state so as to determine possible and desirable path(s) to that state.[68] This is in stark contrast to traditional (Robbinsian) micro-market theory which analyzes (*an*) interrelationship(s) between cause(s) and *subsequent* effect(s) in an attempt to "look forward" to (and predict/explain) likely outcomes.

Such a change in perspective as noted above will imply another "revolutionary" turn—that is, a shift from a type of (mixed) "capitalism" to a type of (pragmatic) "socialism." And the irony here, of course, is that the orthodox analysis of individualist and private enterprise capitalism would find its essential validity and meaning in a type of "socialism"—i.e., a system whose macro

---

Economics, pp. 179-184. For a detailed theoretical treatment of the large firm and market analysis along such post-Keynesian lines, see his *The Megacorp and Oligopoly: Micro Foundations of Macro Dynamics* (London and New York: Cambridge University Press, 1976). Reprinted 1980 by M. E. Sharpe, Inc., White Plains, N.Y.

[68] On this view of the nature and application of economics see Adolph Lowe, *On Economic Knowledge* and *The Path of Economic Growth*.

state(s) would involve the conscious efforts of coherent economic planning. In any event, it is clear that the processes of the Keynesian revolution have run their course. And if we have learned nothing else, it should be that what will come to be identified and widely recognized as a "Post-Keynesian Revolution" will also be a process, the course and details of which are uncertain.

IX. Epilogue: on the timing and pattern of economic revolutions

Dudley Dillard, writing on the periodicity of "revolutions" in economic theory and using the dates of publications of the major recognized treatises as the criterion, has noted that such revolutions have taken place in 1776 (Smith), 1817 (Ricardo), 1848 (Mill), 1890 (Marshall), and 1936 (Keynes).[69] He focuses this sequence on British economists because historically England has been the vanguard of modern capitalist development, and turning points in capitalism have tended to come earlier there than elsewhere.[70]

The intervals between the above-noted "revolutions" are 41, 31, 42, and 46 years, respectively, for an average of 40 years. Dillard goes on to venture the view that this consistency in timing is not merely fortuitous.[71] Economies develop and change as do their key problems and issues, and therefore accepted economic theory, irrespective of how "good" it is, is always on the road to obsolescence. But the change in the economic universe that theory attempts to "explain" is not so rapid as to be very noticeable over a short term, nor is its change teleologically determined. Thus, it is not likely that there will be continuous and synchronized change between an economic system and in its corollary "explanatory" theory. But systemic change does occur and it is both continuous and cumulative, as well as largely unpredictable.

Further, Dillard notes that "revolutionary" theory shifts appear

[69] Dudley Dillard, "Revolutions in Economic Theory," *Southern Economic Review*, April 1978, p. 714.

[70] Ibid., p. 705. (This, of course, neglects Marx by definition, but it nevertheless is a reasonable position, as far as mainstream economics in the United States goes, at least up to the present.)

[71] Ibid., p. 714.

to occur once a generation in response to a once-a-generation cumulation of problems and issues that are successfully grappled with by minds that are not only exceptional, but that are also mature enough to have deeply understood the old, yet are still young and agile enough to recognize the need for change.[72]

Given the forty-plus years since the launching of Keynes's revolution by way of the publication of *The General Theory*, along with the present accumulation and recognition of serious problems in the contemporary economy and in its explanatory theory system, another economic revolution, perhaps even now in process, would be quite in keeping with the pattern discerned by Dillard. One must avoid the lure of determinism, but the various debates, issues, and problems in both vision and theory, discussed in this essay, provide interesting food for thought concerning a possible paradigmatic shift in contemporary economic theory.

[72] Ibid., p. 716. For example, the average age for the "great" economists noted in the text at the time of the publication of their landmark work was 48. Smith was 53 and the oldest, while Mill was 42 and the youngest. Ricardo was 45, Marshall 48, and Keynes 52.

John Blatt

7

HOW ECONOMISTS
MISUSE MATHEMATICS

‖ ‖

ABSTRACT: The mathematical discipline called "optimal control theory" has become fashionable within economics, both in pure economic theory and in economic policy applications based on econometric models. Arguments are given that the pure economic theory applications are frivolous and meaningless and that application to econometric models is entirely premature, in view of the specification errors which plague these models and which have magnified effects on the deduced "optimal" policies. In the final section, we widen the discussion to look at the misuse of mathematics as a whole within so-called "mathematical economics."

I.

Since the late 1950s, mathematicians have been developing what is called "optimal control theory." Control is needed to ensure that a moon rocket takes off properly, goes correctly into its planned orbit, and finally lands on the moon smoothly. There are many ways of "controlling" the rocket so as to achieve this. There are, for example, many possible orbits which lead eventually to the desired landing point on the moon. But some of these are better than others; for example, they may get the rocket to its destination with less total expenditure of rocket fuel and, hence, smaller take-off weight for a given payload. The object of "control theory" is the mathematical study of the possible and sensible control policies. It becomes "optimal control theory" when we wish to find the very best, optimal control policy for the given task (Blatt 1981).

In recent years, economists of mathematical bent have started increasingly to apply optimal control theory to their subject. The scholarly literature in this area is already very extensive and is growing at a rapid pace (e.g., see Pitchford 1977 and Holly 1978).

It is *not* my purpose to survey or review that literature; rather, I propose to criticize and reject the foundations on which this literature rests. Although this paper deals with a highly mathematical subject (optimal control theory), it is not a mathematical paper. Rather, it is addressed to economists, of the nonmathematical variety. Its purpose is to warn against what I believe to be one more example of a serious misuse of mathematics by economists.

Mathematics is, after all, a purely logical subject. One starts from a set of initial assumptions (axioms) and uses the rules of logic to deduce their consequences. When mathematical reasoning is applied to problems outside of mathematics itself, then the results are no better than the initial assumptions. Computer scientists have a telling phrase: "Garbage in, garbage out," meaning that the results which emerge from a computer (or from mathematics) are no better than the initial input. If the initial assumptions are faulty, then the conclusions cannot be accepted as valid, no matter how much and how elaborate the mathematics that lies in between.

There are two main areas of application of optimal control theory within economics. The first is pure economic theory; the second is economic policymaking based on econometric models. A third area, the theory of finance—e.g., the option pricing model (Black 1973) used for optimal investment policy, is microeconomic and less fraught with danger; if (as I believe) the usual assumptions of that theory are rather less realistic than its advocates assert, the only people likely to be hurt are stock market gamblers. One can bear the shock.

In section 2 and 3, we shall discuss these misuses of optimal control theory. Section 4 is devoted to the misuse of mathematics in general, particularly in so-called "mathematical economics."

II.

Pure economic theory has been described by some as the theory of the most efficient utilization of scarce resources toward the attainment of given ends (Robbins 1935). This definition is accepted by many working economists.

Under this definition, all of economics is an optimization problem. In *static* economic theory, we are led to optimize some function of currently available variables of choice. The relevant discipline is called "mathematical programming" and deals with efficient methods for finding the maximum of a function of many variables. One branch, maximization of a *linear* function of many variables, is called "linear programming." It is widely applied in industry and commerce as a model of profit maximization subject to technical and market constraints. Within pure economic theory, however, it is usual to assume that the function we wish to maximize is such that the maximum in question is attained somewhere within the interior of the domain of the function, rather than being a boundary maximum as it is in linear programming. (This is the reason for the common assumption that the functions be concave or "quasi-concave"; the assumption is made in order to obtain the results one wants, *not* because there is an objective reason to believe that the assumption is true.)

If a well-behaved (smooth) function has a maximum somewhere within the interior of its domain, then all first-order partial derivatives vanish at the maximum. Economists use the word "marginal" for these partial derivatives. The mathematical condition that all first-order partial derivatives vanish is the origin of the usual "marginal relationships" in static economics, for example, the equality of price and marginal utility.

Though very much of standard economic theory is restricted to static, timeless systems, not all of it is. There is also a body of theory known as *dynamic* economics, which attempts to study the development of an economic system in time. When the idea of optimal use of scarce resources is applied to optimization over time, the mathematical problem can no longer be formulated as a straightforward exercise in mathematical programming. Some government policy instrument is now the "control variable," and we wish to find the optimal choice for this control variable *as a function of time* (rather than merely a single value, at the present time). This means, mathematically speaking, that the appropriate mathematical discipline is now optimal control theory, rather than mathematical programming. Economists interested in optimization *over time* are therefore drawn naturally to applying optimal control theory to their subject.

To illustrate the sort of problem that arises, and the sort of solution that is produced, take the following very simple case. The national income Y is taken to be some function $f(x)$ of the available capital stock x. This income can be used in two ways: (1) For immediate consumption C, thereby producing utility $U(C)$ per unit time, and (2) for investment, thereby increasing the capital stock x in the future. The "control variable" is the fraction v $(0 < v < 1)$ of current output devoted to consumption; i.e., $C = vY = vf(x)$. For this purely illustrative example, let us ignore such refinements as the need for labor separate from that for capital stock, the need to replace worn-out capital stock, etc. It is usual, however, to include one further consideration, namely, the distinction between utility gained now and utility to be gained at some future time t. The latter utility is to be discounted at some social discount rate ρ, which is some given number. The quantity to be maximized is then the total discounted utility over the entire future (discounting is necessary to make that total come out as a finite, rather than an infinite, quantity).

Let us forego the mathematical equations and turn immediately to the kind of result that one obtains. One typical result is the following: within optimal control theory, there exists a mathematical quantity called a "co-state variable." It can be shown that this co-state variable has the economic interpretation of a price and that this price equals the marginal utility of consumption at each future time t, appropriately discounted at the discount rate ρ. There is no need to pursue this example further. What we have now seen is (1) the sort of problem that is being posed, and (2) the sort of answer that is obtained from the theory.

At this stage, let us turn to criticism.

1. It is characteristic of such problems that they are *not properly specified*. Neither the utility function $U(C)$ nor the production function $f(x)$ are functions in the mathematical meaning of that term. That is, no rule is provided by which, given C, the value of $U(C)$ can actually be computed, and similarly for x and $f(x)$. We may be told that $U(C)$ and $f(x)$ are monotonically increasing and concave functions, but nothing more beyond such general statements. In consequence, there is not enough information to obtain an actual solution, that is, an actual well-defined optimal control

policy. By the very statement (or, rather, incomplete statement) of the problem, it is impossible to solve it! One may indeed obtain general statements about properties which the (unobtainable) solution must possess: The co-state variable is a price and is related to marginal utility, indeed. But we *cannot* know what the optimal price is, or what is the optimal fraction *v* which should be devoted to consumption. The statement of the problem is too deficient to allow such practical conclusions. We are not really given a problem. *We are given bits and pieces of a problem, part of a problem.*

2. This peculiar way of half-posing problems can be traced back to quite early times, but it was given its main impetus by Paul Samuelson (1947) in his very influential *Foundations of Economic Analysis.* I shall have more to say about the effects of this book and its successors, in section 4. For now, let me just note one immediate consequence of this form of problem half-statement, and then go on to ask why problems of pure economic theory should be stated this way.

Such half-problems are extremely difficult to handle, even for professional mathematicians. With a real, specific problem, there are various methods of attack so as to obtain a solution. Some methods rely on the form of the functions, such as $U(C)$ and $f(x)$, providing simplifications if these functions take simple forms or have particular symmetry or other properties. Another whole range of solution methods is numerical in nature, so that the eventual solution is obtained as a set of specific numerical values. All this is excluded before we even start, by the fact that we are not told what these functions are, so we can neither use their specific forms, nor evaluate them numerically. Right from the beginning, therefore, we are faced with the heartbreaking task of fighting our way through some very heavy mathematics with our hands tied behind our backs, and without any hope of getting other than incomplete and partial answers, relationships between different parts of a solution, but never an actual solution, plain and simple.

3. Why are problems of pure economic theory stated in such a peculiar, incomplete fashion? The reason is not far to seek. The utility function $U(C)$ is not given explicitly because it *cannot* be given. It is an artificial construct of the theorist's mind and does not correspond to anything in the real world of men and affairs. Social utility cannot even be defined consistently, to say nothing of being measured (Arrow 1951). The function $U(C)$ is

not given because it does not exist![1]

Exactly the same is true of the production function $f(x)$. It is now more than a quarter of a century since Joan Robinson (1954) demonstrated that the quantity of capital, the "x" of that theory, is impossible to define consistently. Nonetheless, this very quantity still appears, with monotonous regularity, in equation (1) of innumerable papers on pure economic theory, in the initial assumptions on which everything else is based. Garbage in, garbage out, par excellence!

Then again, look at the social discount rate ρ by which future (unmeasurable) utility is being discounted. This is *not* an actual discount rate charged by some bank in a real-world transaction. It has nothing whatever to do with the real world. Rather, it is an entirely fictitious rate at which, supposedly, "society" discounts "social utility" (??) in the future.

All this is *not* the application of mathematics to the economic problems of the real world. Rather, it is the application of highly precise and elaborate mathematics to an entirely imaginary and fanciful economic cloud cuckoo land.

4. The definition of economics as an optimization problem ignores all questions of *economic conflict*. It therefore ignores what are undoubtedly some of the most important influences in the real economic world. Note that the formulation of our simple example quietly passes over the crucial question *whose* utility is being maximized. In the neoclassical cloud cuckoo land, but nowhere else, it may be assumed that employers and labor unions agree completely on how "social utility" of "consumption" (whose society? whose consumption?) is to be measured by some mathematical function $U(C)$. No wonder that the mathematical function cannot be specified properly!

5. The next major point of criticism concerns *uncertainty of the future*. In the peculiar dream world of this problem, certainty

---

[1] In statistical estimation theory, it is not necessary to observe a variable directly in order to estimate it; nor is it necessary to define it fully and explicitly. Examples are "expectation" variables and "fictitious" variables, which are often estimated from the available data, without a precise definition. However, there is a world of difference between (1) a sensible but not directly observed variable, and (2) a "variable" which is logically inconsistent and undefinable in principle. "Estimating" the latter is a flagrant misuse of the statistical method.

reigns for ever and ever. Nothing unpredictable or unexpected will ever happen. Five years from now, ten years, twenty years on— there will be exactly the same relationship $Y = f(x)$ between output and capital stock, there will be the same social utility function $U(C)$ of consumption, the future will then, as now, be discounted at the same social discount rate ρ. No technological progress (other than fully foreseen progress), no unexpected sudden booms or busts, no wars or sudden cessation of wars, no brand new and unexpected industries are allowed to perturb this dull, completely predictable utopia.

In real economic life, the future is extremely uncertain. Uncertainty does *not* mean the "gambles" and "lotteries" which pervade the "economics of uncertainty" of expected utility theorists (Borch 1968). Lotteries are a prime example of what Frank Knight (1921) called "risk" and distinguished sharply from real "uncertainty." Neglect of true Knightian uncertainty is particularly reprehensible in theories involving investment. By its very nature, investment is directed toward the future; any investment evaluation technique *must* allow for the fact that the future is unknown, unknowable, and menacing (Blatt 1979a, 1979b, 1983).[2] Seen in this context, the maximization of future utility from investment on the basis of known certain production functions is utterly meaningless. What purpose can be served by maximizing under the assumption of certainty, when actually uncertainty is the single most important factor in real life (Keynes 1937)?

6. The objections listed so far are standard economic objections raised particularly by post-Keynesian economists. No mathematical expertise is needed for these arguments. What, it may be asked, about the mathematics itself?

By and large, the technical mathematics used in this peculiar game is valid and unobjectionable. Admittedly, some economists use optimal control theory without understanding it fully, and

[2] Many attempts have been made in the past, and continue to be made, to somehow get around this fundamental uncertainty. A recently fashionable example of this tendency is the so-called "theory" of rational expectations. In this "theory" it is *assumed* that "rational" people have expectations of the future which are *correct* on the average. There is no basis whatever for such an assumption. Being "rational" does *not* make a person a prophet. In fact, expectations of the future are very often contrary to what actually is going to happen, and people (particularly rational people!) know this and treat all such expectations, including their own, with a great deal of skepticism.

hence at times get it wrong. But a field should be judged by its best practitioners, not by its worst ones.

However, this does *not* improve matters. If a baby is boiled and served for a meal, it is hardly an extenuating circumstance that the meat is very well cooked and is seasoned with all the skill available to culinary art. On the contrary, most people would feel that this constitutes an aggravation of the crime. When very sound and proper mathematics is misused and misapplied to fairyland problems without any basis in the real world, the fact that the mathematics itself is impeccable makes the whole obnoxious game just that much more offensive.

7. I conclude this section by quoting from John Maynard Keynes (1936, p. 298): "Too large a proportion of recent 'mathematical' economics are merely concoctions as imprecise as the initial assumptions they rest on, which allow the author to lose sight of the complexities and interdependencies of the real world in a maze of pretentious and unhelpful symbols."

Keynes wrote this in 1936, long before the invention of optimal control theory or its application to pure economic theory. But his strictures apply in full force, right here and now.

III.

Let us turn now to the second major area of application of optimal control theory, namely, the area of *economic policy and econometric models*. Here there cannot be any criticism of the aims as being too far removed from the real world. On the contrary, look at this statement, taken from the preface to Gregory Chow's *Analysis and Control of Dynamic Economic Systems* (Chow 1975): "This book presents a set of related techniques for analyzing the properties of dynamic stochastic models in economics and for applying these models in the determination of quantitative economic policy. It also illustrates them with a number of examples and applications. . . ." Nothing could be clearer than such aims, or (at first sight, anyway) more laudable.

To quote Chow some more, the main uses of econometric models are "to provide economic forecasts, to explain the dynamic behavior of the economy in question, and to help make better quantitative economic policies."

The first use, economic forecasting, is not my concern here, but

I shall have something to say about it later on.

The second use, explaining the dynamic behavior of the economy, does not involve optimal control directly. However, it is true that optimal control theory may be used to help in this task: The calculation of an optimal policy, based on an econometric model, may well give valuable insight into the way the equations of the model interact with each other. I have nothing against this use of optimal control theory. But I point out that this is an "internal" use by model builders, to attempt to understand their own models, not a use of interest to anyone else but the model builder himself. Personally, I should not employ optimal control theory for this purpose; it is too much like a sledge hammer used to crack a peanut. But different poeple have different ways of gaining understanding, and, if this scheme helps someone else, fine and dandy.

My real concern is with the third use, "to help make better quantitative economic policies." I submit that this type of work must be looked at carefully and critically. There are two, essentially different, types of criticism: (A) of the aims themselves, and (B) of the extent to which such aims have been realized in practice. Let us take these in turn.

A.

1. Before we can determine an optimal quantitative economic policy, we must first be clear what is meant by the word "optimal." Just what is it that the controllers should maximize? This is not at all a trivial question. On the contrary, it leads right back to the impossibility of giving a consistent definition of "social utility," which we have encountered already in the discussion of pure economic theory. The restriction of economics to an optimization problem is blatantly inadequate in the economic policy area, where the question of exactly what is meant by "optimum" simply must not be ignored (although it is ignored all too often in the literature).

2. The ancient Romans asked: "Who watches the watchmen?" In the present context, they might well ask: "Who controls the controllers?" It is well known within the trade that econometric modeling is by no means purely objective and value-free. The theoretical views of the model builders, monetarist, Keynesian, or whatever, are built into the behavioral equations of the model, of necessity. These views thus affect the "optimal" policies deduced

from the model. It then becomes extremely difficult, if not impossible, for layman politicians or anyone else to contradict these conclusions, since they should need to develop an entire alternative model with different policy consequences. Knowledge is power, even if the "knowledge" is only relative, compared to the ignorance of the laymen. Are we really prepared to let a group of technocrats tell us how something as socially sensitive as our entire economy should be run? If they do take over in this fashion, what then happens to the government which we have elected, supposedly to represent our wishes? Of course, if the technocrats take over, the problem of defining "optimality" is solved at one stroke: Optimal is whatever is best for the technocrats. But do we *want* that "solution"?

3. Within the context of competitive capitalism, there is a clear contradiction between such attempts at control and the very basis of the "free enterprise system." One may opt for the invisible hand of Adam Smith, *or* for the very visible hand of the controller. But one cannot have both within the same system: "The statesman, who should attempt to direct private people in what manner they ought to employ their capitals, would not only load himself with the most unnecessary attention, but assume an authority which could safely be trusted, not only to no single person, but to no council or senate whatever, and which would nowhere be so dangerous as in the hands of a man who had folly and presumption enough to fancy himself fit to exercise it" (Adam Smith 1776, Modern Library edition, p. 423).

4. No contradiction of this sort exists in the context of a socialist economy, which is in any case centrally planned. But there is a different problem there. Socialist planners are not likely to restrict themselves to theories based on competitive pricing. Price control, direct and outright, is not a universal panacea, far from it. But used in moderation, it is much too valuable a tool of control to forgo right from the beginning. Whether socialist planners actually succeed in overcoming the difficulties noted by Adam Smith is a hotly contested subject which need not be debated here. It is incontestable, however, that controlled prices can be found also outside the socialist countries, for example, the prices of crude oil and of refined petroleum products.

These general criticisms are valid, but I believe that they should not be given too much weight. It is surely good to understand how the mechanism of our economic system operates, and any effort in that direction is worth applause rather than censure. This is true especially after the controllers are demoted from all-wise gods to mere human and fallible advisers to equally human and equally fallible politicians who, fortunately for the rest of us, need to worry about being reelected.

B.

Let us now turn to consideration of the present state of knowledge and of practice in building econometric models and using them for control purposes. It is my intention to demonstrate that, in their present state, econometric models are not sound enough to warrant application of the elaborate mathematics of optimal control theory. *Before one can control anything, one must first be able to predict accurately how the system will behave in the absence of controls.*[3] *Next, one must be certain how the system will react to whatever controls are applied.* Only then does it make sense to even start looking for "optimal" controls. It is my contention that existing econometric models and econometric theory are still very far from meeting these preconditions for application of optimal control theory; if that theory is applied anyway, prematurely, then the outcome is likely to be very far indeed from optimal, in any sense of that word.

1. Entirely too much of econometric theory is devoted to the study of *linear* models. For example, of the twelve chapters of Chow (1975), eleven are devoted to that topic. Only the very last chapter considers nonlinear models. Yet linearity is a very severe restriction on a model. There is excellent reason to believe that no linear model can be at all adequate (Blatt 1983). The techniques used for linear models (expounded at such length by Chow) do *not* extend easily, or in most cases at all, to nonlinear models.

A linear model, by its very nature, is unable to generate a truly endogenous business cycle. Thus, an initial restriction to linearity

[3] This statement applies to the type of control envisaged in economic policy making, where government interference with the normal working of the economy is to be kept to a minimum. In engineering control, a tight so-called "feedback control" can be designed to work even for a poorly known system. But then the control mechanism essentially governs what happens, largely independently of the "natural" tendencies of the system. Such tight controls are politically impossible, except perhaps in wartime, and are not what is envisaged by economists or econometricians interested in optimal control.

excludes, from the very start, that whole class of dynamic economic models which alone can fit the observed facts on business cycles (Blatt 1983).

In view of the ongoing debate between conventional econometricians and the advocates of time series and "systems theory" methods (see Sims 1977, for example), it is relevant to point out that these alternative methods are based on the initial assumption of linearity, if anything even more so than conventional econometric methods. This is most unfortunate.

2. Experience with econometric models shows a sorry record of *not* predicting future economic behavior correctly. Only some of them, and those usually not the biggest and most elaborate models, barely succeed in doing as well at prediction as very simple "time series" techniques devoid of any pretense of economic content. In particular, investment is predicted extremely badly (Blatt 1979a); the econometric structural equation for investment is usually the weakest part of the model and fails miserably to predict anything at all unless the parameters within that equation are assigned values which are utterly unreasonable from an economic point of view. Since the economic theory on which these equations are based ignores uncertainty of the future, this is hardly surprising. But it should be a salutary warning against taking such models seriously. With such a very poor record of prediction, there is no reason to believe that these models represent the real economy at all accurately.

3. The econometric treatment of "random shock terms" is strongly suspect. There is no reason to think that these terms are really fully random in the accepted sense of that word. But even to the limited extent that they behave randomly, their conventional treatment by means of a normal Gaussian distribution is *unacceptable* in the economic context. Large shocks occur much more often, and are much more important, than such a treatment implies. Indeed, if something has to be neglected for practical reasons, it is better to neglect the cumulative effect of large numbers of small shocks than the effect of occasional large shocks. Yet econometric theory ignores (by implication, without saying so outright) the large shocks, and places its entire emphasis on cumulative effects of small shocks.[4]

[4] This point is also relevant to the microeconomic applications of optimal control theory in such areas as the option pricing model. This model, in its usual formulation, is based on what engineers call "white noise." This is the

4. The main discrepancies between the deterministic (without shock terms) equations and actual behavior are *not* attributable primarily to random events. Rather, they arise from the unavoidable simplifications and approximations which *must* be made to get workable equations at all. That is, these discrepancies are primarily systematic, not random. In the trade, they are called *specification errors*. They are overwhelmingly important, but econometric theory says very little about them, and econometric practice based largely on such an inadequate theory tends to be helpless in the face of mis-specification.

This criticism of econometric techniques and theory is basic. *If* the analyst mis-specifies his model, *then* the econometric assumptions about the errors *will* be incorrect in fact. Yet, in practical modeling, perfect specification is completely out of the question —thus, the econometric theory assumptions about the error terms are *never* satisfied in practical models!

5. This last point is of crucial importance when it comes to application of optimal control methods. These methods are inherently *not* "robust" against mis-specification of the model. A small change in the model leads to a very large change in the "optimal" control policy. Specification errors which can be tolerated in the context of prediction of future behavior are likely to be intolerably large in the context of optimal control. We quote from an extremely important study by Salmon and Young (1978): "Optimal solutions based in isolation on the dynamic properties of a model will mean little if, as in the economic case, the system is badly defined and the model open to mis-specification." Salmon and Young take the model used by Chow (1975) and demolish it with relentless, devastating logic. They show that Chow's supposedly "optimal" control policy is not even tolerably adequate! The policy fails miserably if the truth differs in the slightest from the

---

ultimate limit of the small shock assumption: infinitely many, infinitely small, shocks. In consequence, this theory does *not* fit real data all that well (Merton 1976). The white noise assumption is prevalent, indeed well-nigh universal, for econometric models specified in continuous time. The reason is that the mathematical literature (for example, see Åström 1970) of stochastic control theory gives the entirely mistaken impression that this is the *only* way of describing random processes in continuous time. The much easier and much more intuitive alternative is presented in Blatt (1981), but is too technical for this paper.

particular equations and parameters adopted by Chow; that is, the policy is highly sensitive to mis-specification. Yet mis-specification of that model is extremely likely: The model in question is by no means the only choice capable of fitting the data used by Chow. Other choices exist, and some of them are considerably more plausible on economic and commonsense grounds. Salmon and Young show that more conventional, non-"optimal" control techniques are actually greatly superior when there is reason to suspect mis-specification.

Let me now *summarize* this discussion of optimal control techniques in the context of economic policy making and econometric models.

In principle, application of control theory to econometric models to generate policy advice to politicians is a laudable endeavor. But at present, and for quite some time to come, this effort is *entirely and completely premature.* The existing models, and the existing econometric theory on which they are constructed, are simply not strong enough to carry such a heavy weight. When the weight is placed on them nonetheless, they collapse.

Politicians and voters ask for economic advice now, and cannot just be put off until better methods of analysis are perfected. They have a right to the best advice available.[5] But the best advice available, in the present state of econometric theory and practice, is *not* the advice produced by optimal control theory. Advice based

---

[5] They also have the right to reject whatever advice is given to them by so-called experts. Nor are they necessarily wrong in rejecting expert advice. Of all countries caught in the Great Depression of the 1930s, it was Hitler Germany which pulled out of that depression fastest and most completely. Without doubt, this resounding success in economic management greatly aided Hitler's rearmament drive in preparation for World War II. After that war, Hitler's minister of finance, Herr Doktor Hjalmar Schacht, was brought before the Nuremberg War Crimes Tribunal, accused of aiding and abetting Hitler's criminal activities by means of his expert and successful economic advice. Schacht was subjected to a trial. But he eventually left the court a free man, found innocent of all charges! This was his defense: "Yes, I was Hitler's finance minister. Yes, I am a recognized economic expert. Yes, I gave Hitler the best, economically correct advice of which I was capable. I told him to balance the budget, to adhere to the gold standard, and generally to stick to proper, accepted, conservative economic measures. But what did Hitler do? He laughed in my face, and did the exact opposite of all my recommendations. My economic expertise was not used at all, and therefore I am innocent." A perfect defense for Herr Doktor Hjalmar Schacht, but hardly for expert economic advice (Galbraith 1975).

on much simpler, more robust theoretical techniques, or on no theory at all (just common sense and compassion for the unfortunate victims of economic management), is certainly much better in the short run and is highly likely to be better in the long run as well.

Until econometric models succeed in producing economic predictions clearly superior to those from simple time series extrapolation methods (we are very far from that situation at present), *these models are totally unsuitable for application of the elaborate techniques of optimal control theory*. Under these circumstances, blind application of that theory to derive "optimal" policies for politicians is little short of criminal negligence.

IV.

Let us now take a wider look at the use, or misuse, of *mathematical methods in general* (not merely of optimal control theory) *within pure economic theory*.

Consider *Foundations of Economic Analysis* by Paul Samuelson (1947). All agree that this book, along with its successors, has been most influential, but the nature of this influence and its full effects are not appreciated as widely as they deserve. That is unfortunate. "The ideas of economists and political philosophers, both when they are right and when they are wrong, are more powerful than is commonly understood. Indeed the world is ruled by little else" (Keynes 1936, p. 383).

In pure mathematics, one works from a set of "axioms," that is, initial assumptions which are accepted without further question (except as regards their internal consistency: axiom 1 must not contradict axiom 2). The pure mathematician is not concerned with whether these axioms correspond to anything at all in the real world. However, chaos results if every individual pure mathematician works from his own private axioms; effective communication then becomes impossible. One needs agreed-upon, generally accepted, and conventional axioms for progress in pure mathematics.

Exactly the same is true for pure economic theory. The axioms used (the "rules of the game") must be substantially the same for all investigators, else progress (in the sense of this word used in pure mathematics) becomes nearly impossible. It is a bit like other conventional rules, for example, on which side of the road a car should be driven. The right side or the left side is equally good, really. What matters is that all cars drive on the *same* side of the road.

Much of early neoclassical writing was rather vague, and almost entirely literary (one must except Walras from this, of course). When one attempts to convert these ideas into precise mathematical statements, it is possible to do so in many different ways. But this will not do. Effective communication and the building up of a proper academic discipline require that the initial mathematical assumptions (the axioms) not only must be clearly stated, but must be the same for all. It is not at all important that these assumptions describe what happens in the real world. Indeed, it is of some advantage if they are rather far removed from reality, since then facts from the real world become irrelevant to the discipline and cannot be used to contradict or discredit the mathematical work which is done. But the axioms must be clear, they must be in mathematical language from the start, they must be consistent with each other (even if with nothing else), and they must allow a wealth of further mathematical developments from the original basis (mathematicians say, the axiom system must be "rich"). Some of the mathematical consequences of the axioms should be simple to obtain and well known to nonmathematical economists, thereby enabling them to recognize familiar features in what might otherwise be an excessively strange landscape. But other mathematical consequences should be hard to deduce, the harder the better, to keep up the interest of mathematically able investigators in playing this particular game.

To put forward such a set of axioms is obviously not an easy task; nor can one man and one book be expected to do it all. In my view, it is the substantial achievement of the *Foundations* to have pointed out the need for such a mathematical approach to pure economic theory and to have gone a long way toward setting out such a system of axioms, in superlative fashion, thereby convincing many other economists to follow this route and to build upon these foundations. Other very influential books have followed, among them Dorfman, Samuelson, and Solow (1958), Debreu (1959), Arrow and Hahn (1971), etc. I shall refer to these works, collectively as the "scriptures." I do not claim canonical authenticity for my list. Some canonical scriptures have probably been omitted; conversely, some of the faithful may dispute that all the books in the above list are truly canonical. It does not matter —some list of this sort can be drawn up on which most of the orthodox mathematical economists would agree.

In any such list, Samuelson's *Foundations* must be number one. This is the book which started it all, which set the tone, laid down the requirements, and inspired others. Others have contributed significantly, but whatever credit, or blame, is attributed to the final result, Paul Samuelson must be assigned the lion's share.

By any reckoning, the *Foundations*, along with the scriptures based on those foundations, have been successful—brilliantly successful beyond the wildest dreams of most authors. For more than one generation now, the scriptures have provided the accepted, conventional truth, the standard of professional judgment and advancement, for all of pure mathematical economics. The economic universe postulated in these scriptures, and only that particular economic universe, is the one in which all students of pure economic theory are taught to live and work, and in which they must live and work if they aim to progress in their chosen profession.

To most of us, at one time or another, there comes the temptation to turn our eyes away from the nasty real world, which is so disconcertingly prone to make hash of our finest mathematical imagination, and instead to develop a world of our own, with rules and axioms which we ourselves lay down, peopled by creatures of our own imagination who can never fight back or vote us out of office. Unfortunately, there is one major drawback to this program: No one else is likely to accept our pet world, to play the game with us. But Paul Samuelson (whether that is what he set out to do is not relevant) has done it! He has postulated an economic universe, and the entire mathematical economics profession has swallowed *his* universe whole and is dancing in accordance with the rules *he* has laid down for that universe.

Of course, this resounding success is not just accidental. For one thing, the time was ripe for a "mathematization" of economic theory, for a new departure after the debacle of neoclassical economics in the Great Depression. For another, the academic fraternity requires an impartial, objective standard of achievement, something for which the study of the real economic world is quite unsuited. When applied economists disagree with each other on how the real economic world operates (as they do often enough), it is by no means easy to decide which of them, if any, is right. No such question arises, or could possibly arise, in the rarefied economic universe of the scriptures. We know precisely, with absolutely perfect pure mathematical precision, how economic agents behave in *that* world. The rules have been laid down, once and for all; we merely need to turn to the appropriate page. If wrong conclusions are deduced from these initial assumptions, they are wrong in the sense of pure mathematics, demonstrably and absolutely wrong, without even the possibility of personal bias or professional favoritism. We have, as a result, a fully objective standard of professional judgment of competence in pure economic theory: The hiring and promotion of young economic theorists can be, and is in fact, decided on the basis of their ability to hack their way through the mathematical jungle defined by the canonical axiomatic system. The entire professional world of these young men is indeed "ruled by little else."

At this point, let me deal briefly with a common excuse. It is said that the ultimate aim of pure economic theory is indeed the mathematical description of the real economic world, but it is necessary to use very simplified models initially since the real world is so very complicated. "We must learn to walk before we can run." This excuse cannot be taken seriously. If the profession really wished to come closer to reality, the basic assumptions underlying these mathematical models should be the subject of lively discussion and frequent alteration and improvement, within the profession itself. Nothing could be farther from the truth. As soon as they hear any basic criticism at all (criticism of the assumptions, rather than criticism of the mathematical manipulations based on these assumptions), the practitioners of the orthodox game somehow lose all interest. They do not oppose or dispute the criticism —they ignore it. The result of this attitude is only too apparent. It is now over thirty-five years since the publication of the *Foundations*. In all this time, there has been *no* significant progress in the direction of economic realism. On the contrary, the dominant trend has been, and continues to be, in the exactly opposite direction, toward ever increasing mathematical abstraction. A good example is current work on so-called general competitive theory. The level of advanced pure mathematics in this literature is heavy going for a professional mathematician. But any resemblance between these exercises in axiomatic set theory and actual markets, competitive or otherwise, is not just purely accidental— it is simply nonexistent! Far from becoming more realistic as time goes on, pure economic theory is moving ever farther away from the real world of men and affairs.

Should any young mathematically inclined economic theorist have the temerity to question the scriptures, to wish to come closer to economic reality in his theorizing, there are excellent reasons for him to forget such wayward impulses and return to the orthodox fold, quickly and expeditiously. For all he should be doing, in effect, is to blight his own future in the profession by persisting in such vile heresy. The departmental heads, who decide on who shall be hired and promoted, either have themselves been brought up on the scriptures, or (if they are not mathematically inclined) will consult the opinion of someone else who has been so brought up. And the very few post-Keynesian or otherwise heretical economists in a position to hire or promote anyone are overwhelmingly nonmathematical and are at least suspicious of, and often directly hostile to, any mathematical work in economics.

This brings me to the last point of success for the scriptures: Not only have they provided the marching orders for the army of the orthodox, but they have also (whether by design or by accident does not matter) succeeded in crippling the hosts of the heathen!

Because mathematics has been used so very badly within economics, those economists who oppose the conventional assumptions have become highly suspicious of and hostile to mathematics as such. There are, sad to relate, working economists of high attainments and great intelligence who are proud of their own ignorance of mathematics and brush aside any mathematical argument whatever. Such arguments must be relegated to a "mathematical appendix," and all these appendixes are skipped as a matter of course, without even an attempt to read them.

The surface justification of this attitude is plausible enough. Mathematical economics, by and large, does live and operate in a universe of its own, with little or no contact with the real world of economic events. It is said that most of the really great economists of the past have been nonmathematical (the exceptions, for example, Keynes, who started as a mathematician, are ignored conveniently).

The sad thing about all this is not merely that these arguments are invalid (the premises may be correct, but the conclusion does not follow from the premises: if mathematics has been misused in the past, it should be used properly and sensibly in the future, not discarded altogether!). Rather, the people who put forward, and accept, such arguments in effect cripple themselves and their own adherents. Mathematics is a very powerful tool, and there is no advantage whatever in handing over such a tool to one's opponents, free of charge. When post-Keynesians avoid all mathematics, the people who misuse mathematics are given a victory of absolutely major order, without even a fight.

Far from opposing mathematics in economics, post-Keynesians should hasten to employ this enormously effective tool for their own ends, to rescue mathematics from bondage to the investigators of economic cloud cuckoo land, to use mathematics the way it should and can be used, to understand the real world in which we live. Until this has been done, economics is not yet a science.

In conclusion, I am happy to acknowledge perceptive and helpful criticism of an earlier draft of this paper by Mr. G. Walsham of Cambridge University and Professor Peter Young of Lancaster University.

REFERENCES

Arrow, Kenneth J., *Social Choice and Individual Values*, New York: John Wiley. 1951.

Arrow, Kenneth J., and F. H. Hahn, *General Competitive Analysis*, Edinburgh: Oliver and Boyd. 1971.

Åstrom, Karl J., *Introduction to Stochastic Control Theory*, New York: Academic Press. 1970.

Black, Fisher, and M. J. Scholes, "The Pricing of Options and Corporate Liabilities," *Journal of Political Economy.*, 81, 637-654 (1973).

Blatt, J. M., "Investment Evaluation under Uncertainty," *Financial Management*, 8, 66-81 (1979a).

_____, "Investment: Fact and Neo-Classical Fancy," Eighth Conference of Economists, Latrobe University, Melbourne, August 1979b.

_____, *Elementary Introduction to Optimal Control*, Sydney, Australia: Computer Systems (Aust) Pty. Ltd. 1981.

_____, *Dynamic Economic Systems*, Armonk, N.Y.: M. E. Sharpe, Inc. 1983.

Borch, Karl Henrik, *The Economics of Uncertainty*, Princeton: Princeton University Press. 1968.

Chow, Gregory, *Analysis and Control of Dynamic Economic Systems*, New York: John Wiley. 1975.

Debreu, Gerard, *Theory of Value*, New York: John Wiley. 1959.

Dorfman, Robert, P. A. Samuelson and R. M. Solow, *Linear Programming and Economic Analysis*, New York: McGraw-Hill. 1958.

Galbraith, John Kenneth, *Money: Whence it came, where it went*, London: Andre Deutsch. 1975.

Holly, S., B. Rustem, and M. Zarrop (editors), *Optimal Control for Econometric Models: An Approach to Economic Policy Formulation*, London: MacMillan. 1978.

Keynes, J. Maynard, *The General Theory of Employment, Interest and Money*, Cambridge University Press. 1936 (reprint: London: MacMillan Press 1973).

_____ , "The General Theory of Employment," *Quarterly Journal of Economics*, *57*, 209-223 (1937).

Knight, Frank H., *Risk, Uncertainty and Profit*, New York: Hart, Schaffner and Marx. 1921 (reprint: Harper and Row, 1957).

Merton, Robert C., "Option Pricing when Underlying Stock Returns are Discontinuous," *Journal of Financial Economics*, *3*, 125-144 (1976).

Pitchford, John D., and Stephen J. Turnovsky (editors), *Applications of Control Theory to Economic Analysis*, Amsterdam: North Holland. 1977.

Robbins, Lionel, *An Essay on the Nature and Significance of Economic Science*, London: MacMillan. 1935.

Robinson, Joan, "The Production Function and the Theory of Capital," *Review of Economic Studies*, *21*, 81-106 (1954).

Salmon, Mark A., and Peter Young, "Control Methods and Quantitative Economic Policy," pp. 74-105 in Holly 1978.

Samuelson, Paul A., *Foundations of Economic Analysis*, Cambridge, Mass: Harvard University Press. 1947.

Sims, Christopher A. (editor), *New Methods in Business Cycle Research: Proceedings from a Conference*, Federal Reserve Bank of Minneapolis. 1977.

Smith, Adam, *The Wealth of Nations*. 1776. (New York: Random House, Modern Library. 1937.)

J. Ron Stanfield

8

INSTITUTIONAL ANALYSIS: TOWARD PROGRESS IN ECONOMIC SCIENCE

Conventional economics, the neoclassical synthesis, has entered an era of sterile formalism in which it is sheltered from destruction at the hands of experience and persists despite its palpable inability to come abreast of the times with respect to the issues of policy and ethics that are of popular concern (see Stanfield, chapters 2 and 9). The sterility of conventional economics and its powerful defense against reality stem from its basic epistemology. The mainstream approach defines the economic process as choice in the face of scarcity. Virtually the entire focus rests upon deductive analysis of the logic of economizing to the neglect of comparative analysis of the actual social institutions and behavior historically associated with production and consumption. The emphasis on calculated choice is intertwined with a pronounced institutional bias toward market exchange. The belief that the exchange process effectively monitors individual values has led to the virtual identification of market prices and social values. This identification has in turn led to policy recommendations and evaluations which distort or impede the fundamental (provisioning) function of the economy. These issues are discussed here by a point-by-point contrast between the formalist perspective that underlies the mainstream approach to economic analysis and the substantivist perspective that underlies the institutionalist approach (see Ayres, pp. 45-62; Polanyi et al., chapter 13; and Kornai, p. 39).

The formalist approach to economic analysis

The formal definition of *economics* emphasizes economizing or

The author wishes to thank, for their helpful comments on earlier drafts of this paper, Hal Cochrane, Bob Keller, and Al Eichner.

maximizing. The axiomatic foundation of this conception starts with the familiar presumption of scarcity: insatiable wants in the face of limited resources imply scarcity. Faced with the ineluctable fact of scarcity, human societies must make choices. Any society and its constituent individuals must by one means or another decide on the allocation and distribution of productive capacity. Given the cultural belief in scarcity with its moral imperative of rationality, economics becomes the *science of choice*, and its typical concern is the logic of maximizing under the constraint of scarcity.[1] In this view, calculated choice oriented toward maximization is *the* economic problem, and the economy consists of a series of choices imposed by scarcity.

Nowhere is this more evident than in the classic formulation of mainstream epistemology provided by Lionel Robbins. Robbins argues that four conditions must be met if a situation is to provide a problem for economic science. There must be various ends or goals, the means for achieving these ends must be limited, these means must be capable of alternative applications, and the ends must be of varying importance. For Robbins, if these conditions are met, the behavior involved necessarily assumes the form of choice. It follows that economic science may not be concerned with concrete productive and consumptive activities at all if the activities do not meet these conditions. It also follows that any activities that do meet these conditions provide scientific problems for economics whether or not the activities are generally conceived of as economic. Robbins' conception of economic science

> focuses attention on a particular *aspect* of behavior, the form imposed by the influence of scarcity. It follows from this, therefore, that in so far as it presents this aspect, any kind of human behavior falls within the scope of economic generalization. We do not say that the production of potatoes is economic activity and the production of philosophy is not. We say rather that, in so far as either kind of activity involves the relinquishment of other desired alternatives, it has its economic aspect. There are no limitations on the subject-matter of Economic Science save this. [Robbins, p. 17]

---

[1] This is not to deny that some scholars, notably Herbert Simon and Oliver Williamson, have endeavored to widen the analysis of choice to include objectives other than maximization. Such writers, however, are justly considered to be outside the mainstream in light of their behaviorist, in many respects institutionalist, orientations.

Interestingly, Robbins also comments that "scarcity of means to satisfy ends of varying importance is an almost ubiquitous condition of human behavior" (Robbins, p. 15).

This formalist view of economics then presumes what in fact should be the subject matter being investigated, namely, the concrete form the culture of a people takes vis-à-vis their economic activities. The formalist view deduces axiomatically that choice is *the* essence of the economy. It would seem that the scientific method would use the inductive record of concrete economic experience to form testable hypotheses about the essential character of the economic process rather than to take this as a given.

Formalism commits what might be called the "economistic fallacy." This is the tendency to raise the concrete culture of the economy in its market capitalist form to a universal constant in human history. The concerns, motivations, and meanings attached to economic activity in a very limited period of human experience are universalized and assumed to represent the essence of human economic activity at all times and places. In a word, this procedure is patently and radically ethnocentric; it sees the entire economic cosmos from the perspective of a single ethnic experience.

The economistic fallacy commits the error of misplaced concreteness. As Alfred North Whitehead defined this fallacy, it lies in "identifying abstract conceptions with reality" (Whitehead, 1925) or "neglecting the degree of abstraction involved when an actual entity is considered merely so far as it exemplifies certain categories of thought" (Whitehead, 1929, p. 11). The economistic fallacy identifies an abstract model with reality and considers empirical behavior only insofar as that behavior corresponds to the postulates of the formalist model. This is very nearly what Schumpeter had in mind when he wrote of the Ricardian vice, that is, jumping to policy conclusions from a highly abstract, almost tautological basis (Schumpeter, 1954, p. 473). One of Ricardo's parliamentary peers, a supporter no less, once remarked that Ricardo argued as if he had just dropped in from another planet. The reference was to Ricardo's insistence upon applying theoretical principles without taking into consideration their qualifications and implications in the context of concrete experience. In other words, Ricardo insisted upon applying his theory to policy considerations without grounding his theory in the context of concrete British political and economic culture.

The remark of Ricardo's colleague indicates the critical problem of the economistic fallacy, namely, the eclipse of institutional analysis in economics. Institutional analysis, as I shall elaborate in more detail below, is concerned with the concrete cultural experience in which the economic activity of a given human group is seated. Economism preempts institutional analysis by presupposing the psychology of economic activity and prefiguring the nature and task of economic institutions. It matters not what the actual motivations and meanings of a given people are; their economic problem is presumed to be one of calculated choice under resource constraints. Economic analysis in the formalist view knows a priori what it needs to know about the economic lives of a human group. In effect, it does not need to know anything about the people whose economic activities it is bent on studying. This eclipse of institutional analysis virtually guarantees that the actual needs, wants, motives, and interests of any given people will go undescribed and unanalyzed.

Robbins is aware that the formalist view is the cultural product of an exchange social economy, but he denies that this limits its applicability.

> But it is one thing to contend that economic analysis has *most interest and utility* in an exchange economy. It is another to contend that its subject-matter is *limited* to such phenomena. . . . [I]t is clear that behavior outside the exchange economy is conditioned by the same limitation of means in relation to ends as behavior within the economy, and is capable of being subsumed under the same fundamental categories. The generalizations of the theory of value are as applicable to the behavior of isolated man or the executive authority of a communist society, as to the behavior of man in an exchange economy—even if they are not so illuminating in such contexts. The exchange relationship is a *technical* incident, . . . subsidiary to the main fact of scarcity. [Robbins, pp. 19-20]

Despite this disclaimer, the formalist view reduces economic analysis to catallactics, preeminently the science of exchange (see Alchian and Allen, p. 5; and Hirshleifer, p. 12). The central focus is on the exchange process which results from a given structure of preferences, capacities, habits, and technology. Empirical analysis of this structure and especially its changing character is given scant attention. The predominant interest is with a set of relative prices established in the exchange process, which in turn guides economic behavior. Virtually all meaning in conventional economics derives from exchange.

For example, the distinction between production and consumption which is vital in the mainstream view is purely a marketing definition. The economist when he uses the term "production" means earning an income, and by consumption he means spending that income. He also sees consumption as the sole end and purpose of production. From the materialist or substantive view, production and consumption are parts of the same process and it is philosophically not meaningful to differentiate them. They are both material processes in which the active element of human imagination, skill, and knowledge is applied to the rest of nature to transform the latter in order to render it more appropriate to human ends. It may be useful to separate production and consumption for purposes of economic accounting and control, so long as people fully understand the limited meaning and purpose of doing so. This condition is not met in the mystified mainstream analysis of the economy.

The exchange focus severely limits the scope and method of conventional economic thought and it is severely misleading as to the actual structure and operation of the economic system. This follows from the fact that much of critical importance to the economic process is hidden or obscured by the exchange view. The exchange process involves the interaction of individuals who are already shaped by the culture and structure of the social economy. Their preferences, capacities, values, and guiding principles are largely given prior to their exchange participation. That is to say, mainstream economics, with its catallactics focus, for the most part takes such variables as data. The conventional theory similarly has no capacity to consider the influence of an exchange economy on these variables. Yet these variables determine the actual content and implications of the exchange process. In effect, conventional economics is content to examine epiphenomena and ignore the underlying phenomenal structure.

Consumer preferences offer the most obvious example. The conventional economist starts with a consumer whose preferences are already given and is seldom if ever moved to investigate empirically the formation, much less the implications, of these preferences. The factor market is equally important. The household reveals not only consumer preferences, but also work or production preferences, and these also receive very little empirical attention. Household sovereignty is celebrated in the abstract but no basis is provided for substantive investigation of consumer and factor owner preferences. Nor is there any basis for examining what makes one exchange economy different from or better than another one in space or time.

The root of the matter can be traced to the conventional theory's approach to typification. Social science proceeds by identifying the characteristics of a phenomenon which are definitive and which therefore set it apart from other phenomena. The typological characteristics of any entity are those without which it would not be itself. Generalization is the scientific process of classifying together those phenomena which satisfy a given set of criteria. The process of differentiation and assembly, or classification, is the incessant tinkering of the scientific craftsman.

In this view the central task of economics is to seek the relevant characteristics appropriate to given economic phenomena. This method demands a working characterization of the economic actor. Economic characterization identifies the traits which are significant to the economic process in a particular context. What are the characteristics or personality traits of a business manager or a consumer? What is the general cultural pattern? How do particular traits fit within the social totality? How is all of this affected by social change?

In short, economics approaches its study without attempting to develop and empirically test a characterization of economic actors. It has traditionally skirted this task by assuming economic man. No doubt there is much to be gained by positing this ideal type but there is more to economic science than using an ideal type to compare "with empirical reality in order to establish its divergencies and similarities" (Weber, p. 43). As Weber noted

> pure economic theory . . . utilizes ideal type concepts exclusively. Economic theory makes certain assumptions which scarcely ever correspond completely with reality but which approximate it in various degrees and asks: how would men act under these assumed conditions if their actions were entirely rational? It assumes the dominance of pure economic interests and precludes the operation of political or other non-economic considerations.
>
> In addition to the formulation of pure ideal—typical formulae and the establishment of . . . causal propositions . . . scientific economics has other problems. These problems include the causal influence of economic events on the whole range of social phenomena. . . . Likewise included among the problems of economics is the analysis of the various ways in which non-economic social events influence economic events. [Weber, pp. 43-45]

Weber's reference is to the area of study known as economy and society. It includes the place of economy in society and the institutionalization of economic behavior by the social process. It evinces a concern for the relation between the way a given human group *lives* and the way it gets its *livelihood*.

The importance of economic character formation becomes evident if society is viewed as an evolving process. The business of society is social reproduction. This involves the production and distribution of goods and services. But this is not so much the end as the means of society. The primary objective is the production of people. The economy is one aspect of society and its proper concern is the economic aspect of social reproduction. Economic character is a dynamic historical concept which is suited to the view of the economy as one aspect of a total social process in which the social status quo is never perfectly reproduced. Social change is incessant and as a part of that change economic character evolves.

The mainstream theory also fails to provide an adequate theory of power and social relations. Given the exchange fixation, social relations are conceived solely as exchange relations, with hierarchy and dominance neglected. The emphasis on the sphere of exchange obscures relations in the sphere of production. The direct social relations involved in the division of labor are obscured and exchange relations stand in their stead. Rather than seeing their technological dependence on one another, people see their pecuniary interconnections. The economist's tool kit fails to penetrate the commodity veil and demystify the underlying social economic relations. This is part of the thrust of Karl Marx's concept of commodity fetishism, Thorstein Veblen's distinction between the ceremonial and technological aspects of human life, and Karl Polanyi's discussion of the market mentality and disembedded economy.

The distortion of power is especially important in the economistic fallacy. The conventional perspective in economics treats power as market power, that is, the ability to influence the price of a commodity one sells or buys. But this neglects a vast area of power, especially the influence over political decisions and the formation of preferences and values. A complete theory of economic power would focus on social reproduction and the formation of economic character. Power is exercised through the relative influence that individuals have on the incessant process of social reproduction. Economic power is the ability to influence those character traits and social relations which are significant in the structure and working of the economic process. Everyone exercises some influence in this process and there are many bases on which this influence rests. Such differential influential is the substantive content of inequality and social stratification.

The substantivist approach to economic analysis

The substantivist view of the economic process defines *economics* in technological or material terms. The economy is the instituted process or culturally patterned arrangements by which a given human group provisions itself as a going concern. The focus is on the provisioning of social reproduction and on the instrumentality of economic activity vis-à-vis the life process. All societies must have economies in this concrete sense and the substantive view emphasizes the actual organization of production and distribution in a given human group.

This is a technological conception of the economy. The economy consists of technology (tools plus knowledge) employed within the context of institutions. This context is one of dynamic interaction: institutions mold technology and technology molds institutions. The characteristic concern of substantive economics is the social organization or patterned arrangements surrounding mankind's relation to the rest of nature, that is, the study of the man-to-man relations by which the materially reproductive man-to-nature relations are institutionalized.

Social reproduction is not simply the reproduction of the status quo because social change is incessant, if here dramatic and there imperceptible. Much of this change revolves around the interaction of technology and institutions, especially the adjustment of institutions to technological changes. Changes in the technical apparata, organization, or knowledge of the social, material process immediately create tensions mandating adjustment in mores, laws, and guiding principles. This adjustment is not simply a matter of one-sided adjustment to technological imperatives. It is also the shaping or restricting of technology by a human group's evaluational imperatives. This institutional adjustment is a focal point of substantive institutional analysis. Indeed, the economic problem in the substantive view is the continuous reinstitutionalization of the technological relations within the social context.

Clearly, the method indicated by this approach to the economic process is one that deals with actual technology and institutions. This is the method of institutional analysis under the aegis of which economic behavior is treated as learned behavior. The stability and recurrence of the economic process results from the way people are acculturated to perform. It is the institutional milieu within which psychological propensities operate that sustains the integration of economic activity. Institutional analysis is more sociological than psychological. If men appear generous at one place, selfish at another, it is not their basic natures that differ but their social organizations. It is not the presence of this or that motive that is significant in institutional analysis, but instead the institutional structure in which the motives operate. Via definite institutional sanctions, this structure promotes some human proclivities and represses others.

The comparative method developed in anthropology is the appropriate method of institutional analysis (see Polanyi et al., chapters 6, 14, 17). This method is highly empirical and deals with events and occurrences rather than man's nature or the timeless necessities. The economy in its concrete manifestations is the subject matter of interest, and the point of departure is not the individual nor any of his various complements of physiological or psychological attributes. The focus is instead on society as a system in which the basic units of analysis are historically achieved patterns of interaction. These patterns of interaction, cultural institutions, then promote or repress the potentialities which inhere in human beings. To understand the economic process or any other aspect of the lives of a given human group, it is necessary to examine these concrete cultural patterns.

The comparative method is not only highly inductive; it is also functional, holistic, and evolutionary. The patterns of interaction must not only be identified in terms of their concrete, historical, and geographical existence, but also accounted for in terms of their function in the social totality. This means that their connection to the other elements of the social system must be explained and the processes which assure their continuity identified. The evolutionary focus is necessary to capture the essential element of continuity. Institutional analysis is not merely descriptive, however, and it must be comparative if a theoretical core is to emerge. The theoretical core of institutional analysis requires that concepts be derived from the general patterns found in the institutionalized operations of different economies.

In this view, then, economic behavior is treated as a cultural process, and the task is to develop a cross-cultural economics. The ethnocentrism of the economistic fallacy makes this impossible because it abstracts from precisely those concrete phenomena which are the pivotal concern of cultural analysis. In contrast, the substantive view, with its emphasis on the institutionalized regularities which vest the economic process with its requisite stability and continuity, insists upon the comparison of carefully documented historical situations. This comparison will enable the institutional analyst to treat economic institutions as culture traits, as expressions of human values stemming from definite patterns of social interaction.

This view insists that much can be learned from the study of past and present economies if their concrete facets are not glossed over by the presumption and abstraction of limited experience. The focus must be on actual behavior and the context of meaning in which people act economically. Utilizing the anthropologist's concept of culture, institutional analysis seeks to examine the context of meaning derived from social interaction that patterns the economic cosmos for people and provides them with a guide for integrating their lives with the behavior of others.

This explains why we so often find institutionalists referring in one way or another to a rewon history or regained historical perspective. The actual social evolution of the economy has been falsely prefigured in the modern period by the predominance of the economistic fallacy. The point is usually made in the context of premarket economies, especially those assigned to the economic anthropologist by the disciplinary division of labor. Cultural ethnocentrism limits the ability of modern social scientists to investigate the actual character of these social economies. The disembedded, autonomous economy of recent vintage is the foundation of the formalist, choice model of the economy. However, precapitalist economies were embedded in the social structure, largely anonymous, and without autonomous logic and laws of their own. Their vital properties are impenetrable to the formalist, ethnocentric approach.

The practical importance of this point emerges when it is recognized that this misinterpretation of past economies severely limits the ability of economists to *imagine* institutional alternatives in light of today's problems. The marketing presumption obscures the nonexchange organization of precapitalist economies. Unable to see the actual alternatives to the market in the past, economists are unable to foresee the possible alternatives to the market in the future.

This is even more important when it is recognized that the paramount problems in the current economic crisis involve the interaction of economy and society. The need is to examine the relation of lives to livelihood and subordinate the economy to the lives it properly should serve—this is to say, to reembed the economy in society! The economics of the market mentality cannot possibly come to grips with this problem because it is preeminently the logic of the disembedded economy.

The economic thought required for such a radical reconsideration of the place of economy in society must draw upon as wide a range of human experience as possible. A thorough and unprejudiced reconsideration of economic anthropology and history is necessary so as to permit a general understanding of the place of economy in society. This rewon history will then provide the best available basis for escaping the market mentality and imagining alternative futures. The promise of substantivism and institutional analysis is to foster the open-minded investigation of the past as a prelude to the open-minded creation of the future.

A comparison of value standards

Institutionalism is not content with positive validation. It also insists that the ultimate validation of inquiry is its usefulness (see Stanfield, chapter 9). Theory and philosophy provide hypotheses or ideas which appear to be significant and are plausibly correct. The scientific method provides ways of bringing the best available cause-and-effect knowledge to bear on these plausible concepts. For example, the falsification principle provides a judgment that a conceptual relation might be true. Such concepts must then pass muster in the ultimate test, the realm of practice and policy.

It is important not to reduce relevance to policy analysis narrowly conceived. Cultural relevance is significant both in its own right and prior to policy relevance. Cultural relevance means bearing a relation to the context of individuals' lives so that they are assisted in their everyday practice. Inquiry is relevant if it works in the context of household and business decisions whether or not it relates specifically to a policy instrument. The test of anxiety posed by John Kenneth Galbraith (chapter 20) is a good statement of the instrumental test with regard to cultural relevance. Galbraith urges that a paradigm be tested by whether or not it relates to the anxieties that people feel about the economy in such a way as to allay their anxiousness. In so arguing, Galbraith implicitly uses institutional analysis with its characteristic emphasis on culture and the concrete context of people's lives.

Moreover, cultural relevance is a prerequisite to policy relevance. Inquiry which fails to capture the essential meaning of people's lives cannot adequately guide policy. If market theory no longer captures the workings of the economy, it will not only fail to be culturally relevant; it will also be of practically no use in the policy context. If economic variables are not explicable in terms of competitive market forces because they are substantially determined by the decisions of the powerful who administer the economy, then the market model will not ring true or adequately inform individuals in their everyday economic activities. The resultant violations of individual expectations would be accompanied by erratic behavior. Under these conditions, the market model would not provide the predictive accuracy required for effective policy.

The institutionalist's different conception of the economic process yields not only a different method but also a fundamentally different value standard. The value standard of conventional economics is, more is better. This follows logically from the conventional theory's axiomatic focus on scarcity. This axiology promotes the disembedded, calculative economy which disrupts lives and stunts individual development in the name of incentives, mobility, rationality, allocative adjustment, and, in a word, efficiency.

This value standard promotes an econocentric culture in which all meaning is read from the process of market exchange. For example, Malthus and other classical economists reduced the vital human function of procreation to a question of market ability. They argued that no individual has a right to subsistence for himself or his children unless his labor will fairly purchase that subsistence in the open market. The vital social function of procreation and its control is thereby turned over to market desiderata. For another example, consider the implications of the celebrated mobility of the factors of production in the case of labor. If labor is to be required to move hither and yon in order to find employment, this will necessitate a highly mobile and restricted family unit, it will make necessary the abrogation of friendships, and it will make it almost impossible to develop a stable working-class community. The justification of alienated labor provides another example. It is the superior goal of production and efficiency that legitimates work that is onerous, boring, and even dangerous. The external, hierarchical control of the labor process is legitimated in the name of productivity. The examples could be expanded indefinitely. Economic progress routinely destroys historical buildings, wildlife habitats, labor skills, small businesses, the economic bases of towns and cities, and so on.

Schumpeter captured the matter very well in his concept of *creative destruction* (Schumpeter, 1950, chapter 7). The economic process regulated by market competition simultaneously creates and destroys. Given the more-is-better standard of value, the inclination is to accept the destruction as the cost of progress. But the destruction of economic values and routines cannot be isolated from human life in general. Economic destruction implies social disruption, especially so given that, in the name of the self-regulating market, vital social functions have been left to the exchange contracts made between individuals.

The value standard of institutional economics is social reproduction and the fuller unfolding of the human life process. Social reproduction means society is reproduced as a going concern. This requires reproduction of its vital occupations and economic functions. Since social change is ever present, this also requires adjustment in the process of this reproduction. Power and coercion are necessary in this view because it is imperative that individuals achieve that minimal cooperation consistent with social reproduction. Sufficiency more than efficiency is the hallmark of this value standard.

The individual is not thereby reduced to a mere functional cog of some social machine. Individual development remains the ultimate value. This requires a focus on the problem of lives and livelihood. Livelihood means the economic process of provisioning. What must be asked of this livelihood is that it reproduce lives without disrupting them and retarding the development of individuals. The acceptance of social disruption and stunted individual development in the name of efficiency is patently absurd from this point of view. Such acceptance, in effect, puts means above ends. In the name of getting as much of the means as possible, the very ends that those means are meant to achieve are sacrificed.

The reproductive value standard implies that distribution is an essential part of the economic function since lives are not maintained unless sufficient income is received to provision them. Distribution is therefore a vital problem that cannot be ruled out of economic inquiry. Here again the end is not sacrificed to the means. Distribution is not sacrificed to efficiency. The maldistribution of income vis-à-vis the sufficiency criterion would mean that the economic process was failing its instrumental function of reproduction.

The implications of this view for everyday life are that first of all the economy is seen as a means to an end, the end being the provisioning of individuals. For households, income and consumption are properly viewed as tools to be used in the furtherance of the life process. This does not reduce consumption to subsistence in a narrow sense. Consumption as a cultural process is not well understood in terms of physiological requirements or given wants. This does not deny the physiological function of consumption. It merely insists that since this is a universal function it is not very helpful in comparative institutional analysis. Instead, cultural analysis suggests a communication theory approach in which consumption is viewed essentially as symbolic interaction (see Douglas and Isherwood). Consumption provides first of all a marking service. The way we dress, the automobiles we drive, the houses we live in, the food we eat, and the places where we vacation are one and the same with primitives' painting of stripes on their faces and their wearing of shell or bone necklaces. In both cases individuals are marking themselves as belonging to this or that group or social status. In addition to group identification these marking services are important to the individual's sense of personal identification. Human self-realization is achieved through the social, material process that includes consumption as well as production, as those terms are normally (mis)used. Consumption is a process of seeking and conveying meaning—literally, participating in culture.

This view complicates but in no way obviates the importance of

Veblen's concept of invidious distinction by which income and consumption become ends in themselves as evidence of superior social status. The differentiation of "instrumental" and "invidious" is to some extent subjective since their meanings depend on the cultural context. Understanding them remains as well, to some extent, a matter of individual judgment. This does not render the concept nebulous, only human. The individual is ethically responsible for examining the meanings he accepts and portrays in consumption. The economic scientist must investigate these meanings and their consequences for the economic function of provisioning society. Invidiousness obstructs the economic function by subverting the instrumental character of the economy and perverting the developmental standard of individual activity.

For the business firm, carrying on economic activity becomes less a matter of profit maximization and more a matter of generating sufficient revenue to remain a going concern. As Charles Dickens attempted to demonstrate in his fiction, business should not be run for profit per se but in the service of a way of life. As John Ruskin noted, business also participates in making culture by the tastes and values its products and organization promote. That this is so much more true of the modern corporation has led to a half-century's discussion of the corporation's social, political, and cultural responsibilities.

For the state, this value standard helps to make sense of a great deal of intervention that is otherwise inexplicable or suspect. The state is involved in a wide range of activities to stabilize the economy, provide social security, protect income, and so on. The state has also become an important instrument of adjustment. Manpower development and training, provision of economic opportunity, targeted investment subsidies, and so on are a part of the complement of state activities aimed at securing the continuous process of provisioning. For most institutionalists, such measures represent the incipient forms of the comprehensive direct intervention mechanism that a mature industrial society requires.

Their fundamentally different conception of the economic process accounts in large part for the institutionalists' leading role in advocating price and incomes policies. From the mainstream view, relative prices established in the market are integrally related to value. The market model with its penchant for marginal niceties predisposes the conventional economist to think in terms of an equilibrium position in which relative prices reflect relative values and provide accurate allocative signals as well as necessary distributive incentives. *Intervention* by the state in relative prices or income flows is viewed askance because it introduces an arbitrary (read nonmarket) element into these all-important market relations. Surely allocative and distributive distortions must follow that are fundamentally counter to the gospel of efficiency.

For the institutionalist, the prices and income flows established by the market are arbitrary in respect to the value standard of social reproduction. There is nothing in the operation of the market as a concrete, historical process that secures consistency of prices and income flows with the reproduction of society. This was, of course, a fundamental point of contention between the medieval and mercantilist world views on the one hand and that of the classical economists on the other. The latter conceptually seized order from chaos with the doctrine of the invisible hand and social harmony, and mainstream economists ever since have upheld the notion of the nonpurposive achievement of the fundamental economic purpose of provisioning society.

Even viewed in respect to the market value standard, the market's pecuniary relations are largely historical accidents because the concrete processes that determine them do not live up to the requirements of the market model. The market view insists that the price system functions so as to incorporate historical events into price and income relations, thereby overcoming their arbitrary character with respect to allocation and distribution. This view is based upon the notion of general equilibrium. Therefore, observations of tendencies to equilibrium in particular markets or of individuals adjusting to relative price changes are not sufficient. The required evidence would have to indicate an effectively functioning process of information flow and adjustment in all sectoral and geographic markets. To the contrary, however, observations of the shifting sands of technology, power, tastes, demography, etc., offer little support for the general equilibrium conception of the economic process (see Pasinetti, p. 20). The institutionalist views the abstract conception of some supreme equilibration of relative prices as absurdly mythic. Unable to understand the technical explosion and changing power relations at the end of the Middle Ages, European minds contrived the invisible hand of the market to replace the divinely guided hands of the clergy and aristocracy.

From the instrumental value standard, price relations and income flows are merely convenient devices of accounting and information. They are useful in recording who wants, has, or got what, where, and when. Their instrumental function is to facilitate the reproduction of businesses, households, and farms. Where an income flow is inadequate to this function, the institutionalist would use the polity to raise it temporarily and provide assistance toward long-term transition and adjustment. The myth that the market can be structurally self-adjusting via automatically shifting incentives has grown progressively less plausible and more dangerous. This is not to deny the usefulness of economic incentives—only to argue that their proper structuring cannot be left to the impersonal market. The institutionalist is not blind to incentive arguments but neither is he blinded by them.

The principle that underlies such income maintenance is less equity, whether based on notions of equality, merit, or humanitarian concern, than it is the need to stabilize the process of social reproduction. For the income flow to serve its instrumental function, it must be balanced. Shortfalls in one sector will multiply through the economy, destabilizing other sectors. Critics of corporate bailouts or pump-priming makework programs usually have an idealized market standard of justice in mind rather than the pragmatic notion of balance in the process of social reproduction.

Their conception of the economic process also accounts for the institutionalists' resistance to other economists' and political populists' demands for vigorous trustbusting. The antitrust strategy is a market concoction which has always paved the way for abdication in the face of power rather than for its effective control. The institutionalist predilection has always been to allow, or recognize the inevitability of, concentration, and then to attempt to control it politically. Concentrated power is more visible and easier to manage in the interest of economic balance and social reproduction than dispersed power.

In summary, the contemporary crises in the social economy and economic thought mandate a fundamental reconsideration of the meaning, place, and function of human economy in society. Substantive institutional analysis provides a basis for this new departure. It offers an alternative definition of the economy, an alternative method for economic inquiry, and an alternative standard of value to vest that inquiry with human meaning.

REFERENCES

Alchian, Armen A., and William R. Allen. *University Economics*. Belmont, CA, 1964.

Ayres, C. E. "The Legacy of Thorstein Veblen," in Ayres et al., *Institutional Economics*. Berkeley, 1964.

Douglas, Mary, and Baron Isherwood. *The World of Goods*. New York, 1979.

Galbraith, John Kenneth. *Economics and the Public Purpose*. Boston, 1973.

Hirshleifer, J. *Investment, Interest, and Capital*. Englewood Cliffs, NJ, 1970.

Kornai, Janos. *Anti-equilibrium*. Amsterdam, 1971.

Pasinetti, Luigi L. *Structural Change and Economic Growth*. New York, 1981.

Polanyi, Karl, Conrad M. Arensberg, and Harry W. Pearson, eds. *Trade and Market in the Early Empires*. Gateway edition, Chicago, 1971.

Robbins, Lionel. *An Essay on the Nature and Significance of Economic Science*. Second edition, New York, 1969.

Schumpeter, Joseph A. *Capitalism, Socialism, and Democracy*. Third edition, New York, 1950.

Schumpeter, Joseph A. *History of Economic Analysis*. New York, 1954.

Stanfield, J. Ron. *Economic Thought and Social Change*. Carbondale, IL, 1979.

Veblen, Thorstein. *The Theory of the Leisure Class*. New York, 1899.

Weber, Max. *The Methodology of the Social Sciences*. New York, 1949.

Whitehead, Alfred North. *Science and the Modern World*. New York, 1925.

Whitehead, Alfred North. *Process and Reality*. New York, 1929.

Alfred S. Eichner

9

WHY ECONOMICS
IS NOT YET A SCIENCE

‖‖‖‖‖‖‖‖‖‖‖‖‖‖‖‖‖‖‖‖‖‖‖‖‖‖‖‖‖

In 1898, the *Quarterly Journal of Economics* published an essay by Thorstein Veblen entitled "Why Is Economics Not an Evolutionary Science?" While one might not agree with the answer Veblen gave, he must at least be credited with having asked the right question. Today, more than eighty years later, the question is even more to the point.

The same neoclassical theory to which Veblen took such strong exception remains dominant. The theory has been supplemented by a Keynesian macroeconomics (quite different from Keynes's own ideas), and the resulting "neoclassical synthesis" has been considerably refined by its translation into mathematics by Hicks and Samuelson, but Veblen would have little difficulty recognizing the core. It is pretty much the theory which ruled in his day—though, of course, with the rougher edges smoothed over.

It is this theory which now, eighty years later, has become intellectually bankrupt. Economic theory can offer no solution to the problem of inflation—except to stifle the very growth of output and employment which should be the greater concern of economists. In this way the problem of inflation, annoying as it may be, has been transformed into the far more serious problem of world stagflation. Politicians and the public alike, impatient with policy recommendations which bring no relief from the malady but instead seem only to make the problem worse, have begun to shun the company of economists, much as any man who cares about his intellectual reputation shuns the company of astrologers, elixir-promoters, and other quacks.

Why, indeed, is economics not yet a science—in the sense of representing a body of knowledge which grows cumulatively over time and which has something of value to teach men and women of practical affairs? One answer is that economists have refused to accept as applicable to their own work the epistemological rules scientists normally follow to avoid falling into error. In particular, they refuse to take seriously the stricture that any ideas or theories they put forward must be empirically confirmed.

The results of this failure to observe the rules of science are only too obvious. Economics as a discipline consists of a body of theory—the same neoclassical orthodoxy attacked by Veblen—which lacks any foundation in reality. Indeed, the theory is little more than an elaborate set of deductions predicated on a set of metaphysical, and hence nonscientific, axioms. Not surprisingly, any public policy based on such a theory simply invites disaster.

But surely, it will be said, this is much too harsh a judgment. Economics as a discipline cannot be so vacuous, so unreliable a guide. Alas, the answer is that this is indeed the case. It remains only to explain why this is so. The first step is to review the epistemological rules of those disciplines which, unlike economics, can be considered sciences.

The epistemological rules of science

It is a common error to think of science as being characterized by a particular methodology, or prescribed way of acquiring knowledge. However, a moment's reflection on the diverse methodologies pursued by scientists, ranging from the highly abstract mathematical models of the theoretical physicists to the carefully controlled laboratory experiments of the biologists and the painstaking field work of the geologists, should suffice to disabuse anyone of this notion. Instead, what uniquely characterizes a scientific approach is a certain epistemology, or way of validating ideas. The modern world is qualitatively different from all previous civilizations, not because a certain group of savants identified as scientists has discovered a new way of adding to knowledge (though it has, indeed, developed an impressive array of new instruments for accumulating data), but rather because the members of that confraternity have evolved a set of rules for discerning what is false and thereby avoiding as much as possible nonproductive lines of research. The set of rules for eschewing what is false is the epistemology of science, and it involves applying a series of tests to what anyone may assert to be true.

One of these tests is the test of coherence. This test consists of determining whether the conclusions adduced follow logically from the assumptions which have been made and thus whether the arguments are internally consistent. At one time, following Descartes, it was believed that this test was sufficient to establish the validity of any proposition. Economists, especially those esteemed by their colleagues as theorists, by and large still believe this test to be sufficient. That is why they tend to favor the exclusive use of mathematics, a language especially suited to logical analysis, along with mathematical "proofs." However, in the wake of Hume's arguments as a skeptic on behalf of empiricism, scientists and philosophers (they were not then differentiated) came to recognize that the coherenece test was only necessary, not sufficient. In addition, a series of further empirical tests was required to validate any proposition. These empirical tests are threefold in nature.

There is, first, the correspondence test. This test consists of determining whether the conclusions which follow from a theory are confirmed by what can be observed empirically of the real world. The greater the ability of a theory to anticipate what can be observed empirically, the greater is the basis for believing that the theory actually corresponds in some way to what happens in the real world. A classic example is provided by Eddington's observations of the solar eclipse in 1919, which confirmed Einstein's prediction, based on his theories of relativity, that the gravitational field of a large mass such as the sun would cause light to bend. Popper (1959), among others, has placed particular emphasis on this test as distinguishing science from other types of intellectual activity, and the classic laboratory experiments associated with science are actually efforts to apply this test.

Then there is the comprehensiveness test. This test consists of determining whether the theory is able to encompass all the known facts pertaining to the class of phenomena under study. The more of these facts the theory is able to account for, the greater the confidence one can have that the theory is comprehensive in nature. The Ptolemaic model of the universe, for example, was able to account for the observable movements of the sun and moon around the earth. But it was less successful in explaining the movements of the planets Venus and Mars. Even more critically, it could not account for the moons around Jupiter which Galileo was able to observe through his telescope. It was therefore eventually judged to be less comprehensive a theory than the alternative Copernican model of the universe. Similarly, Newtonian physics would have been unable to account for the bending of the suns's rays observed by Eddington, and for this reason—as well as for its inability to explain why gravity is proportional to inertia—it, too, was subsequently judged to be less comprehensive than Einstein's theory of relativity.

A theory may fail to meet the comprehensiveness test for either of two reasons: (1) because the theory provides no explanation for certain empirically observable phenomena (such as the bending of the sun's rays which can be seen during an eclipse), or (2) because what is empirically observed is, under certain circumstances, different from what the theory would lead one to expect. An example of the latter is when, because of air resistance, two bodies of unequal weight do not fall at the same speed—as classical mechanics would lead one to expect. A theory which, for either of these reasons, is unable to meet the comprehensiveness test is less likely to be rejected outright than to be relegated to the category of a special case—with the importance of that special case depending on how commonly encountered are the conditions, or assumptions, under which the theory holds. In that event, the comprehensiveness test consists of determining under what circumstances the theory remains valid.

Finally, there is the parsimony test. This test consists of determining whether any particular element in the construction of a theory, including one of its underlying assumptions, is necessary to account for what can be empirically observed. To the extent that the element can be eliminated without reducing the theory's explanatory power, it should be dropped as being superfluous. It is in this way that a theory is purged of its metaphysical elements, and subsequent investigators are not misled into pursuing nonproductive lines of research.

All three of these last tests are empirical in nature. This can be seen more clearly by viewing a theory as a system of interrelated ideas. The inputs into the system are the assumptions, or conditions, under which the ideas become operative, and the output consists of the conclusions, or observable effects, derived from the theory. The internal structure of the theory, meanwhile, is the series of steps by which the conclusions are obtained from the assumptions. The correspondence test, then, consists of checking the theory's output, or conclusions, against the observable reality to determine if they are isomorphic; the comprehensiveness test consists of checking to see whether there is not some part of the observable reality which is left unexplained by the theory, requiring additional inputs, or assumptions, which make the theory a special rather than general one; and the parsimony test consists of checking whether there is not some element of the theory, often based on an input, or assumption, which can be dispensed with entirely in explaining the observable reality. (The coherence test, it should be noted, is merely a check on the logical consistency of the theory's internal structure and involves no empirical question at all.) It is only by meeting all three of these tests that a theory can be said to have been validated empirically.

Social scientists, in arguing that their theories should be accepted without necessarily having to meet all of these tests, point out how difficult it is for them to carry out empirical research. Many economists would be among their number, noting that their subject matter does not lend itself to laboratory experiments, in which other factors can be held constant, and that a reliance on statistical analysis, the only feasible alternative, seldom leads to conclusive results. These points, unfortunately all too true, are nonetheless not a reason for relaxing the insistence on empirical validation of theory. If anything, they are a reason to insist on an even more stringent test in the case of any social science theory. The theory, when translated into one or more public policies, must be shown to make a difference to society in the form of certain clearly distinguishable results. The policies, upon being adopted, must then have the predicted effect. This is the praxis test of a social science theory. It is a form of the correspondence test, but with society itself as the test subject and with the body politic as both the intermediate (should the policy be adopted) and the final (has the policy been successful) arbiter. While it might be argued that this is much too rigorous a test to insist that any theory meet, especially in the social sciences, the present sorry state of economics is evidence of what is likely to be the consequence when, despite its not having been validated empirically in this or any of the other ways, a body of theory continues to remain at the core of a discipline.

The empirical validity of the neoclassical core

The neoclassical core of economic theory is little different from what it was in Veblen's day. That core consists of four basic elements, or theoretical constructs. They are (1) a set of indifference curves, based on a postulated utility function for each and every individual, which, when aggregated for all households, represent the relative preferences for any two or more goods by the society as a whole; (2) a set of continuous, or smooth, isoquants, based on a postulated production function for each and every good that is produced, which, when, taken together, represent all the combinations of labor and other inputs which can be used to produce those goods; (3) a set of positively sloped supply curves for all the different firms and industries which comprise the enterprise sector of the economy; and (4) a set of marginal physical product curves for all the inputs used in the production process, not just the labor inputs but also, even more critically, the "capital" inputs. One or more of these four elements is usually the basis for any microeconomic argument made by economists, and any argument which relies on at least one of these four theoretical constructs can be regarded as being "neoclassical" in nature.

It is, of course, not always clear that one of these four theoretical constructs is the basis for the microeconomic argument being made by an economist. The argument is likely to be couched in less technical terms. Still, the underlying theoretical construct upon which the argument must be based is easily enough identified. For example, any argument based on the notion that households as consumers are "maximizing their utility" or would, under some other circumstance, succeed in "maximizing their utility" is most probably predicated on a postulated set of indifference curves. Similarly, any argument based on the notion that producers have a relatively unlimited choice as to the combinations of inputs they can use, that any and all inputs are readily substituted for one another, is probably predicated on a postulated set of continuous isoquants. Moreover, any argument based on the notion that an increase in supply will not be forthcoming except at a higher price—or, alternatively, that any increase in demand must necessarily lead to a higher price—is assuming a positively sloped supply curve. Finally, any argument based on the notion that workers and others receive as wages and other forms of compensation the value of their marginal product is relying on the presumed existence of marginal physical product curves which exhaust the output produced under any given set of techniques.

What is most startling about these four theoretical constructs is that, despite their vintage, they have yet to be empirically validated by economists. The strong suspicion surrounds them that, rather than serving as the basis for further work in economics, they each represent a source of fundamental error which first needs to be corrected before any progress of a scientific nature will be possible within the discipline.

The indifference curves upon which the orthodox theory of consumer demand is based are suspect because it has proven impossible to derive a set of these curves from the available empirical data, either for individuals or for groups of individuals (Mishan, 1961; Blaug, 1980, chapter 6). The theoretical construct of indifference curves is therefore metaphysical in the same sense that unicorns, ghosts, and the "vital force" once thought to animate human beings are metaphysical: there is no empirical evidence that such things actually exist. Indeed, a skeptic would have to assume they do not exist. When an essential element of a theory has no empirical counterpart in the observable world, the theory itself becomes incapable of empirical validation. Hence, the orthodox theory of consumer demand cannot meet the correspondence test, among the other empirical tests identified above. The evidence usually cited in support of the indifference curve analysis— namely, the negative coefficient often (but not always) observed for the price variable in a fully specified demand equation—only confirms the existence of a negatively sloped demand curve, not the convex indifference curves thought by a majority of economists to underlie that curve. The negative coefficient for the price variable in a demand function is readily accounted for by a much simpler explanation—namely, the tendency of households to alter their speculative inventory of consumer goods as the price varies around the long-period "normal" value. Indifference curves being unnecessary to explain what can be observed empirically, this element of demand theory should, based on the parsimony test, be abandoned.

The isoquants upon which the orthodox theory of production is founded are equally suspect and for the same reason: It has proven impossible to derive these curves from the available empirical data on production by individual firms. The concept of an isoquant is no less metaphysical than that of indifference curves. Indeed, the case against isoquants is even stronger. The implication of isoquants—namely, that firms are able to produce a given quantity of output, even in the absence of technical progress, by employing varying combinations of labor and other inputs—is strongly contradicted by the available evidence. Empirical investigation in a number of manufacturing industries has shown that production requires the use of labor, material, and other inputs in relatively fixed combinations—until such a time as a new plant is built and/or new equipment is installed, at which point a new fixed combination of inputs will be employed. The role of relative prices in determining which combination of inputs will be employed over the long period, as distinct from the short run, is unclear, once the intervening role of technical progress is recognized; and in any case a far more complex set of relationships is involved than that implied by a continuous, or smooth, set of isoquants (Gold, 1971). This element in the orthodox theory of production having consistently failed to meet the correspondence test, and with other, more parsimonious explanations being available (e.g., the Leontief, Sraffa and von Neumann fixed-technical-coefficient models of production—see below), it can readily be dispensed with—if a nonnormative, empirically operational theory is all that is desired.

The purging of indifference curves and isoquants from the theoretical "tool kit" of economists, on the grounds that they are metaphysical concepts without empirical foundation, is fatal to

any neo-Walrasian (actually Hicks-Arrow-Debreu) general equilibrium model. While this would still leave the Marshallian partial
equilibrium theory untouched, this variant of neoclassical microeconomic theory, too, becomes suspect once it is realized that
there is no empirical support, at least outside of agriculture and
mining, for the positively sloped supply curve which is an essential
half of Marshall's famous scissors. The positively sloped supply
curve is based on two assumptions: (1) that firms are price takers
seeking to maximize their net revenue in the short run, and (2)
that production is subject to variable and indeed, beyond a certain
point, to decreasing returns to scale. The available evidence would
seem to contradict both assumptions, at least insofar as the
industrial sector is concerned (Blaug, 1980, chapter 7; Eichner,
1976, chapter 2). Firms in that sector are generally price setters
rather than price takers, and long-term survival and expansion
rather than short-run profit maximization would appear to be
their goal. Moreover, constant and even increasing returns to scale,
rather than decreasing returns, appear to be the rule. At least there
is no evidence that industrial firms encounter higher unit costs as
they expand output (Johnston, 1960; Walters, 1963).

To the extent that the concept of a supply curve is at all applicable to the industrial sector, the curve would appear to be perfectly elastic, at least over the observable range, rather than being
positively sloped. The evidence to this effect is the insensitivity of
prices in the industrial sector to changes in the level of demand
(Coutts, Godley, and Nordhaus, 1978; Eckstein and Fromm, 1968).
The positing of a positively sloped supply curve and, with it, the
conventional supply and demand analysis therefore fails the comprehensiveness test. The Marshallian partial equilibrium model applies, at most, only in the case of agricultural and other interna-
tionally traded commodities. For goods produced in the industrial
sector, an alternative, more general, theory of output and price determination is needed.

The marginal productivity analysis, the basis for the neoclassical theory of income distribution, is immediately suspect because
of the fixed technical coefficients which, the evidence indicates,
characterize the production process in at least the technologically
most advanced sectors of the economy. With fixed technical coefficients, inputs cannot be varied in the manner required to make
the marginal productivity theory applicable. The theory invites

further skepticism because "capital," the marginal productivity of which is central to the explanation offered by neoclassical theory for the distribution of income, turns out to be another metaphysical concept like indifference curves and isoquants. No one would deny the importance of produced goods used as inputs in the production process. The problem is that these capital inputs are heterogeneous, with no common physical measure such as tons, barrels, or BTUs. This means there can be no measure, in real terms, of the capital inputs used in the production process and that therefore, except in the case of a primitive technology, such as agriculture using only seed, the marginal physical productivity of "capital" cannot be determined. It is not possible to aggregate the capital inputs in physical terms, and thus any argument based either on a firm's production function or on an aggregate production function in which an abstract "capital" variable, K, appears as an explanatory variable cannot be validated empirically. The K term, lacking any empirical counterpart, is metaphysical. For this reason, the argument cannot meet the correspondence or any other empirical test (Blaug, 1980, chapter 9; Harcourt, 1972).

The four theoretical constructs discussed so far and found to lack empirical validity are important only insofar as the orthodox microeconomic theory is concerned. This would seem to leave the orthodox macroeconomic theory relatively immune to the same type of criticism, and indeed it is in connection with macroeconomic issues that the bulk of empirical research has been carried out by economists. For this reason alone one can be thankful that at least there has been a Keynesian revolution in economics. It would, however, be a mistake to conclude that, because Keynes's ideas have stimulated a vast body of empirical research, the orthodox macroeconomic theory has been empirically validated. The fact is that the Keynesian revolution was soon negated by a neo-Walrasian counterrevolution led by Hicks (1939) and Samuelson (1948). What elements of Keynes's own ideas were retained were then vitiated by the neoclassical microeconomic theory to which they were joined as part of the "neoclassical synthesis" which has become the prevailing orthodoxy, at least in the non-Communist world, since the end of World War II. To the neoclassical microeconomic core already lacking empirical validity have been added two new theoretical constructs, no less suspect on empirical grounds. These two additional theoretical constructs are (1) the

Hicks-Hansen LM-IS model, which makes the level of national income depend on whatever is the interest rate consistent with both real sector and monetary equilibrium, and (2) the Phillips curve, which makes the rate of growth of money wages, and thus the price level, a function of the unemployment rate. While the concepts underlying the Hicks-Hansen model and the Phillips curve are not metaphysical —unlike the several other components of the neoclassical synthesis—they must nonetheless be rejected as having failed to meet even the correspondence test, not to mention the praxis test.

The Hicks-Hansen model places the primary emphasis on the interest rate as the factor determining the level of macroeconomic activity. Not only will a change in the interest rate lead to a new monetary equilibrium, according to the model, but, even more importantly, it will, because of the effect on business investment, lead to a change in the level of national income. The latter proposition is a fairly easy one to test empirically and, as numerous studies have shown, is unsubstantiated by the available evidence. A change in the interest rate will, at most, have only a slight effect on the level of business investment (Nickell, 1978, pp. 299-300; Forman and Eichner, 1981, p. 123). This being the case, there is no basis for positing, as the Hicks-Hansen model does, that the level of national income depends on the interest rate. Indeed, governments which have formulated their macroeconomic policies on that premise have been uniformly disappointed in the results.

Moreover, there is reason to be skeptical as to whether monetary equilibrium depends on the interest rate either—or whether there is even such a thing as a monetary equilibrium one can observe empirically. The proposition that the interest rate determines monetary equilibrium has usually been assumed rather than justified by reference to any evidence. What evidence does exist—in the form of unsatisfied credit demand and flow-of-funds movements—would seem to suggest that it is monetary disequilibrium, and not equilibrium, which is the prevailing condition. Indeed, an empirically operational definition of monetary equilibrium has yet to be offered in connection with the Hicks-Hansen model. Once the notion of an LM curve representing all the points of possible monetary equilibrium is abandoned, the rest of the Hicks-Hansen model, and especially the notion of a uniquely determined level of income, Y, based on the balance between real and monetary factors, disappears with it. The Hicks-Hansen model, it turns out, is largely fatuous. This does not mean that large-scale macroeconomic models have not been constructed starting from a Hicks-Hansen framework (Klein and Burmeister, 1976). It merely means that, when the empirical work of constructing the models is complete, very little of the original theoretical framework is likely to remain.

The Phillips curve has been grafted on to the Hicks-Hansen model for much the same reason the Hicks-Hansen model has been added to the core of the orthodox neoclassical theory: to explain what cannot otherwise be accounted for. Just as it is not possible, within a neoclassical framework, to explain fluctuations in real output and employment without introducing the Hicks-Hansen model or some similar bastardization of Keynes's arguments, so, too, it is not possible, within the context of any of those orthodox Keynesian models, to explain the inflation which has bedeviled the world's economies since the end of World War II without positing an inverse relationship between the rate of growth of prices and the unemployment rate. Orthodox Keynesian models can explain only the level of income, Y, undifferentiated between price and quantity movements. To explain changes in the price level, separate from the movement of real output and employment, a Phillips curve must be added. Monetarist models, it should be noted, also need to posit a Phillips curve—if they are to distinguish a short-period change in real income from a short-period change in nominal income. These models, too, can explain only the level of income, Y, undifferentiated between price and quantity movements. The difference is that monetarist models use the Phillips curve to convert the nominal magnitudes into real magnitudes rather than the reverse. Both the orthodox Keynesian and the monetarist models, then, must rely on the Phillips curve to separate out the price and quantity movements. The problem is that the Phillips curve, like the Hicks-Hansen model, has consistently failed to meet either the correspondence or the praxis test.

Although the unemployment rate is often specified as the principal factor determining the rate of growth of prices, it turns out, when the matter is investigated empirically, that other factors are actually more important. The predominant influence on the price level, by far, is the rise in unit labor and material costs. The unemployment rate, like the interest rate in the case of business investment, adds only marginally to the explanatory power of the price equations which econometricians have developed, and, with the influence of rising labor and material costs properly taken into account, that variable can be all but ignored. It would seem to be merely a proxy, and a poor one at that, for the level of demand in certain commodity markets. Thus, when governments, acting on the assumption implicit in the Phillips curve that the unemployment rate can be used instrumentally, have attempted to curb the rise in prices by deliberately engineering a slowdown in the level of economic activity, they have succeeded only in transforming the troublesome problem of inflation into the even more serious problem of stagflation.

Moreover, the somewhat weak inverse relationship between the unemployment rate and the growth of prices which can be observed once the more important, other determinants of the price level have been taken into account would appear to be an unstable one—the presumed trade-off between unemployment and inflation having apparently become less favorable over time. More recent studies suggest that it now requires a higher rate of unemployment to prevent prices from rising by a certain percentage than it previously did. This evidence is, of course, consistent with the explanation frequently offered in defense of continuing to assume the existence of a Phillips curve—namely, that the curve has shifted outwardly to the right over time. But the same evidence is also consistent with a quite different hypothesis—namely, that the Phillips curve is actually a figment of the economists' imagination, invented to fill a hole in the neoclassical line of argument. Indeed, the Phillips curve, like the Hicks-Hansen model, would appear to be fatuous.

It will, of course, be argued in response that if all six of the key theoretical constructs just identified were to be purged from the economics textbooks on the grounds that they have not been validated empirically, very little would remain and what was left would lack coherence. This, however, is not a compelling argument for retaining the six key elements of the neoclassical synthesis. Rather it is a measure of how intellectually bankrupt the dominant orthodoxy has become. If economics is to establish itself as a scientifically based activity, it has no choice but to purge all six elements from the core of its discipline. This is an essential first step to revitalizing economics as a field of study—however painful an adjustment it may require in accustomed modes of thinking. As for what should be taught in their place, there is, it turns out, a ready answer.

The alternative paradigm

A comprehensive, and robust, alternative to the orthodox neoclassical theory in economics has emerged in recent decades. This new paradigm has been termed post-Keynesian—in part because it is based on Keynes's own ideas, with the clear intent of carrying those ideas through to their logical full development, and in part because, drawing on the ideas of other economists no less outside the mainstream of economics, it seeks to transcend the limitations of even Keynes's own analysis. In other words, the new paradigm has as its principal objective the completion of the aborted Keynesian revolution in economics (Eichner and Kregel, 1975). Thus, to the principle of effective demand and the role ascribed to money in *The General Theory* have been added the growth dynamics of Roy Harrod and John von Neumann, the production theory of Wassily Leontief, the value theory of Piero Sraffa, and the distribution and pricing models of Michal Kalecki (Eichner, 1979, 1980). It was Joan Robinson who, in *The Accumulation of Capital* (1965), first succeeded in synthesizing many of these ideas within a single coherent model, and it was Luigi Pasinetti who, more recently in *Structural Change and Economic Growth* (1981), has succeeded in producing an even broader synthesis.

Post-Keynesian theory is intended to provide a causal explanation of how a real economic system, with advanced institutions, operates. It is therefore set in historical time, with an immutable past and an unknowable future, both of which play a critical role in determining the present. This is in contrast to the orthodox theory, which abstracts not only from time but also from most other important aspects of reality. The orthodox theory is concerned with optimization criteria rather than with explanation. Indeed, to the extent that the orthodox theory amounts to little more than the specification of the conditions that must be met if resources are to be optimally allocated under various hypothetical states, it makes no pretense of being an explanatory science in the tradition of physics, chemistry, and biology. The trouble, of course, is that not all economists imbued with a neoclassical perspective recognize this limitation of the theory, and they then mistakenly attempt to apply it to the real world. This is especially true of the many economists who offer their advice to political leaders and other men of practical affairs based on one or the other version of the neoclassical synthesis, either the orthodox Keynesian or the monetarist one.

To each of the elements of the neoclassical synthesis previously identified as being without empirical validity, post-Keynesian theory offers an alternative formulation, one that has yet to be discredited on empirical grounds and indeed, in several cases, already has a considerable body of evidence behind it. In place of the metaphysical indifference curves which underlie the neoclassical theory of demand, post-Keynesian theory starts with the price and income elasticities of demand which economists are actually able to estimate. Based on that substantial body of research going back to Engels's work in the nineteenth century, post-Keynesian economists generally assume that, in an economy that is expanding over time (though not necessarily at a constant rate), it is the income effects which will predominate over the relative price, or substitution, effects. Indeed, any substitution, based on a change in relative prices, is likely to be of only minor importance and, if ignored altogether, will be less disastrous to the argument than if, as in the typical neoclassical model, the income effects are instead ignored.

The reason for the lack of substitutability, in the case of the inputs used in production, will be gone into shortly. As for the items of final consumer demand, the lack of substitutability reflects the importance of social convention, and thus of acquired tastes, in determining each household's normal consumption pattern. In a line of reasoning that can be traced back to Veblen (1899), Mitchell (1937), Duesenberry (1949), and other institutionalists, consumer preferences are viewed as being the result of learned social behavior rather than being innate at birth or, in some other sense, exogenous to the analysis. These preferences are likely to be modified over time, not just by advertising and other selling techniques but also, even more significantly, by the growth of income levels within each of the social groups, or classes, which comprise the society so that an increasingly more affluent life-style comes to be viewed as the norm. A household's normal consumption pattern, at any given point in time, thus reflects the life-style of the other households which constitute its social reference group. What must be purchased is what is required to maintain the household's relative position in society, the items customarily bought being reducible to a standardized shopping list that changes but slowly over time, and then for reasons that have little to do with relative prices. Consumer preferences are, in this sense, lexicographically ordered (Canterbery, 1979a; Earl, 1983). This means they come in discrete bundles, with both the composition of the bundle at any one point in time and the change in the bundle over time depending more on income levels and prevailing social norms than on any hedonistic calculus.

However, it is on the supply side rather than on the demand side that post-Keynesian theory departs even more radically from the orthodox neoclassical theory. In this respect, post-Keynesian theory marks a resumption of, rather than a break with, the classical tradition in economics. As opposed to the isoquants which are the starting point for the analysis of production, such as can be found in neoclassical models, post-Keynesian theory begins by positing the prior existence of a set of labor and other technical coefficients (which constitute what is generally termed the **A** matrix), as a reflection of the prevailing technology. By assuming a fixed set of technical coefficients, post-Keynesian theory is able to draw on the path-breaking work of Leontief insofar as the interindustry effect of a change in the composition of final demand is concerned, of John von Neumann insofar as the growth dynamics of a multi-industry economy are concerned, and of Piero Sraffa insofar as the distributional impact of a variation in the real wage is concerned. Indeed, the substantial body of empirical work that has been carried out, based on input-output analysis, serves to validate the theory of production underlying the post-Keynesian approach. It is the inverse of the **A** matrix, the so-called Leontief inverse, which plays the key role in the long-period analysis of both output and prices. Using the inverse, one is able to determine the differential effect on each of the economy's many industries from a change in the composition of final demand, and thus the differential effect produced by the uneven growth of those very industries over time. Meanwhile, relying on the dual solution to the input-output model, one is able to use the same inverse to determine the set of relative prices which must prevail in the long period if each industry is to earn sufficient revenues to cover the cost of all required inputs, including any additions to the capital stock when the system is expanding. In this way, it is the A matrix, or set of technical coefficients, which determines relative prices in the long period, and not the reverse, as is usually assumed in a neoclassical model.

This theory of the relative prices which must prevail in the long period, if the system of production is to be able to reproduce itself, becomes a theory of absolute price levels, in both the long period and the short, once a numeraire in the form of the wage rate is introduced. The wage rate, rather than being just another price, as in a Walrasian general equilibrium model, plays the key role in determining all other value relationships within the production system. Here post-Keynesian theory is careful to distinguish between the real wage—which consists of the actual basket of consumption goods workers can purchase with the income they earn—and the money wage. The latter is simply a nominal rate of compensation and, as opposed to the real wage, depends on the bargaining strength of workers and other factors which are extrinsic to the production process and therefore labor productivity (Piore, 1979; Canterbery, 1979b). Indeed, this distinction between the real and the money wage underlies the post-Keynesian theory of inflation, it being the growth of money wages in excess of the real wage that necessarily leads to an offsetting rise in the price level (Weintraub, 1959; 1966). What is significant about this theory of inflation is that it does not depend on any excess-demand condition. It therefore does not rest on the assumption that industry supply curves, especially within the industrial sector, are positively sloped.

Indeed, the post-Keynesian theory of production and prices suggests a specific alternative to the positively sloped industry supply curve upon which the orthodox explanation for inflation is based. Whatever the time frame of the analysis, the prices at which goods are sold in the market will depend on the cost of producing those goods—including the cost of any capital inputs. Firms in the industrial sector are generally price setters, rather than price takers, and the prices they set are the prices dictated by their costs of production plus a certain margin, or markup. The markup, instead of rising and falling with the level of demand, tends to remain fixed over the cycle, with the size of the markup dependent both on the amount of external debt that must be serviced as a result of past capital accumulation and on the amount of internally generated funds that is required to finance the firms' planned future capital outlays. This markup, or full-cost, pricing model is the only one that has been substantiated, at least insofar as the industrial sector is concerned, by empirical studies, and indeed the model itself was first put forward by Gardiner C. Means (1962), the Oxford Pricing Group (Wilson and Andrews, 1951), and other empirical investigators as a generalization of the pricing practices they observed. What it implies is that, to the extent an industry supply curve can even be said to exist (Wiles, 1956; R. Robinson, 1961), it is within the observable range, perfectly elastic rather than positively sloped. A change in the industry price is produced only by a change in costs, and thus by a shift of the supply curve itself. It means that the price is unaffected by a movement along the supply curve, and thus by a shift of the demand curve, both at the industry and the aggregate level.

The markup pricing model specified at the industry level can then be generalized to explain the change in the aggregate price level over time. The costs of production for the economy as a whole are, with the exception of whatever raw materials must be imported, entirely costs of labor, since, in a vertically integrated model of production (Pasinetti, 1981), all costs can be reduced to the labor costs incurred at some earlier stage in the production process. The aggregate price level, then, depends on the average unit costs of labor plus whatever markup generally prevails. The average unit costs of labor depends, in turn, on the growth of output per worker relative to the growth of money wages. The size of the markup which generally prevails has already been explained in terms of the rate at which firms need to generate funds internally to finance their expansion over time as well as to service their past debt, while the growth of money wages has been explained in terms of the bargaining strength of workers and other factors extrinsic to the economic system. To explain the rate of growth of the aggregate price level, and thus of inflation, it is therefore necessary to explain only the growth of output per worker and the other determinants of the real wage. This, however, requires that the theory of income distribution favored by neoclassical economists, based on the marginal physical product of labor and other factors of production, be replaced by an alternative explanation of relative income shares.

Within a post-Keynesian model, the distribution of income is explained primarily by a set of macroeconomic conditions. This is in sharp contrast to the neoclassical theory, in which the explanation depends on a set of microeconomic relationships—in particular, on the ability of firms to substitute one type of input for another at the margin. The most important of the macroeconomic factors explaining the distribution of income is the growth of output per worker, itself largely the result of the technical progress made possible by the application of science and other forms of knowledge to the problem of wringing a material existence from a stingy natural endowment. The rate of technical progress may be exogenous to the model, at least in part, but its profound effect on all economic relationships is not ignored. To the extent technical progress takes the form of product innovation, it leads to the emergence of entirely new industries over time and thus to the basic dynamic quality of modern economic systems. To the extent technical progress takes the form of process innovation, with the labor coefficients of production falling, it leads to the observed growth of output per worker. This growth of output per worker, in turn, serves as the basis for the secular rise in the real wage (Pasinetti, 1981). For it is only from the increase in output per worker that, other things remaining the same, the per capita consumption of workers can be increased. Still, the growth of real wages does not depend solely on the growth of output per worker. Indeed, this is one of the reasons that an incomes policy, as an alternative to the more conventional demand-management policies for controlling inflation, is so difficult to implement.

The growth of the real wage depends, in addition, on the rate of investment, or accumulation. Other things, including the rate of technical progress, remaining the same, it can be shown that the greater the rate of investment, and thus the more rapid the pace of economic expansion, the lower will be the *relative* share of income going to workers. This occurs because wages will need to be depressed, at least compared to profits, so that resources can be diverted from consumption into capital formation. Of course, the real wage need not fall in *absolute* terms. The growth of the real wage merely has to be less than the growth of profits so that the disproportionate increase in investment can be financed, both in money and in real terms. Moreover, the rate of technical progress will not necessarily be unaffected by the rate of investment. With technical progress to a significant extent capital-embodied, that is, dependent on the introduction of new types of capital goods, an increase in investment can be expected to lead to a higher rate of technical progress as measured by the growth of output per worker. It is just that, in the absence of any offsetting factors, an increase in the level of economic activity, as induced by a higher rate of investment, can be expected to lead to a decline in labor's relative share. This can be observed, both in the long period and in the short, whenever the pace of economic expansion quickens. What it means is that, if trade unions and the other representatives of labor insist on workers' obtaining a constant share of the national income, any shift to a more rapid growth path will set off a wage-price spiral as trade unions first obtain higher wages to match the disproportionate increase in profits and then business firms, especially the large corporations or megacorps, insist on price increases to match the rise in unit labor costs.

The growth of the real wage depends on one other factor. This factor is the amount of consumption out of profits, that is, the share of profits that is used for other than private investment purposes. An increase in the amount of consumption out of profit will, as an increase in investment would, serve to reduce the share of national income going to workers—except that, in contrast to an increase in investment, it will not have the effect of increasing at least the future income of workers by expanding the productive capacity of the economic system. While it might seem that the amount of consumption out of profits is limited to any dividends paid out and other forms of rentier income not reinvested, this item actually encompasses a much broader set of income flows. The government, through the taxes it collects from business, receives a share of all profits. Moreover, the foreign suppliers of raw materials, through any increase in the prices they are able to charge, can also siphon off a share of the profits being earned domestically. Thus the share of national income that goes to workers will be reduced, not just by a more rapid rate of investment but also by an increase in the size of the public sector and by rising raw material prices. Indeed, it is because of these last two factors that the rate of inflation, at least in the United States, has quickened since 1965, first as a result of the Great Society programs and then later as a result of the rapid rise in oil and other commodity prices.

Post-Keynesian theory thus not only provides a specific alterna-

tive to each of the four elements that constitute the microeconomic core of neoclassical theory; it also offers a plausible explanation for the stagflation, or simultaneous inflation and recession,
the American economy has experienced recently—an explanation
that suggests the need for some form of incomes policy to take the
place of the singular reliance on conventional monetary and fiscal
policy instruments that is the best advice orthodox economists can
offer at present. Indeed, post-Keynesian theory does not need to
postulate a set of dubious LM-IS and Phillips curves to explain inflation and thereby plug a hole in the analysis (Eichner, 1980).

One could elaborate in much greater detail, both on the points
already covered and on the other elements of post-Keynesian theory. Still, enough has been said to demonstrate that, if economists
are reluctant to abandon the neoclassical theory, despite its well-
known shortcomings, it is not because there is no better alternative with which to replace it, one that seems more likely to meet
the empirical tests that distinguish science from mere metaphysics
or superstition. The explanation must lie elsewhere. Indeed, it
lies in the nature of economics as a social system.

The economics profession as a social system

That its structure is difficult to discern makes the economics profession no less a social system. It is just that the structure, and
thus the system itself, is easily lost sight of—and its importance
overlooked.

The structure of the economics profession appears, at first
glance, to be a simple pyramid. At the bottom are the greater
number of economists who teach outside the universities with
Ph.D. programs in economics or who, alternatively, work for private firms and the government. Though they constitute the bulk
of the profession, they are likely to have the least influence on the
discipline. Their time is usually so consumed by instructional and
other duties that they find it difficult to carry out research—let
alone succeed in having it published. Moreover, only a very small
number of their students—if they should have any—are likely to
continue on with economics beyond the undergraduate level and
in this way reflect the influence of those who have taught them.

Somewhat higher up in the pyramid are the economists who
hold professorships at universities with second- and third-rank

graduate programs. They are in a slightly better position to have a long-lasting effect on economics. They have more time and institutional support to carry out research, while the greater reputation of their schools gives them a better chance to have their work published. Even so, their research is likely to go unnoticed except by their own students or by others working in the same narrow specialty. Moreover, while they have some access to graduate students, it is unlikely, when those students themselves become economists, that they will rise above the bottom level. The best the economists at this level can hope for is that either they themselves will one day be offered an appointment at a more prestigious institution or, that being out of the question, their own department will rise to the first rank. (Holding an appointment at a university with a graduate program in economics but still being restricted to teaching undergraduates is not enough. One is still at the bottom level—though with a better chance of rising to the next level than those relegated to lesser institutions.)

At the top of the pyramid, at least in the United States, are the small number of economists who teach in the graduate programs of the dozen-and-a-half leading universities, and among this elite the most influential are the ones who teach the required core courses at MIT, Harvard, Chicago, and perhaps one or two other universities. They constitute the economics "establishment." It is they who will largely shape the perceptions and values of the next generation of important economists, for the economists at the top of the profession, and indeed even well down into the middle level, are likely to come from the ranks of their students. Moreover, it is they who will largely determine the future directions of research in economics, in part through their own large volume of published work—facilitated by the reputation and resources of their own university—and in part through the judgment which they are continually being asked to pass on the work of others within the field. Finally, it is they whose work is most likely to be read, and cited, by other economists—beginning with their own students and continuing with their students' students. In Great Britain, the same role is played by the economics faculty at Cambridge, Oxford, and the London School of Economics.

The structure of the economics profession described so far is not really different from that of other academic disciplines, including the natural sciences. Nor is the means by which power is exercised within that system so different.

The most important source of power, as in any social system, is the ability to influence how positions which carry a salary, that is, jobs, are filled. In this regard, the economists at the top of the pyramid are clearly the most powerful within the profession. It is not just in filling the highly coveted positions within their own departments that their judgment is likely to prove decisive. It is also in filling positions throughout the economics profession, within other leading departments as well as at lesser institutions. It is they who are most likely to learn when an important position opens up, it is they who are most likely to be asked to suggest possible candidates, and it is they whose letters of recommendation are likely to carry the greatest weight. This disproportionate influence which the economists in the leading graduate departments exert in determining how positions are filled is, in turn, important in explaining why it is that their students are more likely to rise to the top of the profession. The two, a powerful mentor and a favored protégé, go together, with each providing support for the other—the one through patronage and the other through tribute in footnotes, prefaces, and the other coinage of the academic community.

It is this last point which, when fully appreciated, leads to an awareness that the structure of economics is more than just a pyramid with an "establishment" at the top. The structure also reflects a series of personal relationships, not unlike those between liege and vassal under feudalism, which links a group of lesser economists to each person of prominence within the profession. In some cases, the lesser figures are simply students, past and present. In other cases, they are colleagues whose own position within the profession, whether because of the approach they have decided to follow in their research, because of the job they have succeeded in obtaining, or both, depends on the individual to whom they have chosen to pay homage. Whatever may be the group forming the entourage—and prestige within the profession reflects both the size of the entourage and the reputation of those involved—its existence needs to be recognized in identifying the structure of the economics profession. Indeed, with the lesser members of a given entourage likely to have their own entourage in turn and with involvement as a lesser member in more than one entourage not uncommon, there exists a complex set of interrelationships among economists that cuts across both the several levels of the pyramid and the different institutions found at each level. What holds the entire structure together, like the wire mesh of a concrete form, is the power which the economists of note at the center of each entourage are able to wield.

How jobs are filled is not the only source of that power. It is also how articles are chosen for publication in refereed journals, especially the premier ones, and how research is chosen for support by the National Science Foundation and other funding agencies. These last two considerations are, of course, not unrelated to how jobs are filled. A substantial list of publications is essential for advancement to tenure, if not for initial appointment, within the better economics departments, while the ability to obtain research grants counts heavily in determining one's standing with colleagues, university administrators, and students. Here, too, the economists at the top—the establishment—exert a disproportionate amount of influence.

Still, this is not what distinguishes economics from the disciplines which are considered to be sciences. It is rather that this pyramidal structure and the power that is exercised through it is used to support and reinforce an ethos that is opposed to science. In other words, the culture of economics as a social system is a nonscientific one. In part, this is simply a reflection of the economics profession's intellectual heritage, its rooting in the antiempirical tradition and political ideology of the classical economists who followed Adam Smith. But it is also the result of more recent developments in economics—in particular, the neoclassical counterrevolution which Keynes provoked.

No sooner had the Keynesian heresy surfaced than it led to a response that would effectively contain the threat to the established way of thinking in economics which *The General Theory* posed. First Hicks and then, even more definitively, Samuelson laid down the foundations of a new "neoclassical synthesis" which, like the Thomistic synthesis six centuries earlier, could serve to reconcile faith with reason. One key aspect of this neoclassical synthesis has already been touched upon. This was the reformulation of Keynes's ideas in such a way that, taking the form of the now conventional LM-IS curve analysis, the idea could serve as the macroeconomic counterpart to the older microeconomic theory, now transformed along neo-Walrasian lines. That the two parts were incompatible with one another, that they created a duality no less than that between the Christian soul and the Greek mind, was beside the point. What mattered was that the orthodox body of theory could now account for so undeniable a phenomenon as the business cycle—and that phenomenon explained as the exception, when wages and/or prices were downwardly sticky, to the more general case in which resources were being optimally allocated by the market.

An even more significant aspect of the neoclassical synthesis, however, was its reformulation of all of economic theory, macro as well as micro, into a more precise mathematical language. In the process the Marshallian partial equilibrium analysis, which had been dominant in the Anglo-Saxon world, was supplanted by a neo-Walrasian general equilibrium approach as the ideal in pure theory. This reformulation of economics—actually translation of theory into mathematic language—was to have a number of important consequences, not the least of which was to make economics appear to be more scientific. After all, mathematics was the language of physics and the other hard sciences (though not, it should be noted, of biology, to which economics and the other social sciences are more closely related). More substantively, one could argue that, until the theory was first reformulated in a more precise mathematical language, the empirical testing of the theory could not begin. Unfortunately, economics would proceed along entirely different lines in the post–World War II period, eschewing empirical validation for mathematical formalism.

The reasons for this development are not entirely clear. It could have been that the ascendency of those trained in mathematics, at the expense of those trained in more historical methods, simply reinforced the long-standing penchant within economics for purely deductive modes of analysis—what Wiles, following Schumpeter (see his essay in this collection), has termed the Ricardian vice. Or it could have been that, meeting with so little success in validating empirically the key elements of the neoclassical synthesis, the theorists simply retreated into mathematical formalism as a refuge. Whatever the reason, the effect on economics as a discipline has been disastrous.

There is first the continued adherence to a non-scientific epistemology which the mathematicization of economics has encouraged. Economists as a group have adopted the view that formal, or mathematical, proofs are entirely sufficient to establish the validity of a theory rather than being just necessary. This is the only conclusion one can draw in view of the fact that economists are generally permitted to put forward various theories—in journal articles, books, and other forums subject to peer review—without having to provide any evidence in support of those theories. All they need do is adduce some mathematical proof starting from given (and, drawing support from Friedman's "positive methodology," not entirely plausible) assumptions.

The insistence that formal proofs are sufficient has led to two further transgressions against scientific norms. One is the sharp distinction that is drawn in economics between "theorists," those who employ formal (mathematical) methods, and "applied" economists, those whose work is based on statistics and other means of analyzing actual data. The former are usually absolved from having to concern themselves with empirical issues and, whether for that reason or not, are generally held in higher esteem within the profession. Indeed, it is possible for a theorist in economics to set up a model in such a way that the postulated behavior runs counter to all that is known about actual economic systems without this fact impugning either the argument or the economist's reputation. The more "simplifed" (i.e., unrealistic) the assumptions made by the theorist, the "purer" the theory is judged to be. The responsibility for testing the realism of the model is said to lie with the applied economists, it being the function of the theorists only to supply the models for testing. Such a sharp distinction between theory and empirical research, it should be noted, is unknown in the natural and biological sciences, and for good reason. It leads to an outpouring of useless theories which simply waste the time and energy of empirical researchers. At the same time, with the theorists largely innocent of what the data actually reveal, the theoretical models never become any better at explaining the observable phenomena. Nor is it clear that explaining observable phenomena is always their aim or main interest.

The sharp distinction that is drawn between theory and empirical research is then given a further twist away from reality by the argument that the purpose of theory, at least in economics, is not to explain what actually happens under observable conditions but rather to determine, logically, the conditions that must be satisfied if a certain goal, to wit, the optimal allocation of resources, is to be satisfied. It is with this stated purpose in mind that economists like to think of their discipline as the "science of optimal decision-making." In fact, however, the shift away from explanation, with the focus instead on rational decision rules, is a further transgression against scientific norms. It is not that the decision rules, if their allocative effects could be tested, would not be worthy of scientific investigation. It is rather that the allocative effects, since they occur only under hypothetical conditions never actually observed, are simply another metaphysical concept that, like the indifference curves and isoquants which underlie this type of analysis, defeat any hope of economics ever becoming a true science.

With the shift in purpose away from explanation, the position of the "pure" mathematicians among economic theorists has become the dominant one, especially at the leading graduate schools where, as the teachers in the required core courses, they are able to exert a particularly strong influence on the profession. The result is that, in economics, the imperatives of mathematics—with the emphasis on formal rather than on empirical proofs and on elegance rather than on relevance—have replaced the norms of science. Under the circumstances, it is not surprising to see economic theorists turn to increasingly more powerful mathematical tools to arrive at the same, familiar results. The plaudits, and recognition, go to those who can do so either as a more general case or in fewer logical steps. It is in this way that they display their skill as "theorists." Indeed, the development of more sophisticated mathematical modes of analysis has become an end in itself, whether the argument reveals anything about the real world or not. This emphasis on technique for its own sake, devoid of any explanatory power, is what constitutes the mathematical formalism by which economic theory is at present chiefly distinguished.

The objection here is not to the use of mathematics—or even to the mathematicization of economics. It is rather to the misuse that has been made of mathematics in economics—and in particular to the way mathematics has been used to give a pseudoscientific facade to a body of theory which can meet none of the empirical tests by which science is distinguished from mere superstition or crude ideology.

Disturbing as these developments may be to those who look to economics for intellectual guidance in dealing with pressing social problems, they have, quite apart from that consideration, enabled economics as a profession to solve a number of problems that might otherwise undermine its privileged position in society. One is the problem of making the neoclassical core of economic theory intellectually respectable. The retreat into mathematical formalism has surrounded that core with a protective layer that, to the scientifically naive at least, gives economics the appearance of being a science. It also, of course, makes it more difficult for the uninitiated to challenge the arguments based on that theory or, if they should attempt it, to gain command over those arguments. Indeed, mastering the mathematics needed to understand the core theory, once it has been reformulated using point set typology or even the calculus, can be quite a challenge; and it is difficult not to believe, once the challenge has been successfully met, that something useful has been learned. In this way, economists themselves are likely to become persuaded that the theory which sets them apart from the lay public has scientific merit.

The other problem which the retreat into mathematical formalism has helped ameliorate is finding an objective basis for judging the relative merit of economists and the work they do. Instead of focusing on what can be learned substantively from a particular line of research—an assessment which, if the research sheds any light on actual social conditions, will tend to be politically controversial—the emphasis is placed on the extent to which the work being done has led to an advance in technique. Relying on this criterion, not only are economists encouraged to add to the discipline's "tool kit" to the benefit of the profession as a whole, but, in addition, economists can be depicted as being like other scientists in that the work they do is above "politics." Economics is, from this perspective, simply the application of optimization techniques to a variety of problems. While the problems chosen for study may reflect a particular political perspective, the optimization techniques which are then used do not. They represent the "positivistic," and hence scientific, component of economics.

The reason why the retreat into mathematical formalism, following the neo-Walrasian counterrevolution orchestrated by Hicks and Samuelson, is viewed so favorably by the majority of economists should now be clear. It has enabled economics to retain the neoclassical core of its theory while still appearing to be both scientific and above politics. Indeed, the two elements—the mathematical formalism and the neoclassical core—reinforce one another. The neoclassical core provides the basis for learning mathematics, and the mathematics then vouches for the scientific nature of the theory. But why should retention of the neoclassical core be so important? The answer to this question has two parts. One has to do with the role the neoclassical core plays in enabling economics as a social system to maintain and reproduce itself without change; the other, with the role the same body of theory plays, as part of the ruling set of ideas, in enabling the larger society—as distinct from just the economics profession—to do the same. The two parts are, of course, not unconnected.

The neoclassical core is the essential glue by which the economics profession as a social system is held together. The neoclassical theory is more than just the theoretical constructs previously identified. It is, even more fundamentally, a particular way of looking at the world, involving the use of a particular type of language and, no less important a particular type of metaphor (based on a fictional market). Without that language and without that metaphor, economists, given the enormous diversity of viewpoints represented among them, would have no way of communicating with one another—and thus of carrying out the everyday business of the economics profession: setting up curricula, choosing textbooks, conducting research, judging one's peers, and filling academic and other posts.

The neoclassical core also serves as an effective instrument for raising the economics profession above the level of the untutored masses—and thus of effectively restricting entry into the profession itself. This use of the neoclassical core can, of course, be justified by the role it plays in holding the profession together. How, indeed, is the neophyte economist to make his way in the field if he cannot communicate in the language of his elders? Still, this use of the neoclassical core serves a second, no less important, purpose. It ensures that only those who have come to accept the limitations of economics at the present time—including its nonscientific epistemology and the entire body of empirically unvalidated ideas—will be certified as being competent in the subject. It therefore helps to insure that the social system represented by the economics profession will be able to reproduce itself without change.

At every stage in the development of an economist, beginning with the first introductory course, the neoclassical theory serves as a screening device to filter out the disbelieving. Usually, just an exposure to the subject is sufficient to divert into other fields those hoping to understand economic and other social processes. The unrealistic nature of the assumptions, proudly proclaimed, are a clear warning that those seeking knowledge should steer clear of the field. But some students will have teachers who nonetheless succeed in making the subject seem relevant—they are most likely to be members of the faculty known for their unorthodox viewpoint—while other students will be so strongly motivated that, despite what they are exposed to, they will persevere in their study of economics, hoping that more advanced courses—or at least courses at a more prestigious university—will finally shed some light on the problems which attracted them to economics in the first place. All the same, long before an individual who makes it that far has completed his or her doctoral training, he is likely to find himself faced with a hard choice. To win the praise, and support, of his teachers, he will need to embrace their perspective. In almost every case, this means adopting a neoclassical framework for analyzing problems in economics.

For some, of course, adopting a neoclassical framework poses no dilemma. They are content simply with logical answers, whatever the limited relevance of those answers. For others, however, the dilemma is a real one. They can either pretend to accept the neoclassical framework, keeping to themselves any reservations they have, or they can voice their skepticism. What happens to those who fall into the latter habit serves as a powerful lesson to the others. Students who evidence difficulty accepting a neoclassical framework inevitably receive lower grades in their courses, are less likely to pass their qualifying exams, can expect more criticism and other forms of resistance to the research they want to carry out, and in every other way will find their progress as a student impeded. Worst of all, unless they come around to a more sympathetic view of the dominant theory, they are likely to become known as "not quite sound" and thus will be eliminated from serious consideration whenever their mentors are asked to recommend someone for an important position in economics. It is not surprising therefore that by far the greater number of fledgling economists choose to keep to themselves any reservations they may have about the neoclassical framework in which they are forced to work.

These younger economists, if they do not immediately abandon themselves to cynicism, will say that they are simply holding their reservations in check until they can complete their doctorate (or obtain tenure, or receive an endowed chair, or . . .), and thus can speak out more freely. They can meanwhile comfort themselves with the thought that this is how the game must be played if their career in economics is not to come to a premature end. Unfortunately, long before they reach their final goal, whatever that goal may be, they will become so practiced in the neoclassical framework that they will be unable to think in any other terms. Indeed, they are likely to come to regard as somewhat "odd," and therefore somewhat suspect in their views, those who reject that framework. In this way, they will become part of the next generation of economists that makes sure the generation which succeeds them is firmly schooled in the same neoclassical framework. There are only two alternatives to this path of least resistance. One is to turn away from economics altogether, deciding to make one's contribution to society in some other way. The other alternative is to accept the handicaps, and thus the reduced career prospects, that go with working outside the neoclassical mainstream.

The advantage to the economics profession from using the neoclassical core as a screening device is clear enough. It enables the profession to meet head on and defeat the most potent challenge to the dominant orthodoxy—the greater skepticism of the younger minds drawn to the study of economics. This function of the neoclassical core takes on a special significance once it is realized that the purpose which economics serves insofar as the larger society is concerned is not so much to provide an explanation of how the economic system actually works—indeed, for this purpose, it is largely useless—but rather to provide support for a certain set of ideas which have been important in the historical development of Western civilization.

Economics as a political philosophy

Viewed as an explanation of how a modern, technologically progressive economy actually operates, the conventional economic theory makes little sense. Indeed, how can a model which abstracts from production, money, and almost every other identifiable feature of economic life explain anything about how the members of an advanced industrial society satisfy their material needs? The conventional economic theory begins to make sense only when one realizes that it is a political, and not an economic, argument which is being made. The argument runs as follows: The economic system can be viewed as a self-regulating mechanism, one that requires little or no interference by the government to insure the best possible results. Indeed, government intervention is likely to impair the economy's performance since any decisions based on the dynamics of the political system will probably be inferior to those made impersonally through the market. From the largely self-regulating nature of a market economy, it then follows that the role of the government in economic matters can, and should, be sharply limited.

Economics, as part of the system of ideas which has ruled the world's leading industrial countries for over 200 years, is concerned only with the first half of the above syllogism. Ever since Adam Smith's anticipators first pointed it out, those schooled in "political economy" have been fascinated by the systemic, self-regulating nature of a market-based economy. They have sought to demonstrate, on purely logical grounds, that reliance on the market leads to an allocation of resources which cannot be improved upon, that it produces what economists refer to as "Pareto optimality." The general equilibrium models of Arrow and Debreu, as the culmination of the neo-Walrasian revolution initiated by Hicks and Samuelson, are simply the latest, and mathematically most elegant, efforts among these lines. Whether any "Pareto optimality" will actually be achieved is beside the point. So too is the realism of the models themselves. As long as the models provide a sufficiently convincing case for limiting the role of the government in the economy, they more than serve their purpose. Those who constitute the "establishment" within economics are more concerned about the worst-possible outcome in politics than they are about the worst-possible outcome in economics—especially now that a Keynesian macroeconomics has been grafted on to the neoclassical core to explain, and help counter, the fluctuations in output and employment to which a market economy is prone. The first danger to be guarded against is too great an accrual of power by the state. The economy, it is believed, will take care of itself.

This fear of an all-too-powerful state is not an unwarranted one. As the historical record bears out, it is the greed and ambition of individuals operating under the guise of the state rather than the same greed and ambition, operating through the market, which has been the greatest source of human misery. The experience of the twentieth century, whether in Hitler's Germany, Stalin's Russia, or some other, more recent site of political extermination, amply attests to this fact. Moreover, one can argue, again citing the historical record, that it was precisely the weakened condition of the political authority which permitted first science and then an industrial mode of production to emerge in Western Europe. Indeed, it would appear that individual initiative, whether it be in the realm of ideas or in the sphere of production, is soon extinguished if the state is permitted to grow too powerful. Still, it is one thing to develop an argument in political theory, based on a model of the state that can be empirically validated by the historical evidence, and quite another thing to develop a myth about the efficaciousness of the market so that the rest of the society will not be tempted to turn to the state for a solution to its economic problems. The former is the task of the political scientist while the latter, however justified it may seem by the concerns economists have as witnesses to history, defeats any hope of economics ever becoming a science. A myth, be it God's creation of the world in six days or the self-regulating nature of the market, cannot be the basis for the scientific study of anything except the nature of myths themselves.

As for the market being a self-regulating mechanism, the reality belies this notion. The market can fail, with disastrous consequences, in any number of ways economists have identified. These include the provision of unsafe products, an indefensible distribution of income, the contamination of the environment, and, at times, even the collapse of the economy itself. To make the case for the market being a self-regulating mechanism, economists must posit the existence of indifference curves, isoquants, positively sloped supply curves, and marginal physical product curves—in other words, precisely the elements of neoclassical theory which cannot be empirically validated. At the same time, they are forced to ignore the existence of large corporations, trade unions, and many of the other institutional features of an advanced industrial society—including the intrusive role of the government in the economy—which represent an effort to cope with the problem of market failure. Only in this way can the myth of the market as a self-regulating mechanism be sustained.

It can now be seen more clearly why economics is not yet a

science. Economics, viewed as a social system, is unwilling to purge from the body of theory that defines professional competence certain key elements—despite the inability to empirically validate those theoretical constructs. It is unwilling to do so because those key elements, aside from being the means by which the discipline is held together and orthodoxy maintained, are essential to preserving the myth of a self-regulating market system. The myth serves as an important bulwark against too great an accretion of power by the state; and continuing to preserve that myth is more important, at least to those who carry the greatest weight within the profession, than a better understanding of how the economic system works.

This refusal to abandon the myth of the market as a self-regulating mechanism is not the result of any conspiracy on the part of the "establishment" in economics. It is not even a choice that any individual economist is necessarily aware of making. Rather it is the way economics operates as a social system—including the way new members of the establishment are selected—retaining its place within the larger society by perpetuating a set of ideas which have been found useful by that society, however dysfunctional that same set of ideas may be for a scientific understanding of how the economic system works. In other words, economics is unwilling to adhere to the epistemological principles which distinguish scientific from other types of intellectual activity because this might jeopardize the position of economics within the larger society as the defender of the dominant political faith. The situation in which economists find themselves is therefore not unlike that of many natural scientists who, when faced with the mounting evidence in support of, first, the Copernican theory of the universe and then, later, the Darwinian theory of evolution, had to decide whether undermining the revelatory basis of Judeo-Christian ethics was not too great a price to pay for being able to reveal the truth.

The fallacy, creating the dilemma for economists, lies in the belief that only the myth of a self-regulating market mechanism can protect a society against the heavy hand of the government. The fact is that the case against too intrusive a role by the government in the economy can be made without having to invoke that or any other myth. All that is necessary is to point out the various sources of government, as distinct from market, failure. The myth of a self-regulating market mechanism can then be abandoned, along with the neoclassical core of economic theory which is used to sustain it. Both economics as a discipline and the larger society as a separate body in need of solutions to its economic problems would, as a result, be better off.

The responsibility of the individual economist

The explanation which has just been offered, though it may go far in accounting for the present sorry state of economics, leaves at least one point still somewhat up in the air. The emphasis on the failings of economics as a social system, however necessary and more sophisticated a view this may be, ignores the responsibility individual economists have for what the discipline has become. While the fault may lie with economics as a social system, only the actions of individual economists can bring about a change for the better. The responsibility for seeing to it that economics becomes a body of useful knowledge therefore rests with each and every member of the profession. The repsonsibility is, of course, greatest for those who have risen to the top of the profession and therefore constitute its "establishment." The responsibility, however, is only slightly less for every other economist holding a tenured position.

An individual economist may, of course, come to believe—with deep conviction—that a better understanding of how the economic system actually works is far less important than preserving the myth of the market as a self-regulating mechanism, this so the state will not grow too powerful. However, this position, whatever else can be said for it, clearly fails to meet the responsibility the individual economist has as a professed member of the scientific community. That responsibility requires, first and foremost, that each economist recognize and accept the validity of the critique that has been offered in this and the other essays in the volume— or at least accept the need to address the issues that have been raised.

Once the correctness of that critique can no longer be denied, it is then incumbent upon each and every economist to do whatever is within his or her power to replace the present ethos in economics with a scientific one. This means insisting that any argument, before it is passed on to others as part of the cumulative body of economic knowledge, be empirically validated—and that any argument which cannot meet this test be viewed as at best only a tentative hypothesis, if not rejected outright. At the same time it means giving due weight to any and all alternative arguments until, by one empirical test or another, only a single explanation remains. While this set of rules will probably mean that economics will finally have to abandon the neoclassical core of its theory—along with the myth of the market as a self-regulating mechanism—nothing less will suffice if the present ethos in economics is to be replaced by a scientific one. Not only must each individual economist adhere to this set of rules personally but, in addition, he or she must be willing to invoke whatever sanctions he or she can—even if it is only the withholding of praise—against any colleagues who refuses to abide by the same code. Only in this way can economics ever hope to become a science.

REFERENCES

Mark Blaug. 1980. *The Methodology of Economics. Or How Economists Think*, Cambridge University Press.

Ray Canterbery. 1979a. "Inflation, Necessities and Distributive Efficiency," in J. H. Gapinsky and C. E. Rockwood, Jr., *Essays in Post-Keynesian Inflation*, Ballinger.

_____. 1979b. "A Vita Theory of the Personal Income Distribution," *Southern Economic Journal*, July.

Kenneth Coutts, Wynne Godley, and William Nordhaus. 1978. *Pricing in the United Kingdom,* Cambridge University Press.

James S. Duesenberry. 1949. *Income, Saving and the Theory of Consumer Behavior,* Harvard University Press.

Peter Earl. 1983. *The Economic Imagination*, M. E. Sharpe, Inc.

Otto Eckstein and Gary Fromm, 1968. "The Price Equation," *American Economic Review*, December.

Alfred S. Eichner. 1976. *The Megacorp and Oligopoly: Micro Foundations of Macro Dynamics*, Cambridge University Press. Reprinted 1980 by M. E. Sharpe, Inc.

_____. 1979. *A Guide to Post-Keynesian Economics*, M. E. Sharpe, Inc.

_____. 1980. "A Post-Keynesian Interpretation of Stagflation: Changing Theory to Fit the Reality," U.S. Congress, Joint Economic Committee, *Stagflation: The Causes, Effects and Solutions*, Special Study on Economic Change.

Alfred S. Eichner and J. A. Kregel. 1975. "An Essay on Post-Keynesian Theory: A New Paradigm in Economics," *Journal of Economic Literature*, December.

Leonard Forman and Alfred S. Eichner. 1981. "A Post-Keynesian Short-Period Model: Some Preliminary Econometric Results," *Journal of Post Keynesian Economics*, fall.

Bela Gold. 1971. *Explorations in Managerial Economics, Productivity, Costs, Technology and Growth*, Basic Books.

Geoffrey C. Harcourt. 1972. *Some Cambridge Controversies in the Theory of Capital*, Cambridge University Press.

John Hicks. 1939. *Value and Capital*, Oxford University Press.

John Johnston. 1960. *Statistical Cost Analysis*, McGraw-Hill.

Lawrence R. Klein and Edwin Burmeister. 1976. *Econometric Model Performance*, University of Pennsylvania Press.

Gardiner C. Means. 1962. *The Corporate Revolution in America*, Crowell-Collier.

Edward Mishan. 1961. "Theories of Consumers' Behaviour: A Cynical View," *Economica*, February.

Wesley C. Mitchell. 1937. *The Backward Art of Spending Money and Other Essays*, Kelley.

S. J. Nickell. 1978. *The Investment Decision of Firms*, Cambridge University Press.

Luigi L. Pasinetti. 1981. *Structural Change and Economic Growth, A Theoretical Essay on the Dynamics of the Wealth of Nations*, Cambridge University Press.

Michael J. Piore, ed. 1979. *Unemployment and Inflation, Institutionalist and Structuralist Views*, M. E. Sharpe, Inc.

Karl Popper. 1959. *The Logic of Scientific Discovery*, Harper.

Joan Robinson. 1956. *The Accumulation of Capital*, Macmillan.

Romney Robinson. 1961. "The Economics of Disequilibrium Price," *Quarterly Journal of Economics*, May.

Paul Samuelson. 1948. *Foundations of Economic Analysis*, Harvard University Press.

Thorstein Veblen. 1898. "Why Is Economics Not an Evolutionary Science?" *Quarterly Journal of Economics*, July, reprinted in Veblen, *The Place of Science in Modern Civilisation*, Huebsch, 1919.

_____. 1899. *Theory of the Leisure Class*, Modern Library edition, 1961.

Alan A. Walters. 1963. "Production and Cost, An Econometric Survey," *Econometrica*, January.

Sidney Weintraub. 1959. *A General Theory of the Price Level, Output, Income, Distribution, and Economic Growth*, Chilton.

_____. 1966. *A Keynesian Theory of Employment, Growth and Income Distribution*, Chilton.

Peter J. Wiles. 1956. *Prices, Cost and Output*, Basil Blackwell.

_____. 1979-80. "Ideology, Methodology and Neoclassical Economics," *Journal of Post Keynesian Economics*, winter, reprinted in this volume.

T. Wilson and P. W. S. Andrews. 1951. *Oxford Studies in the Price Mechanism*, Clarendon Press.

INDEX

‖ ‖ ‖ ‖ ‖ ‖

ABOUT THE CONTRIBUTORS

‖ ‖

John M. Blatt, Professor of Applied Mathematics at the University of New South Wales, is the co-author, with Viktor Weisskopf, of *Theoretical Nucelar Physics* and the author of *Dynamic Economic Systems*.

E. Ray Canterbery, Professor of Economics at Florida State University, and Robert J. Burkhardt, Professor of Philosophy at the University of Kentucky, are the co-authors of the study "Economics: The Embarrassed Science," completed in 1979 for the National Science Foundation. Professor Canterbery is, in addition, the author of *The Making of Economics*.

Richard X. Chase, Professor of Economics at the University of Vermont, has written extensively on the impact of Keynes's ideas on economics.

Peter E. Earl, Lecturer in Economics at the University of Stirling, is the author of *The Economic Imagination* and the co-author, with Sheila Dow, of *Money Matters*.

Alfred S. Eichner, Professor of Economics at Rutgers University, is the author of *The Megacorp and Oligopoly* and the editor of *A Guide to Post-Keynesian Theory*.

Wassily Leontief, Director of the Institute for Economic Analysis at New York University, received the Nobel Prize in Economics for his work in developing input-output analysis.

J. Ron Stanfield, Professor of Economics at Colorado State University at Fort Collins, is the author of *The Economic Surplus and Neo-Marxism* and of *Economic Thought and Social Change*.

James A. Swaney, Assistant Professor of Economics at Wright State University in Dayton, Ohio, has written on methodology and the history of economic thought. Robert Premus, staff economist for the Joint Economic Committee of Congress, has written on migration and other topics in regional economics.

Peter Wiles, Professor of Russian Social and Economic Studies at the University of London, is the author of *Economic Institutions Compared* and the editor of the conference volume *Economics in Disarray*.